Three Against One

Churchill, Roosevelt, Stalin
vs
Adolph Hitler

Three Against One

Churchill, Roosevelt, Stalin
vs
Adolph Hitler

by

Vance Stewart

SUNSTONE
PRESS

SANTA FE

Sunstone books may be purchased for educational, business, or sales promotional use. For information please write: Special Markets Department, Sunstone Press, P.O. Box 2321, Santa Fe, New Mexico 87504-2321.

Library of Congress Cataloging-in-Publication Data:

Stewart, Vance, 1929–
    Three against one: Churchill, Roosevelt, Stalin vs Adolph Hitler / by Vance Stewart.
        p. cm.
    ISBN: 0-86534-377-2 (softcover)
        1. Churchill, Winston, Sir, 1874–1965. 2. Roosevelt, Franklin D. (Franklin Delano), 1882–1945. 3. Stalin, Joseph, 1879–1953.
    4. Hitler, Adolf, 1889–1945. 5. World War, 1939–1945. I. Title.

    D736 .S785 2002
    940.53'092'2—dc21   2002030916

Published in
SUNSTONE PRESS
Post Office Box 2321
Santa Fe, NM 87504-2321 / USA
(505) 988-4418 / *orders only* (800) 243-5644
FAX (505) 988-1025
www.sunstonepress.com

Table of Contents

Chapter 1   **The Beginning**   **13**

The Four Players   13
The Mystique of Germany—How Did They Do It?   15
Adolph Hitler—The Beginning   17
Hitler—Goals and Motivations   23
Hitler—The Master Race   25
Internal Struggles—Hitler and Roehm—Showdown   27
The International Scene—Hitler's First Moves   29
Franklin D. Roosevelt   31
Winston Churchill   35
The Making of a Hero   36
Churchill—The Dardanelles 1915   40
Churchill—1930s   44
Munich   50
Stalin   55
Roosevelt—United States   59
Post–Munich   60
World War II Begins   66

Chapter 2   **Hitler Strikes—Blitzkrieg!**   **71**

Hitler's Greatest Triumph—The Fall of France   71
The Manstein Plan   72
Allied Plans   73
Charles de Gaulle   77
Hitler vs Churchill   79
Operation Catapult—British Attack the French Fleet   80
The Battle of Britain   81

1941   88
The Mediterranean Front   89
Hitler—Frame of Mind—June 21, 1941   92
Barbarossa—June 22, 1941   94
Roosevelt—1941   99

Chapter 3   The War comes To America   102

Pearl Harbor   102
America and Hitler—After Pearl Harbor   105
Allied Coalition Formed—By Hitler!   108
Japan on a Rampage   109
The Prince of Wales and the Repulse   109
To Lose an Empire—Malaya and Singapore   111
Wake Island—Bataan and Corregidor   113
Wake Island   113
Bataan–Corregidor   114
Japanese Americans   115
Americans Bomb Tokyo—The Doolittle Raid   117
The Coral Sea   118
Midway—The Turn of the Tide   120

Chapter 4   Europe and Africa, 1942   124

Basic Strategy of England   125
Churchill's Chief Adviser—General Brooke   127
Anthony Eden—Foreign Secretary, Adviser to Churchill   128
Churchill and Roosevelt   129
Russia 1942—The Turning Point on the Russian Front   132
Stalin—Man of Steel   137
El Alamein   139
Dwight D. Eisenhower—Operation Torch   143
Personal Notes on Eisenhower   148
Military—United States and Great Britain   151
Planning Operation Torch   153
French North Africa—1942-1943   154
The War at Sea—Atlantic   157
The Bismarck   158

The U-Boat Menace   160
Arctic Convoys—Aid to Russia   160
The Casablanca Conference   162
Overall Strategy—Middle of the War—The Four Players   164
The Pressure Mounts   166
Anzio   170
Russia—Westward Ho!   173
Teheran—November, 1943   175

Chapter 5   1944: Year Of Decision   179

Normandy   179
Wray   182
The Beaches   183
Hitler—June 6, 1944   184
1944 Post-Invasion   189
July 20, 1944   192
The Invasion of Southern France   193
The Resistance Movement   195
Defense Stiffening   197
Market Garden   198
The Russian Front 1944   201
Surprise Attack—The Ardennes   202
The Air War   208

Chapter 6   The Pacific War   218

Roosevelt and Churchill   218
Chiang Kai-shek   219
Guadalcanal   221
The Death of Yamamoto   222
Japan on the Defensive   223
Across the Pacific   224
Churchill and the Pacific   226
Leyte Gulf   227
Kamikaze   229
Post-Leyte   230
MacArthur—The Pacific War   231

Iwo Jima—The Last Steps to Japan   235
Okinawa—Final Stepping Stone to Japan   237
Five Americans   239

Chapter 7   War In Europe—The Beginning Of The End   241

Roosevelt and Hitler—The Atomic Bomb   241
The (Decision) to Use the Atomic Bomb   243
The Yalta Conference   244
Industrial Production—USA Arsenal of Production   246
Hitler and the Death Camps—The Final Solution   249
Roosevelt—Warm Springs, Georgia   252
Harry S. Truman   253
Germany Crushed   256

Chapter 8   The Reckoning   260

The Final Days of Hitler and Nazi Germany   260
Final Tally—Strategical Mistakes in World War II   264
Adolph Hitler   269
The Greatest Leader Was . . .   272
Churchill, Roosevelt, and Stalin vs Adolph Hitler   274

References   279
Index   283

This book is dedicated to my brother,
Lt. William C. Stewart, Jr.,
a bombardier on a B-17.
He was killed in a raid on Berlin on
September 12, 1944.

Preface

At the end of the war in November, 1918, people looked back over the death, carnage and destruction of the past four years. After all that had happened they couldn't quite remember what had started it all.

There was no such problem with World War II. What started it all was one man—Adolph Hitler. It seems impossible but it was true. This tormented personality brought death and destruction over most of the world. Churchill, Roosevelt and Stalin were called on by history to stop this menace. This is the story of that struggle—the fate of the world was at stake.

The Second World War was the most colossal event in history—it did indeed cover the whole world. Locations that were mostly unknown such as Bataan, Guadalcanal, Anzio, Bastogne, and Stalingrad now became places that were given the utmost attention. The magnitude of the violence on all fronts was incredible. It is estimated that in Russia alone there were 20,000,000 military and civilian casualties. There has never been anything like this war, and let us hope that there never will be again.

The focus of this book is mainly devoted to the highest leadership, that is, Churchill, Roosevelt, Stalin, and Hitler. Their personalities, their backgrounds, and their decisions are what made the decisive difference in World War II.

This book is also a tribute to the many millions of people who put their lives at risk to stop and destroy evil forces. Many of these people made the ultimate sacrifice. Theirs was a good and noble cause. The graves all over the world are a testimony to their mighty effort and courageous actions against forces that were bad almost beyond comprehension.

In a horrific struggle the heroic endeavors of millions of good people were ultimately successful. It was their battle and it is their victory.

1

The Beginning

The Four Players

When you see the title Churchill, Roosevelt, and Stalin vs. Adolph Hitler, at first it seems a little unfair. That is, three against one. But, then you have to ask yourself, "How did this happen?"

It happened because one man, Adolph Hitler, had managed to bring it about. Hitler, the master of one country at a time, had managed to bring his three possibly largest opponents all in against him at once.

Overconfidence? Arrogance? Egotism? Poor judgment? Yes, all of these, coupled with a very inadequate educational background. Hitler had the intelligence; he did not have any kind of world view such as Churchill had. He had failed to defeat England, and then he had failed to defeat Russia, and then he took on America.

At the beginning, I think it advisable to give a thumbnail sketch of each individual involved.

Winston Churchill—Churchill was, in the opinion of the author, the greatest Englishman that ever lived. He embodied everything that was great about England. He was courageous, brilliant, and had an extraordinary vision of the future. He had a great deal of experience in high level positions in World War I. His use of the English language was unequaled. He inspired the British people when they had nothing other than his inspiration to keep them going. Churchill knew good from evil, and he viewed Hitler as the worst form of evil. Hitler fooled a lot of people for a long time, but he never fooled Churchill. Churchill knew what he was and resolved to stop him at all costs.

Churchill's main goal was to somehow get the United States involved in the war. He felt with the United States out, England could not win. With the United States in, England could not lose. Japan and Hitler accomplished Churchill's goal for him.

Franklin D. Roosevelt—Roosevelt became President of the United States in 1933 at the worst time possible. The Great Depression just about had America on its back. If ever there was having the right man at the right place and time, Roosevelt was it.

Roosevelt, by nature, was an optimistic, cheerful type of person, and that was just what America needed. As he said, "The only thing we have to fear is fear itself." Roosevelt did not immediately improve conditions, but he set a course that over a period of time brought America back again. He was ready and willing to use the power of government to alleviate and improve the lot of the average citizen. Although he was suffering from a disability, his personality, charm and attitude made it seem of little consequence.

In international affairs, Roosevelt was very much akin to Churchill in seeing the menace of Hitler's Germany early on. Just as Churchill was, Roosevelt was frustrated in not being able to do anything about it. Although he was President, he knew the American people did not want to go to war unless they were directly threatened.

Roosevelt was a very intelligent man and a terrific politician. Maybe that is why he was elected President four times. Roosevelt was a larger-than-life person. When he died, Americans couldn't believe it. They thought he would be there forever. Roosevelt will go down as a giant in American history.

Joseph Stalin—Stalin was somewhat of an inscrutable man. But what we do know about him is, as his name implies, that he was as tough as steel. Tough and ruthless. Stalin did not become the dictator of the Soviet Union by being a nice guy. From a lowly background, he fought himself up inch by inch to the top, over the prostrate forms of many other people. Most of them had underestimated him to the forfeit of their lives.

Stalin was brilliant in the fact that he had goals and succeeded by doing whatever it took to achieve them. His primary goal was absolute power for himself over the Soviet Union. He ruled by fear and intimidation, and it worked. His secret police knew everything about everybody, and the camps of Siberia awaited. He had a fervent belief in Communism and wanted to take it as far as it could go or as far as other people would let him go. However, his main goal was not power to the people. It was power to Stalin.

Strength, decisiveness, and ruthlessness were Stalin's main assets. They actually were exactly what was going to be needed to save the Soviet Union from Hitler.

Adolph Hitler—What can one say about Hitler other than he was everything bad and evil rolled up into one man? This one man caused World

War II. In the history of the world, the world is lucky that someone like Hitler only comes along about once in every one thousand years. Genghis Khan may have been the last, and he was nowhere near as bad as Hitler. Hitler caused more casualties and damage than anyone in the annals of history. It is very probable that the Second World War caused by Hitler, combined with the First World War, accounted for more deaths than all of the previous wars in history put together.

No one can conceive of a human being killing six million people just because he did not like their race or religion. Hitler did it. Hitler had no remorse; he was a cold-blooded killer on a massive scale. He was a homicidal egomaniac with an obsession against the Jews. Hitler's strength was his own unwavering belief in himself and his ability to convince the German people of that belief also. What a terrible man and cause they fought and died for. Hitler's other strength was audacity. He did what no one else would consider doing and got away with it...for a while.

In many ways, Hitler was a very smart, resourceful man, but he was not as smart and resourceful as Churchill or Roosevelt or Stalin. That's why he lost. There is no question that Hitler was a man of extraordinary talents, among them fanatical determination. He wouldn't have gotten where he was without them. It was too bad at that time in German history that he used his talents in such a terrible way. Directed in a positive manner, Hitler could have done a great deal for Germany. Instead, he started World War II and all the calamities that it caused. It is safe to say that the personalities and personal characteristics of only four men had a huge effect on the outcome of the greatest war in history and on history itself.

During the early years of the war a coalition of Churchill, Roosevelt and Stalin seemed impossible. Stalin, early on, had acted with Hitler in devouring Poland. He then absorbed the Baltic states and brutally attacked the small country of Finland. Stalin was shipping war materials on a massive scale to Hitler—they were in effect allied. Yet at the end of 1941, Hitler was in a life or death struggle with . . . Churchill, Roosevelt and Stalin, the strongest coalition of all time. How dumb can you get? What seemed impossible, Hitler had made possible. This is the story of these incredible events.

The Mystique of Germany
How Did They Do It?

To understand the Second World War, it is necessary to understand the psychological impact of Germany on the rest of Europe.

Beginning in 1939, how did Germany, the losing country of the First War, manage to create an empire that stretched from the Atlantic in the west to the Volga in the east? From the Arctic on the north to North Africa in the south? In fact it was the greatest military achievement since Khan. Germany was a country with only 80 million people, and they did it in a few short years.

The fact is, in the 1930s and early 1940s, the countries of Europe were scared to death of Germany, particularly under the brutal leadership of Adolph Hitler. It all goes back to World War I. The Germans came very close to defeating all of Europe and probably would have except for the intervention of American troops in France. Having defeated Russia, the Germans in 1918 were able to concentrate the bulk of their army against France and Britain on the Western Front. They mounted a series of attacks designed to finish off the Allies before American troops arrived. As mentioned, they came very close to succeeding. They were turned back at the Marne again this time by American and French troops. After that, the Allies went over to the offensive all along the Western Front. The Germans were forced to retreat; the morale of the Germans on the front and at home deteriorated. With their allies all folding around them, the Germans asked for an armistice on November 11, 1918. The war was over.

The punishment that Germany had inflicted on all of its neighbors was immense, in particular on France, Britain, and Russia. On this Western Front, after the first battle of the Marne in 1914, the Germans were basically on the defensive, except for Verdun, from 1914 to 1918. This was because they had a large army tied up on the Eastern Front opposing Russia. During this period, the French and British were on the attack and sustained horrendous casualties. Frontal attacks against massed machine guns and artillery were suicide. The Allied generals seemed oblivious to this fact over and over again. Some say that the generals and their staffs were too far behind the lines to know exactly what conditions the troops were under. It is said that at one point a staff officer went to the front lines and, amid the mud, rats in the trenches, and dead and wounded men, said, "And we ask our men to fight in this."

The British sustained 60,000 casualties in one day on the Somme, catastrophic losses. The French in their attacks in 1917 under General Nivelle, sustained hundreds of thousands of casualties. So much so that some French troops mutinied. General Petain saved the situation mainly by discontinuing offensive attacks.

As Britain and France were much smaller countries than Germany, it meant they sustained greater casualties proportionate to their population than Germany. While Germans also sustained large casualties in this period, the fact that they were in defensive positions made their casualties less than those of the French and British. Thus, as the war ended, you had France and Britain with the flower of their young men cut down on the fields of Northern France. They had given it their all to achieve victory. There was not much left to give.

Russia also had sustained millions of casualties. At Tannenberg, in one day, an army of over 100,000 men was destroyed. In fact, the Germans with only minimum forces on the Eastern Front destroyed the Czarist Empire which was replaced by the Bolsheviks under Lenin. The Germans had actually aided Lenin in order to undermine the Russians. When Lenin took over, Stalin came with him. This came back to haunt the Germans later.

After the war, the statesmen, politicians, and public looked back on the war with horror. They vowed, "Never again." Thus, in 1933, with Hitler assuming power in Germany, the rest of Europe did not even want to think about another war. They would go to any limits to prevent a repeat of 1914-1918. Peace at any price. Thus, this fear, which was intensified by their fear of Hitler, laid the groundwork for the success of Hitler's Germany. The French and British in particular, because of their huge manpower losses, were anxious not to have another conflict with Germany—they barely survived the first one. This affected the attitude of the statesmen and the public as well and played right into Hitler's hands. He wasn't afraid of anything or anybody—at this stage.

Hitler knew that at some point there would be another war; however, this time Germany would win. In the meanwhile, he would take whatever anyone would give him.

Adolph Hitler—The Beginning
The Formation and Growth of the National Socialist Party (NAZI)

What were the origins of this man, Adolph Hitler, a man who would shake the world? A man whose attitude and thinking would affect and shatter millions of lives. After looking at his drab early life and youth, it seems almost impossible that someone could come out of such lowly and forlorn beginnings to change the course of history.

Hitler was born on April 20, 1889, at Branauam Inn, a small town in Austria near the German border. His parents were German—Alois and Klara Hitler. Alois Hitler was a minor civil servant, a custom official who retired early, and often moved from place to place. By the time Adolph was fifteen, he had attended five different schools, one being a Benedictine monastery where he spent two years and sang in the choir.

Later, one of his teachers, Professor Eduard Huemer, commented on Hitler as a student:

> Hitler was certainly gifted, although only for particular subjects, but he lacked self-control and, to say the least, he was considered argumentative, self-opinionated and bad tempered, and unable to submit to school discipline. (These traits would follow Hitler all his life and, in the end, proved to be his undoing.)

Hitler's stern father was insistent that Adolph become a civil servant like himself, but Hitler detested the idea of being confined in an office shuffling papers. He decided to become an artist, which greatly upset his father. At sixteen Hitler had a lung ailment which kept him out of school for a year. Together with his own lack of interest, Hitler drifted away from school and never graduated high school. Thus, he had a very limited view of the world.

At sixteen, after his father's death, Hitler and his mother moved to Linz. Hitler lived an aimless, carefree life. He made no attempt to help his impoverished mother. The thought of a regular job was repulsive to him and remained that way the rest of his life. Hitler did develop a consuming interest in politics and began reading, particularly German history—he became a fanatical German nationalist.

In 1906, aged seventeen, Hitler went to Vienna to seek his fortune in art. Unfortunately for him and for the world, he failed the entrance exam at the Vienna Academy of Arts and failed again the next year. His work was judged insufficient.

When Hitler was nineteen, his devoted mother died and now he was alone and penniless. The next five years in Vienna were a time of misery and destitution for Hitler. The man who in later years would inflame the world was reduced to doing odd jobs, living in flophouses, and frequenting charity soup kitchens. Living in the festive and beautiful city of Vienna, Hitler's own life was as dismal as possible. Sometimes he received meager funds from selling small, mediocre drawings he made of Vienna's landmarks.

Hitler still continued his interest in politics, and he began reading anti-Semitic literature. Considering his own miserable existence, perhaps Hitler was looking for a scapegoat and fixed on the Jews. His own violent and anti-social personality only added to the fixation.

In 1913, Hitler left Vienna and went to live in Germany at Munich. He was now twenty-four and was a total failure. His situation seemed hopeless. Then the war came, a wonderful deliverance for Hitler from his dreary life.

But for the war, Hitler would, no doubt, have faded into obscurity. But the war saved him and set him on a new course which would change the world.

The war, and the way it ended, transformed Hitler's life. The German people were angry and bitter over losing a war they almost won. The timing for Hitler was perfect. Over many yes of degradation and war, under Hitler's very ordinary exterior, there was brewing a hurricane of large proportions waiting for the moment to be unleashed. Now, at the end of the war, that moment had come. The inner force that swirled within Hitler came to the fore and from nothing Hitler went on to become the total leader of Germany and threatened to become master of the world. Hitler was a phenomenon almost beyond understanding—a man of explosive, dynamic and diabolical force. Beneath all is an undercurrent of rage at everything—a rage which manifested itself in violence. Hitler was a very frightening man. This all adds up to a lethal combination that would disastrously affect the whole world. Hitler's story is incredible but, unfortunately, is all too true. The road to the top for Hitler began on August 1, 1914.

On August 1, 1914, Germany declared war on Russia. In the next few days, a number of countries joined in the war. It was France, Great Britain, and Russia on one side and Germany and Austria-Hungary on the other. The crowds went wild with joy. Why, no one quite knows for sure. Troops were marching, bands were playing. In Munich, a large crowd gathered to celebrate. In the crowd was Adolph Hitler—his face was jubilant—he was ready to march.

Hitler joined a Bavarian regiment and was sent to the Western Front. His regiment was decimated by the British at the first Battle of Ypres. Hitler served courageously for four years on the Western Front. He was wounded twice and also was promoted to Corporal—his highest rank until he assumed command of the entire German army in 1942.

For his service during 1914-1918, Hitler received the Iron Cross, First Class. He wore it proudly to the end of his life. During the war, Hitler showed evidence of a growing hatred for Jews and Marxists, particularly the Jews. He blamed them for all of Germany's troubles—an irrational attitude which became an obsession.

On the night of October 13, 1918, Hitler's unit was hit by a heavy British gas attack. "I stumbled back with burning eyes. A few hours later my eyes had turned into glowing coals. It had grown dark around me." Hitler was hospitalized and gradually recovered his sight. On November 10, 1918, he first heard that on the next day Germany would sign the armistice at Compeigne in France. Germany had lost the war.

Hitler almost fainted on hearing the news. All of the suffering he and his comrades had endured had been useless. He said he broke down and wept. He found the news incredible. He felt that Germany had not lost the war, but that it had been betrayed from within. The army had been "stabbed in the back." Millions of Germans came to believe this even though it wasn't true. The German army had been beaten in the field and was on the verge of surrender. It called for an armistice to prevent a total collapse.

This did not faze Hitler. He believed what he believed, and that was what counted. A belief that would affect millions of people. Hitler determined at this dark time to go into politics. A fateful decision for Hitler and the world, as William L. Shirer would say in his tremendous book, The Rise and Fall of the Third Reich.

Hitler remained in the army and returned to Munich, a hotbed of revolutionary activity. His anti-Semitism pleased his superior officers, and he was placed in a unit to combat dangerous ideas—pacifism, socialism, and democracy. During meetings, Hitler found out he had exceptional oratorical skills which he later used with tremendous effect.

One day in September, 1919, Hitler received orders from the army's political department to have a look at a tiny political group in Munich called the "German Workers Party. He went to the meeting, which was in a beer hall with only about 25 people present. Hitler was not impressed. He was about to leave the dull meeting when one of the speakers began talking about Bavaria breaking away from Germany and becoming part of Austria. This caught Hitler's attention and made him furious. He rose and gave an impassioned speech opposing such an idea—to the astonishment of everyone there. Then he left.

Later the next day, Hitler was surprised to receive a post card saying he had been accepted into the German Workers Party. "I didn't know whether to be angry or cry," he remembered later. "I had no intention of joining a ready-made party but wanted to found one of my own."

Yet there was something about these shabby men in an ill-lit room that attracted him. That evening in the barracks, "I faced the hardest question in my life." The very unimportance of the small organization would give a man of energy and ideas an opportunity to express himself.

"After two days of pondering and reflection, I finally came to the conviction that I had to take this step. It was the most decisive resolve in my life. From here on there was and could be no turning back."

All the ideas in Hitler's mind which had been bubbling since his youth came to the surface and burst forth. Gradually, by his hard work he was able to increase the number of people who came to the meetings. On the night of

Hitler's first "public" speech, one hundred eleven people showed up. Hitler spoke for thirty minutes and electrified the audience. On February 24, Hitler organized a meeting to be held in a hall with a capacity of two thousand people. Hitler's fellow members thought he was crazy. However, it marked a significant turn in the fortunes of Hitler.

During the tumultuous meeting Hitler outlined his program in detail. Number one was "that all Germans should be in union with Greater Germany (seeds of things to come!—author's note). The Jews were to be denied office and even citizenship in Germany. The abrogation of the Treaty of Versailles. The creation of strong central power of State."

It is remarkable that here in 1920, Hitler had outlined his plan which he strictly followed and put into place when he became Chancellor of Germany many years later. In 1921, Hitler formed a group within the party which was essentially a strong-arm group of ruffians. They became known as the S.A.— storm troopers dressed in brown uniforms. Also in this period, Hitler was looking for an unusual symbol to rally around. He decided on the swastika— a hooked cross used in ancient times. The colors were red, white, and black. Hitler spent a great deal of time on this, and when he got it exactly like he wanted, he was exultant. It was used extensively and helped bring in many new members to the Party. The swastika seemed to appeal to something in the German beyond understanding.

In 1921, Hitler took over undisputed leadership of the Party. Money began to come in, and the Party bought a newspaper. Most of the men who became Hitler's closest subordinates came into the Party about this time. Rudolph Hess, stirred by Hitler's oratory, joined the party and became one of his most zealous supporters. Alfred Rosenberg also joined at this time.

The major figure that joined the party in 1921 was Hermann Goering. Goering was a great war hero, the last commander of the famed Richthofen Fighter Squadron and a holder of the Pour le Merite, the highest war decoration in Germany. Goering added a great deal of prestige to the Party. He became, along with Ernst Roehm, a leader of the S.A.

Goering was vain and on the heavy side, and some did not think highly of him. But Goering was a highly intelligent and ruthless man. Later he would command the German Air Force, "the Luftwaffe," and become second to Hitler in command of Germany. He was a much tougher and smarter man than the image that has come down.

Joseph Goebbels joined the Party and became head of propaganda. He was ideally suited for the job. He believed the bigger the lies the better, and just to keep repeating them over and over, louder and louder. It seemed to work. Goebbels was a fanatic and a follower of Hitler, and stuck to him to the very end. Heinrich Himmler was a nondescript, mild looking man who joined Hitler in 1925. He had worked as a fertilizer salesmen and then as a poultry farmer.

He also became close to Hitler and became head of the S.S., an elite unit of zealous Nazi followers. By 1936, he was head not only of the S.S., but also of the newly unified nationwide police—the Gestapo. These units exerted great power in controlling and terrorizing huge numbers of people. They were fanatical followers of Hitler and would stop at nothing to sustain and strengthen him. Hitler told them what to do, and they did it, no matter what it was.

Later, the S.S. would branch out into the Army. S.S. Panzer divisions were formed. These were considered the crack German units in the Army; they were given the most difficult assignments. Their infiltration of the Army also undermined the German General Staff. The S.S. was an army within an army.

In the late 1930s, Himmler and the S.S. were put in charge of the "Final Solution," the elimination of the Jews. Vast concentration camps and execution chambers were built.

◆ ◆ ◆

So we have in the 1920s the formation and growth of the Nazi Party. The top organization was complete—Hitler, Goering, Goebbels, Himmler, and, yes, Rudolph Hess. Their apparatus of terror and propaganda was in place.

Germany in the tumultuous times of the 1920s and early 1930s was in a ferment; inflation was astronomical at times. Different groups including the Communists were inciting trouble and turmoil. A vacuum of power at the top was developing. The head of the government, von Hindenburg, was in his eighties and was bordering on senility. With the Depression of 1929, things only got worse. Unemployment was high and kept getting higher.

The situation was perfect for Hitler and his Party. They were tough, strong, organized men. They had a simple message—put Hitler in charge and he would produce order and stability. He would get the country back where it used to be. At a time when everything else seemed to be falling apart—Hitler was one constant. He led the strongest organized group in the nation. His opposition was weak and fragmented.

The opposition parties were so busy fighting and scheming for power, one against the other, that they left the door wide open for Hitler. The Nazi Party, the largest in the Reichstag, began to disrupt the operations of that body.

Nazi hooligans, the Storm Troopers, took control of the streets of Germany. Goebbels turned up the heat on the propaganda front, clamoring that Hitler was Germany's only salvation. Hindenburg, seeing chaos approaching, decided to solve the problem by giving Hitler the powerful office of Chancellor of Germany on January 30, 1933. Hindenburg thought that making Hitler a part of the establishment would moderate the situation. What a terribly absurd idea! This powerful position and situation is exactly what the violent Hitler wanted. Hindenburg was trying to put a hurricane in a box. When the dust settled, the box was gone along with the democracy and most of Hitler's opponents. Hindenburg became merely a figurehead and died several months later. Adolph Hitler was master of Germany.

Hitler with his iron will and fanatical followers had done the impossible. He had taken over Germany. From a small obscure party of 25 followers, Hitler now was in command of potentially the strongest and most efficient state in Europe. His first priority was to begin rearmament. While his potential enemies were still sleeping, Germany began to make guns, shells, and planes. For Hitler, World War II had already begun.

Hitler—Goals and Motivations

Let us examine Hitler's goals and motivation which made him act as he did—actions that brought on the greatest war in history.

Hitler's goals were:

1. To avenge the First War. Hitler sincerely but erroneously believed that Germany had not actually lost the war on the battlefront but had been betrayed from within by the Jews, Communists, and other traitors. To Hitler, "perception was reality." Despite the results of the war, Hitler believed Germany was invincible.

To avenge the First War, there was only one way to do it—to replay it. If this involved another war, which it surely would, with Britain and France—so be it. All of Hitler's actions in the 1930s led to the final conclusion in September, 1939—another great war—which was not surprising to him at all. Why else would a violent man create a huge army and air force if not to use it? Hitler's actions made war inevitable. It was just a matter of when. Probably when his adversaries were pushed into a corner and there was no way out. To have weak and vacillating opponents was a big help to Hitler. They were scared to death of him, and rightly so.

In this second war, Hitler felt confident that under his dynamic and ruthless leadership, Germany would win. This time there would be no problem on the home front—Hitler would see to that by gathering the fanatical support of the entire German nation around him, which he did.

2. The bringing together within the German state all German and German speaking people. This would include the Sudetenland in Czechoslovakia, Austria, and Danzig including the Polish Corridor—this last named precipitated the Second World War.

3. To eliminate or exterminate the entire Jewish population of Europe. This seems to be a thought beyond human comprehension, but not to Hitler. If ever there was someone who was Satan's gift to the earth, it was Adolph Hitler. Human life and suffering meant nothing to him. No rational person could commit the atrocities that Hitler committed.

4. To establish German ascendancy over all of Europe. The frightening thing about this is that with proper leadership, the right decisions and good execution, Germany and Hitler had a good chance of achieving it. After this occurred, Hitler, being Hitler, would not be satisfied. Most likely, he would turn south and take over the oil fields of the Middle East, occupying the Suez Canal while doing so.

With his partner, Japan in East Asia, Hitler would then be the predominant force in the whole world. He would then no doubt turn Germany's highly efficient scientific community to making inter-continental ballistic missiles to neutralize his last remaining adversary, the United States of America. These plans may seem far-fetched, but given everything going right for Hitler, they were attainable. There were very high stakes involved in the coming fight for the world. It was winner take all and the loser destroyed.

What motivated Hitler in these endeavors? Certainly he was a very egotistical man (some said an egomaniac) and had a strong lust for power. However, his motivation was his belief in Germany and the destiny of Germany. "Deutschland uber Alles." He actually believed in his own propaganda, although he didn't think it was propaganda—he thought it was truth. Perhaps that is what made him such an effective orator.

He did indeed believe that the Germans were a superior race and all other races were inferior, especially the Slavs of Eastern Europe, whom he thought of as sub-human. The fanatical belief that Germany was superior to all other countries, coupled with the burning desire to avenge and overturn the results of the First War, were the two motivating factors that drove Hitler. As mentioned, these motivations led to the greatest war and probably the greatest catastrophe in world history.

The fact that he had contempt for his enemies and potential enemies encouraged Hitler to aggressively pursue his goals. If he could take on his enemies one by one, it would be even easier. To intimidate, frighten, and divide his adversaries was a natural progression of thought for Hitler. It had worked in Germany—why not all of Europe?

Evidently, Hitler appealed to everything bad in the German people, still smarting from the loss of the First War. His powerful oratory had almost a hypnotic effect on them. It was not only that he said what they wanted to hear, but also his dynamic delivery and body movement seemed to overwhelm them—bordering on a state of mass hysteria.

Without the people's fervent support, Hitler could do nothing—with it, he could go a long way to achieving his goals. When he began to build one success on top of another, his power over the people expanded by multiple effect—to reach a point where he had virtually the entire German nation behind him in unquestioning and fanatical obedience. The German people were in lock-step with a lunatic and there was no looking back.

Hitler achieved a momentum that seemed irresistible—not only to the German people, but to much of the world as well. The power of Hitler's personality plus the unwavering, strong and efficient support of the German people produced a war machine that had not been seen in the history of the world.

It is true that Hitler did not have a world view, but he was very good at smashing what was in front of him. If you continue doing this successively over a period of time, it makes no difference if you have a world view—you become so powerful that the world is overcome.

Hitler—The Master Race

As strange as it may seem, the idea of the Germans being the "Master Race" came from an Englishman—Houston Stewart Chamberlain. Chamberlain wrote the book *Foundation of the Nineteenth Century* in 1898. In it, Chamberlain's main thesis is that the key to civilization was race. He extolled the Aryan (German) race as superior to all others and is contemptuous of Jews. The book created a sensation, particularly in Germany as one would expect, and sold over 250,000 copies.

Kaiser Wilhelm II was particularly enthused over Chamberlain's book and they became friends—exchanging many communications. At the outbreak of World War I, Chamberlain wrote the Kaiser:

Once Germany has achieved the power—and we may confidently expect her to achieve it—she must immediately begin to carry out a scientific policy of genius. . . superior to all in art, science, technology, industry, finance in every field, in short; teacher, helmsman, pioneer of the world, every man at his post, every man giving his utmost to the holy cause—thus Germany . . . will conquer the world by inner superiority.

(For such thoughts as these the Kaiser made Chamberlain a naturalized German citizen in 1916and presented him with the Iron Cross.)

Chamberlain's theories were enthusiastically embraced and taken over by the Nazis. They called Chamberlain the "spiritual founder" of the National Socialist Party. Chamberlain was swept off his feet by Hitler; he told Hitler, "You have mighty things to do," and he joined the Nazi Party. In articles he wrote in 1924, Chamberlain hailed Hitler as destined by God to lead the German people. Chamberlain died in 1927—Hitler was the only public figure at his funeral.

Friedrich Nietsche was also one from whom Hitler drew some of this thinking that Germany was looking for a superman, highly gifted in intellect and will. This man and the elite around him will become "lords of the earth." Hitler, writing in *Mein Kampf*, quotes Nietsche extensively and knows that he, Hitler, is the man Nietsche is looking for. Another theory of Nietsche that Hitler embraced was that a genius with a mission was above the law.

Hitler did believe the Germans were a master race and that other races were inferior. This is one of the central tenets of his philosophy, if not the central tenet. With his oratorical genius he convinced the German people that they were the master race—that their destiny was unlimited.

On assuming power in 1933, one of the first things Hitler did was to take over the educational system of Germany. Through this system, his beliefs were inculcated into young Germans in particular that they were the master race. Jews and Slavs were sub-humans. The Hitler Youth under Baldur von Schirach was created; in 1938 it had over 7,700,000 youths enrolled.

Thus, Hitler wrapped his hold over the Germans and the German youth. The more fanatical they became, the better. The more immune they became to other people's suffering, the better. Hitler believed that with this type of spirit he could conquer Europe and anyone else that got in his way.

The Germans found out in World War II that they could be killed by bullets and bombs just as easily as anyone else—that their country could also be destroyed—unfortunately, they did not realize this until 1945.

Internal Struggles
Hitler and Roehm—Showdown

In 1933, Adolph Hitler was Chancellor of Germany, virtually in full control. One of his closest friends and supporters was Ernst Roehm, the leader of the S.A.

Roehm had been an original member of the Nazi Party in Munich, which Hitler joined and then became its leader. Ernst Roehm was a thug. He was a brutish and zealous believer in National Socialism. If anything, he was more radical than Hitler. He believed in the elimination of anyone connected with the old order, businessmen, office holders of any kind. He became the leader of the S.A., the Storm Troopers, whose terror tactics had helped make Hitler the leader of Germany.

In 1933, Roehm had control of two and a half million storm troopers. He wished to make the S.A. the foundation of the new German Army replacing the regular army. This naturally infuriated the members of the German General Staff. Relations between Roehm's S.A. and the German generals became very tense. It was the survival of one or the other.

Unknown to Roehm, Hitler came down on the side of his generals. He knew that at some point a war would break out to overcome the results of Versailles. He would need professional army men, not the street thugs of the S.A. Roehm had become obsolete. Hitler worked out a deal with the General Staff assuring his support for them in exchange for their support of him, the "Pact of the Deutschland." The highest officers of the German Army unanimously endorsed Hitler as successor to the dying President Hindenburg. They put their fate and Germany in Hitler's hands.

A struggle for power began within the Nazi Party. Goering and Himmler turned against Roehm. Himmler was chief of the black-coated S.S. and also the Gestapo. Rumors began to circulate (perhaps started by Goering) that Roehm was plotting with Gregor Strasser and others to take control of the Party and the government. Hitler believed that "Roehm began preparation to eliminate me personally."

At this point, von Papen, who was still vice-chancellor, made a speech denouncing violence and calling for order and a return to civility, an attack on the S.A. and possibly on Hitler himself. The German generals approved this speech, which was a warning to Hitler: Roehm and the S.A. must go or else. On June 25, General von Fritsch, the commander in chief, put the Army in a state of alert, canceling all leaves. On June 28, Roehm was expelled from the German Officers League. The Army was putting more pressure on Hitler to do something about Roehm and the S.A. Hitler's power was in jeopardy.

On June 29, Hitler was in the town of Godesberg on the Rhine. Goebbels arrived and told Hitler that Roehm was about to start a violent putsch and take over the government. At 2 o'clock in the morning, Hitler flew to Munich. At this time, Roehm was in a hotel at Wiesse nearby, an unlikely spot to start a revolution.

Shortly after dawn, an armed Hitler and his party sped out of Munich toward Wiesse in a long column of cars. They found Roehm and his friends still asleep. Hitler entered Roehm's room and confronted him. An argument ensued. Hitler left the room and gave orders that a pistol be left on the table for his old comrade, but Roehm refused to make use of it. Thereupon, two S.S. officers entered and fired their revolvers at Roehm point blank. Roehm, one of Hitler's oldest and strongest supporters, was gone.

In Berlin, in the meanwhile, Goering and Himmler were at work. Some 150 S.A. leaders were rounded up, stood against the wall, and shot by firing squads of the S.S. All over Germany, former enemies or potential enemies of Hitler were rounded up and shot. With one swipe, Hitler had eliminated anyone and everyone who stood in his path—a ruthless but brilliant stroke.

On July 2, President Hindenburg thanked Hitler for rescuing the German people from a great danger. The head of the Army, General, von Blomberg, congratulated Hitler on his actions in defense of the state. The S.A. was disbanded. The German generals were pleased; they had made an alliance with Hitler and Hitler fulfilled his part of the bargain. From here on, they were subservient to Hitler and became a part of his march to destruction. They even took an oath swearing their loyalty to Hitler.

This episode in Hitler's career represents Hitler's shrewdness, his resourcefulness, and his ruthlessness. He had eliminated a serious rival and secured the full support of the highest officers of the Army.

With his home base secured and under control, Hitler could turn his eyes outside Germany. He had secured his foundation at home; now it was time to make Germany's presence known in the world outside. The Versailles Treaty would be avenged. Germany would again have its place in the sun. Any means necessary would be used by Hitler—violence, terror, fear, and manipulation. The world had no idea of what it was in for.

The International Scene
Hitler's First Moves

On March 1, 1936, Adolph Hitler made a momentous decision. He would occupy the Rhineland with military forces. The Rhineland had been set up after the First War as a demilitarized zone, a buffer between France and Germany. It had been part of Germany before the war.

To occupy the Rhineland was in direct violation of the Versailles Treaty and also previous promises by Hitler not to do so. The world was to find out that Hitler's promises meant nothing; they would find out the hard way and almost too late.

This order to occupy the Rhineland terrified the German generals. The German army was in no way at this time prepared for war against France. The move by Germany would only be a huge bluff. There was really very little to back up the few battalions sent into the Rhineland. France had a large standing army of over a million men which could have easily crushed the small German units in the Rhineland. In fact, the German orders were that if France intervened, the German troops were to beat a hasty retreat back across the Rhine.

The French did nothing. General Gamelin, the Chief of the General Staff, advised his government not to take any action. He was afraid of starting a whole new war with Germany. Certainly, he may have been correct, but it was a war which would have been over very quickly with an easy French victory. General Gamelin was certainly no Marshal Foch; if he had been, in all probability there would have been no Second World War.

Hitler said later, "The forty-eight hours after the march into the Rhineland were the most nerve-racking in my life. A retreat on our part would have spelled collapse."

Hitler was correct in this regard, and in fact, World War II could have been prevented if Hitler had been opposed in the Rhineland. As William L. Shirer has written, the consequences of this action by Hitler and the non-action by the French, were immense. It strengthened Hitler immeasurably in his popularity with the German people. Also, he asserted his authority over the German General Staff.

Great Britain had been approached for support by France at the time of the occupation. Great Britain advised doing nothing. Even Anthony Eden, the Foreign Minister, counseled caution. As some pacifist Englishmen would say, "After all they are only going into their own backyard." As Shirer, the foremost authority on Germany of this period, has written, the failure of the Allies to act was a disaster. This was their best chance to stop Hitler and they failed. Hitler believed the Allies would not react, and he was right. It encouraged him in his contempt for them and gave him confidence to take further aggressive action. The other countries in Europe took note. Germany was on the rise and France was evidently afraid to do anything to stop it. For France, it was the beginning of the end. The thought of another war paralyzed France and its leaders.

For Austria, too, it was the beginning of the end. They were next on Hitler's agenda, as they realized, in particular, Dr. Schuschnigg, the Chancellor of Austria.

On February 12, 1938, Dr. Schuschnigg was summoned to meet with Hitler at Berchtesgaden. Hitler, in a rage, gave Schuschnigg an ultimatum which amounted to a virtual takeover of Austria by the Nazis. With no support in sight from anywhere, Schuschnigg signed. Austria was gone. Hitler had won again.

It has to be said that many in Austria welcomed the German takeover. Many were of German heritage, and also there were many who were sympathetic to Germany.

On March 12, 1939, Hitler made a journey to the country where he was born. Hitler, of German heritage, was born at Braunau Am Inn, a small town in Austria near the German border. On his way to Vienna, Hitler was met by jubilant crowds everywhere along the route. He made a triumphal entrance into Vienna on March 14. Vienna, the same city where Hitler had been rejected and ignored when he was a penniless youth, now greeted him with delirious acclaim. Adolph Hitler had come a long way.

The Gestapo immediately began to operate. Over 79,000 people in Vienna were arrested including Dr. Schuschnigg. The Jews were singled out especially for rough treatment.

Austria ceased to exist as a country and was incorporated into the German state as a province. By his annexation of Austria, Hitler gained seven million more people to add to Germany's strength. Many divisions of soldiers were raised from Austria. In addition, another avenue was added to surround Czechoslovakia, his next victim. Hitler was on the march.

There was one man Hitler didn't even consider during his ascent and eventual grasp and use of power. This man, to Hitler, was so far away that he did not appear on Hitler's limited horizon and was therefore of no consequence. With his hungry eye on all the states of Europe and in what sequence to take them over, Hitler did not think about the man across the Atlantic Ocean— Franklin D. Roosevelt. If he ever did think about him, he should have put a little more time and thought into it. Unknown to Hitler, Roosevelt would play a big part in Hitler's and Germany's future.

Franklin D. Roosevelt

Franklin D. Roosevelt was born to James and Sara Delano Roosevelt at Hyde Park in New York State. He was an only child of wealthy parents and was doted on by his mother his whole life; in fact, to a certain extent, Franklin was her whole life. Franklin attended the best schools, Groton and Harvard. While popular, he did not quite seem to fit in; he was not an athlete, and possibly that explains some of it. On graduating from Harvard, Franklin went into law practice.

He met Eleanor Roosevelt, the niece of President Theodore Roosevelt, and after a brief courtship they became engaged. They seemed a somewhat unlikely pair. Franklin was handsome, talkative, and dashing, while Eleanor was quiet, withdrawn, and somewhat plain. In any event, they seemed to get along well; both were very intelligent.

In the Democratic Convention of 1920, the Democrats nominated James Cox as their presidential nominee and Franklin D. Roosevelt for Vice President. This was a considerable achievement by a young man with little political experience. It is said that Franklin was causing the Democratic Party bosses in New York so much trouble that they helped nominate him to get rid of him. In fact, the Democratic Party didn't have a chance in 1920. The Republicans promised a return to normalcy, and that's what the public wanted—Cox and Roosevelt were defeated in a landslide.

Strangely, the whole thing had a positive effect on young Franklin's career; since he was only the vice presidential nominee, the loss was not directed at him. Indeed, his vigorous campaigning had made him many friends all over the country; he was a likable, friendly, and handsome young man. There were, however, some people at that time who considered Roosevelt, even with all his charm, something of a lightweight.

In 1923, at his family vacation retreat on Campobello Island, Franklin was suddenly stricken very ill. In fact, he was almost completely paralyzed. Doctors came and studied him and finally concluded that he had been stricken with infantile paralysis—polio. This terrible disease hit thousands of Americans each year, many of whom died or were seriously handicapped. (The younger brother of the author contracted polio in 1950 at the age of six. It was a life-or-death matter; fortunately, he survived with only a moderate handicap and has lived a very productive life since).

Over a period of time, Roosevelt regained control over his arms and upper body, but he had very little feeling from his waist down. This was a terrible blow to him, his wife, mother, and family. A vital, ambitious young man struck down in the prime of his life. His mother wanted him to end his public life and retire to the estate at Hyde park.

Franklin, Eleanor, and his friend Louis Howe refused to give up. They moved back to New York City and took residence there. Roosevelt continued with all kinds of exercises to improve his condition. It helped to a limited extent; he still could not walk. He took up stamp collecting and still continued to keep up with events. He corresponded with a number of friends and supporters all over the country. In short, he continued an active life. It was a major triumph for him when he gave the nominating speech for Al Smith at the Democratic National Convention, the "Happy Warrior" speech. (When Roosevelt was president, he began a charitable campaign, The March of Dimes, to do research on eliminating polio. A number of years later, this resulted in the Salk and Sabin vaccines, which did eliminate polio.)

Roosevelt and his family and aides took great pains to conceal the extent of his disability from the public. For instance, he was never photographed in a wheelchair—most Americans never thought he had a major disability. His warm smile and charming personality was what came across to the people.

Because of his condition, Franklin became a changed person, both internally and externally. He was more mature; he had more sympathy for people with handicaps and was also more sympathetic to people in general, especially poor people. Although he came from a wealthy background, he seemed to connect with the average people. He and his wife Eleanor were both especially concerned with the plight of Black Americans—Roosevelt can be said to have started the growth of the Civil Rights Movement in the United States. His attitude toward everyone was more considerate and understanding. It was this change of personality and attitude that helped him become President of the United States.

In 1928, Al Smith, the governor of New York, decided to run for President, and he won the Democratic nomination. He wanted Franklin to run for Governor to replace him. This was Roosevelt's big chance; he accepted Smith's request. Smith was resoundingly defeated for President by Herbert Hoover, as 1928 was definitely a Republican year. Prosperity was at its zenith. Contrary to the trend, Roosevelt was elected Governor of New York by a narrow margin. The fact that the Democrat Roosevelt had been elected despite an overall Republican landslide was noted by many people, and the Democrats in particular. Roosevelt looked like a winner, the best asset a politician can have.

In late 1929, the Depression struck. Wall Street virtually collapsed. The country went into a tailspin. Hoover seemed powerless to do anything about it. In 1930, 1931 and 1932 the Depression worsened. Meanwhile, in New York, Roosevelt was doing everything possible to alleviate the suffering of the people. With the limited power he had, he was doing all that he could to help the people. In particular, his attitude of really caring meant a great deal—this was in stark contrast to Hoover, who seemed paralyzed and unfeeling. Hoover seemed to have no idea how to stop the Depression. In 1932, whoever won the Democratic nomination was sure to be President. Roosevelt had gained considerable support by his activist and caring policy in New York, and he had many supporters from his earlier days also. The fact that he was the governor of the largest state in the Union was also a big plus for Roosevelt. The focus of Democrats all over the country seemed to center on Roosevelt.

Franklin D. Roosevelt was nominated for President by the Democrats and won the election in a landslide over Hoover. The Democrats also won the House and Senate by large majorities. Roosevelt, who had been considered by many a few years earlier to be finished, had become President of the United States.

Beginning his presidency in March, 1933, Roosevelt took over at the worst possible time. Twenty-five percent of the people were unemployed; banks were failing left and right. Thousands of farms were being foreclosed while crops rotted in the fields—the country was in a crisis situation.

The main thing Roosevelt as President brought to the people was a sense of optimism and hope. That things were going to get better, slowly but surely. He surrounded himself with the best brains in the country. "Eggheads." He put in the W.P.A. to give people work on public projects, the Social Security system, unemployment insurance, the Wage and Hour Law, assistance for the farmers, and the Tennessee Valley Authority, which built power and hydroelectric plants in the South, the poorest part of the country. He improved the banking and financial systems, which helped bring confidence back to these institutions. Roosevelt believed in the free enterprise system and with government help was trying to get it back on its feet along with everyone else. His overall program was called The New Deal. He believed in trying things; if it didn't work, try something else. The country slowly began to get better. In 1936, Roosevelt was reelected in another landslide, one of the largest in American history. People knew that Roosevelt was doing everything he could to improve the condition of the country. His attitude of optimism, in itself, was a big help to the country.

Roosevelt had another big asset. Radios were now in most homes in the country. Ever so often, Roosevelt would deliver a speech to the country over the radio. A "Fireside Chat." This reached millions of people. Roosevelt had a great voice and a wonderful delivery; he told people the problems and what he was trying to do about them. He exuded a sense of calm confidence that it could be done. In short, he lifted the spirits of the people during the crisis. The author can recall as a young boy in the 1930s and 1940s listening to Roosevelt's chats along with his family. When his speech was finished, I was sure we were going to win no matter what—particularly with F.D.R. in charge. The country was gradually but surely working its way out of the worst depression ever, and it was due to the efforts of Franklin D. Roosevelt. It can definitely be said that Roosevelt was anything but a lightweight. He was a strong, effective leader and a tremendous politician. In fact, he was the greatest politician in American history.

Some people may say Roosevelt was a great actor and there may be a grain of truth in that, but he was essentially a charming and powerful personality that one sees once and may never see again. The following is a speech given during the 1936 election which illustrates Roosevelt's masterful blend of ridicule and humor to demolish his opponents, the me-too Republicans. The Republicans had previously opposed Roosevelt's social reforms, but now seeing they were popular, wanted to jump on the bandwagon. This speech was Roosevelt's reply and was delivered in a low key, mocking tone, which was very effective.

Let me warn the nation against the smooth evasion which says, 'Of course we believe in all these things; we believe in Social Security; we believe in work for the unemployed; we believe in saving homes. Cross our hearts and hope to die; we believe in all these things; but we do not like the way the present administration is doing them. Just turn them all over to us. We will do all of them—we will do more of them—we will do them better; and, most important of all, the doing of them will not cost anybody anything.

In the 1936 election Roosevelt won 46 states, the Republicans 2. Roosevelt, the paternal aristocrat, had somehow bonded with the average man on the street. (Churchill was not like Roosevelt in this respect. Churchill, the eternal aristocrat, lived in an entirely different world from the average Englishman, in fact, he was somewhat appalled at the life of ordinary English people.)

To illustrate Roosevelt's belief that the Government should make every effort to make life better for the average person, Roosevelt said: "Better the occasional faults of a Government that lives in a spirit of charity than the constant omission of a Government frozen in the ice of its own indifference."

Roosevelt marked a turning point in American history. He would forever change the role of Government and the Presidency in American life. Roosevelt would leave his mark not only on America, but on the world as well—the United States would emerge as the foremost power in the world.

There were some political observers who said that Roosevelt had no administrative talent. That he presided in an ad hoc, chaotic way. At times he would give one of his aides an assignment and then later give another aide the same one. There was a sense of a great deal of activity in many directions. Through it all, Roosevelt remained calm, cheerful and optimistic. There was one thing that came through—that his pragmatic way of operating seemed to work. Despite what his critics said, Roosevelt was a highly intelligent man— he knew what he was doing and where he was going at all times.

Surrounded by people and under the umbrella of his charming demeanor, Roosevelt actually lived in his own world, a world that was on such a high plane that only one man shared it—Winston Churchill. The single most important thing they shared was their awareness of the gravity of the world situation. They had to save the world from the worst tyranny in history. If they failed, the consequences were unimaginable.

In 1940, with war clouds gathering, Roosevelt was elected to an unprecedented third term. Wealthy people mostly hated him, while most ordinary people loved him. He cared about them and was trying to help them. Roosevelt had become President in one of the direst times in the country's history, both domestically and in foreign affairs. He met both of these crises head-on in a wonderful and brilliant way. Just as Churchill had come at the right time for England, so Roosevelt had come at the right time for America.

Winston Churchill

There was one man who could have stopped Hitler and prevented the catastrophe of World War II. That man was Winston Spencer Churchill. Unfortunately the British ignored his early and repeated warnings of the menace of Hitler's Germany. They did not call on the genius in their midst until May, 1940, when the roof was falling in on them. It was almost too late.

It might be well to note here that at a very early age Winston showed no promise at all. In fact, it seems his father, whom he adored, had a very low opinion of Winston. He noticed young Winston played with toy soldiers a lot; it seemed to be his one interest. So, Randolph Churchill sent his son to

Sandhurst, not knowing what else to do with him. Winston went to India as a young officer to serve the Empire.

Winston, as he matured, became a very well-informed, ambitious young man. As his mother was an American, he was particularly drawn to the United States. His mother was a great help and a strong supporter of Winston.

The Making of a Hero

"How unhappy is that poor man who loses his liberty! What can the wide world give him in exchange? Before I had been an hour in captivity I resolved to escape." These are the words of young Winston Churchill as he was imprisoned by the Boers during the Boer War.

The author recounts an episode in the life of Churchill that seems to sum up what he was all about. Character, courage, perseverance, and resourcefulness.

The Boer War started in October, 1899, when the Orange Free State joined the South African Republic in declaring war on Britain. Bad feeling had existed for some time between the Boers, or Dutch farmers, and "Uitlanders," foreigners, mainly the British. When gold was discovered, it brought more British into the region. Continued conflicts between the Dutch and the English settlers resulted in the Boer War. The English Army went in on the side of the British emigrants. The Boers were initially successful, and the British brought in more troops; it then developed into a full-blown war.

How did young Winston wind up in a Boer prison camp? It began on October 14, 1899, when Winston sailed from Southampton. His destination was Cape Town. Winston was sailing as a war correspondent for the *Morning Post*. They had made Winston a handsome financial proposal, and Winston told his mother, "I am at their disposal." This trip was, in the end, to gain him international fame, a seat in Parliament, and led him eventually to be Prime Minister of Great Britain.

Churchill made his way as best he could toward Ladysmith, which by that time had been cut off. He was forced to put up at the outpost town of Estcourt with other fellow journalists, including his long-time friend, Leo Amery. Leo Amery was to later point at Neville Chamberlain in Parliament in May, 1940, and utter the unforgettable words, "In the name of God—go!" This was the end of Chamberlain as Prime Minister who was replaced by Winston Spencer Churchill.

Another friend at Estcourt was Captain Aylomar Haldane, who was on duty there. There indications that the Boers might attack Estcourt. Haldane was ordered to take out the armored train as a reconnaissance. Haldane was not too happy with this assignment. While the armored train looked impressive, it was very vulnerable to any obstacle placed in its path. The soldiers regarded it as a "death trap." Naturally, Captain Haldane was going to carry out his assignment and asked Winston to come along. Churchill realized that this was not a healthy venture but decided to go along. He asked his friend, Leo Amery, to come with them. Amery was definite in his reply that he had no reason to go on such a risky operation—he could end up in an enemy prison camp.

"That is perfectly true," agreed Churchill. "But I have a feeling, a sort of intuition, that if I go something will come of it. It's illogical, I know."

The train steamed out of Estcourt early on the morning of November 15 with Haldane, Churchill, and 120 soldiers. A few hours later, they steamed into Chevely Station. Churchill spotted a column of mounted Boers toward the railway at their rear, and at the same time a row of black spots lining a hill above the station. Haldane was instructed by telegraph to return. The train was put into reverse. Two miles later, Churchill again spotted the enemy, who opened fire. The train was careening down a steep grade when it came to a jolting and crashing stop. Rifle fire was peppering the train from three directions. Jumping into the hail of fire, Churchill tried to determine the extent of damage to the train.

One car of the train was half on and half off the tracks. It was obvious to Churchill that the car had to be pushed aside by the engine for them to get away. First, he had to persuade the engineer, who in the midst of the gunfire was trying to make his own escape. Although the engineer's face was bloody, Churchill talked him into getting back into the cab.

The engineer had a very difficult time getting the damaged car off the rails. Churchill ran up and down the line, under fire, rapping out orders to the men and the engineer. He was phenomenally calm. Everyone present paid tribute to his cool courage. Without him, all would be lost.

The only thing that could be moved out the chaos was the engine and the tender. This was crowded with as many men as possible. Haldane and a number of his men were left behind. Churchill, unintentionally, was caught on the engine as it steamed away; he was wedged among wounded men. The engine finally stopped at Freer Station; Churchill jumped out and started to run back to the scene of action.

Haldane with fifty of his men by that time had been forced to surrender. Unaware of this, Churchill came running down the line. He saw two civilians approaching who opened fire. He was trapped in a small gorge. Churchill decided to run towards more open ground and escape. As he jumped up, a horseman came riding up towards him, aiming his rifle and shouting to Winston to stop. Churchill reached for his pistol, but it was gone. The Boer had him covered. He had no alternative but to give up. Years later, more than 43 different Boers claimed to have been the horseman who captured Churchill.

Churchill was joined with Captain Haldane and the other captured British. He tried to explain to his captors that as he was a newspaper correspondent, he should be released. Unfortunately, one of his captors recognized Winston's name and connected it with Lord Randolph Churchill, his father. Winston was now, unexpectedly, a prized prisoner.

Meanwhile, back at Estcourt, Leo Amery and his friend J. B. Atkins had heard the sound of gunfire when the train had been attacked. They started towards the scene and shortly met the engine coming back. The soldiers on the engine were full of praise for Churchill, especially his coolness under fire. They gave him credit that they had come back alive. They also told Amery and Atkins that Winston had been captured going back to help Haldane and his men.

Word from Amery and Atkins sped quickly by telegraph to England. Instantly, Winston became a national hero. Several newspapers suggested that he be given the Victoria Cross. No longer Lord Randolph's son, he was now a hero in his own right. Unfortunately, this instant fame made him an even more valuable prisoner to the Boers.

On the long, arduous march into captivity at Pretoria, Churchill and Haldane were generously treated by all who came in contact with them. Churchill had been shot in the hand, and a doctor noticed it and treated it. Churchill began to feel a certain admiration for the enemy. Later, one of the top Boers, Jan Christaan Smuts, became one of Churchill's best friends and a confidant.

In prison at Pretoria, Churchill continued to no avail to demand his release because he was a newspaper correspondent. Although captivity for the British prisoners was very boring, they were treated well. Churchill, however, hated being confined. His fiery, free spirit rebelled against it. Escape became his foremost thought.

Haldane and a Sergeant-Major Brockie had a plan to escape, and Winston convinced them to add him to the plan. The plan was to escape through the lavatory and then scale a six-foot corrugated iron fence. The risk was that periodically, sentries patrolled the area.

On December 12, they decided to make the escape that evening. However, in the lavatory at the appointed time, they noticed sentries nearby. Haldane and Brockie decided it was too risky to attempt the escape and left the lavatory. Churchill remained and waited. Half an hour passed. Then, one sentry strolled over to talk to his companion. Their backs were to Churchill. Standing on a ledge, he gripped the top of the fence and with all his strength was able to pull himself over. He crouched on the other aide and decided to wait for Haldane and Brockie.

Haldane was not aware that Churchill had escaped. He looked for him in the prison but couldn't find him. However, another officer told him that Churchill had escaped as planned. Haldane then tried to escape, but a sentry saw him on the roof of he lavatory and at rifle point ordered him down. Incidentally, the guards made no attempt to see if any other prisoners had escaped. Churchill strolled through the gate of the prison. A sentry was there nearby, but did nothing. Churchill was free—to some extent.

Walking through Pretoria, he headed south and came to a railway. He decided to wait for a train heading north. Eventually, a train did come along, and Winston was able to haul himself into a moving car. It was carrying empty coal sacks back to the colliery. Winston buried himself in the sacks and went to sleep.

When he awoke, he decided to jump off the train before daylight. The train was traveling at a fair speed, but Winston jumped off and was unhurt. He holed up for the day and that night waited for another train, but none came. Dispirited, he began to walk. After several miles, he came upon a mining camp. Hungry and miserable, Winston decided to take a chance and knocked on the nearest door. By an incredible streak of luck, the man that opened the door was English. He name was John Howard, manager of the coal mine. The Boers were aware that he was English, and he was under close scrutiny; he could be shot for aiding an escaped prisoner. Churchill told him of his plight, and Howard offered to help him escape.

Howard took him to the mine, where he led Winston to the bottom of the pit. Churchill felt safe at the bottom of the mine, even though the rats were his only company.

Meanwhile, back at the prison camp, Churchill's disappearance was finally noted. Churchill left a letter thanking the Boers for their hospitality. The Boers were outraged. Word of his escape was announced far and wide. A poster was distributed with his picture and the words, "Churchill dead or alive 25 pounds." Winston was in the bottom of the mine for three days. Finally, the close confinement and his friends, the rats, were beginning to get on his nerves. Howard moved him to a storeroom at the back of the house.

After a discussion, it was decided to hide Winston in a shipment of wool consigned to Lourenco Marques in Portuguese West Africa. Churchill was smuggled onto the train and set out on the long journey of 300 miles. After many hours of travel and suspense, the train crossed the border and Churchill was really a free man. He went immediately to the British Consulate, where he was royally treated. Churchill sent a wire to the Boer government announcing his safe arrival. On December 22 he boarded the SS Indiana, which docked at Durban, where he was given a hero's welcome.

Churchill had by now become famous. His escape had captured the imagination of the world. Even in America, where pro-Boer feeling ran high, his courage and daring evoked widespread admiration.

Churchill went on to be elected to Parliament in 1902 and quickly became one of its leading members. In 1911, at the age of thirty-seven, he was appointed First Lord of the Admiralty. Truly, Churchill's intuition that a ride on an armored train would somehow be to his advantage proved to be absolutely correct.

All of the traits that a great leader needs were shown by Churchill in his episode in the Boer War. Included are courage, determination, high intelligence, and perseverance. These traits were to serve England well in the dark days of 1940 as Prime Minister of Great Britain.

Churchill refused to give up in South Africa, and he refused to give up facing the might of Hitler's Germany alone. The world is indebted to him.

Churchill—The Dardanelles 1915

An important episode in Churchill's life, possibly the most significant one until May, 1940, was the Dardanelles operation of the First War. It cast a cloud over his reputation that continued for many years. It is very possible that Churchill would have become Prime Minister much earlier, say in the 1920s, if not for the failure of the Dardanelles operation.

The Dardanelles is a narrow strait between Europe and Asia and was part of Turkey. As Turkey was now allied with Germany in 1915, it was enemy territory to the Allies, very valuable territory.

Churchill is regarded as the main proponent of the attack on the Dardanelles, but the operation was backed by almost all of the members of the government. They were looking for a way to defeat Germany without sustaining the heavy casualties that were mounting on the Western Front. Each yard of ground there was bought in blood with no end in sight.

It was actually Admiral Fisher, First Sea Lord of the Admiralty, who in a note to Churchill on January 3, 1915, first proposed using the Navy to free the Dardanelles and occupy Constantinople at the eastern end. Churchill had previously felt that the Army should be used in the undertaking. Now, his chief naval adviser was telling him that the Navy could do it. Lord Kitchener would not support the operation with troops, saying he had none to spare. Time would show this was not an accurate statement, but at this time in 1915, that was Kitchener's reply to Churchill. According to Kitchener, it was a naval affair.

The goals of the Dardanelles operation were:

1. To establish communication with Russia. Vital supplies could be sent to Russia, who was floundering, to keep her in the war. An Eastern Front was vital to the Western powers, because if it did not exist, all of Germany's power could be turned on them—possibly with terrible consequences. The war could be lost, in fact.

2. To knock Turkey out of the war—one less ally for Germany. This would allow resources used against the Turks to be turned against Germany and Austria.

3. To draw Greece and then Balkan and Mediterranean countries into the war on the Allied side. A new front could be opened to attack the Central powers from the south.

All in all, the Dardanelles operation, if successful, would be a large step toward winning the war. The most momentous decision in regard to this operation was whether it could be done by naval action alone or whether ground troops would be needed also.

Churchill's position was that his navy said they could do it alone, and meanwhile Kitchener would offer no troops to make it a joint undertaking. It was either try it with the Navy alone or call off the operation.

Enthusiasm was high in nearly all concerned. It was decided not only by Churchill but also by the War Cabinet to undertake the operation with the Navy. This was on January 28, 1915. Unfortunately, when the operation did not succeed, it was considered a Churchill operation. He was made the scapegoat, while everyone else headed for cover, Lloyd George and Fisher included.

Admiral Carden was in charge of the attack, and he felt it would be successful. A large fleet of British and French ships was gathered and the bombardment of the outer forts began on February 19. In the meanwhile, the Turks were very concerned and had called in German advisers to help, and they played a critical role in the battle. Admiral Tirpitz said the war was at stake.

The bombardment of the outer forts was successful, and they were destroyed—a good beginning. Admiral Carden decided to make the main attack on March 18. However, under severe strain, Admiral Carden collapsed and was succeeded by Admiral John de Robeck.

In the days before the attack, mine sweeping operations were conducted to ensure the safe passage of the fleet. Here it was that fate took a hand. Many of the navy personnel were inexperienced in this type of operation. However, all seemed well until shortly before the operation began, a small Turkish steamer, the Nourset, laid twenty mines parallel to the shore. Unfortunately, the Allies were not aware of this critical development.

On the morning of the 18th, six British and four French battleships began the attack. They were met with artillery fire from the Turkish batteries directed by their German advisers. The French battleship Bouvet was hit by a salvo and sunk. In quick succession, two British battleships and one French ran into mines left by the Nourset. The British ships sank, and the French battleship was also seriously damaged and had to be beached. Disaster had struck in just a relatively few minutes. De Robeck prudently withdrew the remainder of his fleet. The Turkish loss was minuscule, but they had almost run out of ammunition.

De Robeck intended to renew the assault the next day; however, bad weather intervened. In the meanwhile, General Ian Hamilton was on the scene. He was Lord Kitchener's observer. He wired Kitchener that he didn't believe the Navy could do the job by itself and that troops would be needed.

Churchill was ready for another try by the Navy but was overruled. Kitchener was now in the saddle, and Churchill was relegated to the sidelines. Naval activities were suspended while a large army under General Hamilton was organized. The surprise element was all over; of course, the Turks were building up their forces as well as including more Germans. General Leman von Sanders arrived to direct the Turkish army. It was a whole new ball game. By the time the British were ready to attack, General von Sanders had 84,000 troops ready to meet them, six times more men than were there March 18. General Hamilton assembled approximately 70,000 British, French, Australian, and New Zealand troops.

The invasion attack took place on April 25 at several different beaches at Gallipoli. Most of the landings were virtually unopposed. However, at V Beach many casualties were caused by machine gun fire. As Turkish reinforcements rushed up, heavy fighting began all along the invasion front. At one point, it looked as if the British would prevail and achieve victory, but their commander hesitated to take advantage of the opportunity.

A savage battle now developed with General von Sanders and the Turks determined to drive the Allies into the sea. Reinforcement rushed in from both sides. The Allied landing had succeeded but appeared to be confined to a small area. The hope for a quick victory for the Allies at the Dardanelles was over. Their objectives had not been achieved. The operation was a failure.

Meanwhile, British naval forces were taking losses. The battleship Goliath was torpedoed and sunk by a Turkish destroyer; 470 seamen were killed. Twelve days later, the battleship Triumph was sunk by a German submarine. Two days after that, another U-boat sank the battleship Majestic. The Dardanelles was turning into a nightmare for the British.

About this time, Admiral Fisher despaired over the operation and wanted to pull out. A row erupted between Fisher and Lord Kitchener. Fisher resigned.

At the same time, reports of a shortage of shells on the Western Front became known. Because of this and the failure of the Dardanelles campaign, Prime Minister Asquith was put under pressure to form a new cabinet and a coalition government. As a price for joining the new government, the Conservatives insisted that Churchill had to go. This was done, and thus Churchill was out of the government. Eventually, the Allies had to withdraw from Gallipoli after suffering thousands upon thousands of casualties.

Of course, all this amounted to a tremendous failure. Churchill became the target of nearly all of the criticism. Somehow, his name was linked to the Dardanelles. It was very convenient for all the other politicians and military officials. Remember that Churchill at no time had complete control of the operation. He had to work with others, but he wound up receiving the blame. If the naval attack had been supported by army units at the beginning, it had a good chance of being successful. Bad luck such as the newly laid mines also played a part.

In any event, Churchill left the government and went to the front lines in France as a major. It seemed his career was over.

However, as time passed, cooler heads prevailed. David Lloyd George became Prime Minister. He brought Churchill back into his government as Minister of Munitions, where Churchill did an excellent job. The invention and use of the tank was Churchill's idea. However, the cloud of the Dardanelles seemed to have wrapped itself around him. This held him back from advancing to the highest post in government. On May 10, 1940, his chance came. The British were looking for a fighter, and Churchill was there.

Churchill—1930s

After the First War, Churchill held several important offices in the conservative government, including the high office of Chancellor of the Exchequer. His father, Randolph Churchill, had held this same office forty years earlier.

Many who have held this office have gone on as the next step to become Prime Minister. However, the Conservatives lost in the 1929 election, and Churchill left office not to return to a cabinet position until 1939. During this period, he was an active member of Parliament. As the years progressed and he was not in a prominent position, Churchill's star seemed to wane. By his positions on the fear of a rising Germany, the Indian question, and the abdication of Edward VIII, Churchill became somewhat isolated, even within his own party. His followers were few.

At this time, Churchill also had to consider his own financial situation. With a large family and the fact that he liked a high standard of living, Churchill had to struggle to keep everything going financially. Fortunately, he was an excellent writer and wrote a number of books, including a four-volume history of the war entitled *World Crisis*. As to his high standard of living, Churchill would say, "My wants are simple, I only want the very best of everything." And he managed somehow to live that way.

Although he was not in office, Churchill very actively kept abreast of world affairs, particularly European affairs. He made many speeches in the House of Commons. Although most members didn't agree with him, they appreciated his remarks. Churchill had a skillful command of the English language and a sharp sense of humor, sometimes at the expense of the other members and officials. At any rate, Churchill was so much better and more interesting as a speaker than anyone else, that the Parliament members all looked forward to his discourses. They didn't agree too much with what he said, but they liked the way he said it.

Churchill's preoccupations during the 1930s were, in order: (1) Germany; (2) the possible breakup of the Empire which was focused in India; (3) Communist Russia. Of the three, his main interest, by far, was Germany. He noted that at the end of the war the German state that had caused so much trouble was still virtually intact. What was there to prevent Germany from taking the same course over again?

Churchill highly respected Germany and the German people. They were tough soldiers; they were efficient and determined. If someone who was smarter than the Kaiser became the head of this potentially very effective war machine, then things could turn grim in a short time. Germany had come close to defeating almost all of Europe in the First War—what would happen if she tried it again with better leadership?

So, Churchill never took his eyes off the main threat to England—a resurgent Germany. In particular, he was alarmed by attempts at disarming the French Army. The French Army was the one thing that stood between Germany and England.

In May, 1932, Churchill gave his first warning of approaching war. (What vision he had!—author's note). In a speech to the House of Commons, he said at the conclusion:

> I should very much regret any approximation in military strength between Germany and France. Those who speak of that as though it were right, or even a question of fair dealing, altogether underrate the gravity of the European situation. I would like to say to those who would like to see Germany and France on an equal footing in armaments 'Do you wish for war?' For my part, I earnestly hope that no such approximation will take place during my lifetime or that of my children. To say that it is not in the least to imply any want of regard for the great qualities of the German people, but I am sure that the thesis that they should be placed in an equal military position with France is one, which, if ever emerged in fact, would bring us within practical distanceof almost measureless calamity.

This in 1932. Churchill was so far ahead of everyone else, it is mind-boggling. Too bad, too bad they didn't listen.

Churchill was particularly interested in the air situation. He perceived that the air could become a decisive factor in a future war. On learning the British Air estimates of March, 1933, he was alarmed by the lack of comprehension of everyone involved. On March 14, 1933, he said:

> I regretted to hear the Under-Secretary say that we were only the fifth air power, and that the ten-year programme was suspended for another year. I was sorry to hear him boast that the Air Ministry had not laid down a single new unit this year. All these ideas are being increasingly stultified by the march of events, and we should be well advised to concentrate upon our air defenses with great vigour.

In another speech on March 23, 1933, Churchill said:

Thank God for the French Army. When we read about Germany, when we watch with surprise and distress the tumultuous insurgence of ferocity and war spirit, the pitiless ill treatment of minorities, the denial of normal protections of civilized society, the persecution of large numbers of individuals solely on the grounds of race—when we see all that occurring in one of the most gifted, learned, and scientific and formidable nations in the world, one cannot help feeling glad that the fierce passions that are raging in Germany have not yet found any other outlet but upon themselves.

This was in 1933, when Hitler was just getting started! Churchill says that he particularly remembers the look of pain and aversion which he saw on the faces of members in all parts of the House when he said, "Thank God for the French Army."

It must have been intensely frustrating for Churchill. He could foresee what was going to happen even then at the beginning of Hitler's reign, but he could do nothing about it. However, there may have been one man across the Atlantic who was listening, and a very important man—Franklin D. Roosevelt, President of the United States.

Again, in March, 1934, on hearing that the R.A.F. would be increased by only forty planes that year, Churchill said:

I dread the day when the means of threatening the heart of the British Empire should pass into the hands of the present rulers of Germany . . . I dread that day, but it is not far distant . . . This is the time we should take the necessary measures. No nation playing the part we play and aspire to play in the world has a right to be in a position where it can be blackmailed [1938 Chamberlain at Munich].

Stanley Baldwin, the Prime Minister, replied, ". . . that this government will see to it that in air power this country shall no longer be in a position inferior to any country within striking distance of its shores." Churchill took this to heart and hoped the government would fulfill its pledge. The life of Great Britain could depend on it.

When later in 1934 the government made a belated and inadequate proposal for strengthening the R.A.F., the Labor Party, supported by the liberals, attacked the government for doing so. The attack was made by the Labor Party leader, Clement Attlee (future Prime Minister). Mr. Attlee said, "We deny the need for increased air armaments. We deny the proposition that an increased British air force will make for the peace of the world, and we reject altogether the claim to parity." In later years, the Labor Party blamed the Conservative government for failure to provide for national security. No wonder in 1940 they all turned to Churchill. He was one of a very few not responsible for getting Britain into such a peril that is life was at stake. In fact, he had tried his very best to avoid this dangerous situation and had been jeered for his efforts.

In regard to the air, on May 22, 1935, Mr. Baldwin admitted that he had been mistaken about the German air force and that now they had caught up and were surpassing the strength of the R.A.F. The Labor Party was undaunted by this confession. Mr. Attlee said, in effect, that they weren't concerned about armaments; they were concerned about disarmament. Their aim was the reduction of armaments. This would be fine indeed if Hitler would do the same on his own. Of course, in the meantime, while Mr. Attlee was making these statements, Hitler was in the midst of a vast rearmament program, especially in the air.

Evidently, Mr. Attlee was counting on that very strong institution, the League of Nations, which had in its lifetime accomplished absolutely nothing— pitiful. In fact, Germany no longer even belonged to the League of Nations. What fools we mortals be.

Churchill, in a letter to his wife Clementine, sarcastically points out the cynicism and defeatism that permeates the higher circles in England at this time:

Rothmere rings me up everyday. His anxiety is pitiful. He thinks the Germans are all powerful and the French are corrupt and useless, and the English hopeless and doomed. He proposes to meet the situation by groveling to Germany. 'Dear Germany, do destroy us last!' I endeavor to inculcate a more robust attitude.

On June 8, 1935, Stanley Baldwin asked Churchill to become a member of the Air Defense Research Committee, which Churchill accepted. During this period, research scientist Professor Watson-Watt had developed the idea of detection of aircraft by radio waves (radar). This plan, under urging by Churchill, was adopted, and by 1939 the Air Ministry had constructed the so-called coastal chain, which enabled Britain to detect approaching aircraft while they were still many miles distant. Also, an elaborate network of telephonic communication had been installed, linking the twenty radar stations with the headquarters of Fighter command.

What would England have done without this system in 1940? Lost, perhaps.

On March 7, 1936, another momentous development occurred. Hitler marched into the Rhineland. The British and French governments reacted vigorously. . . . They made a strong complaint to the League of Nations! Take that!

French Foreign Minister Flandin flew to London. Mr. Flandin, representing France, was ready to act against Germany. If Germany weren't stopped now, it would be too late—it would be all over. Flandin believed he needed the support of England before acting. Baldwin replied that the British people did not want war; they wanted peace. No support from England would be given. With that, Flandin gave up. Hitler had been right about the allied reaction, and he had succeeded in his daring gamble.

With this development in the Rhineland, Churchill's stock began to rise. In fact, there was much talk of bringing him into government. Then, a completely unrelated and unexpected event cast Churchill down again, somewhat of his own making.

Churchill was a personal friend of King Edward VIII. He liked the King and felt himself bound to support him. The King had fallen in love with a divorced woman, Mrs. Simpson. Since the Church of England would not marry them, it put the whole country in a huge state of turmoil. Some were for the King, some against. No one was neutral. Controversy covered the country—everything else stopped.

Churchill expressed his support for the King. In the meanwhile, Prime Minister Baldwin had deftly moved behind the scenes to settle the explosive situation. He forced the King to abdicate. The King's brother, George VI, assumed the throne in May, 1937.

At the end of all this, Churchill's career had hit rock bottom. His strong defense of Edward VIII had brought about universal criticism of Churchill. Some felt that Churchill was at last finished. In any event, Churchill's drive to re-arm and face up to the Germans was given a huge setback. The hero was Stanley Baldwin. The episode of abdication was a big distraction to the main dire events building up in Europe, and it set back England's intentions to focus on these much more important events.

On May 28, Baldwin retired. His successor was Neville Chamberlain, the Chancellor of the Exchequer. While Baldwin had held the office of Prime Minister, Chamberlain was, in effect, running the government. Now, he was officially in charge.

In many ways, he was quite different from the colorless Baldwin. Chamberlain was vigorous, forceful, and self-confident. Actually, some people thought he was too self-confident. He had his own opinions and seemed impervious to any other advice.

However, he did agree with Baldwin in international affairs. That is, the appeasement of Hitler. Chamberlain also believed in a tight control of military expenditure; unfortunately, just the opposite of Hitler. Chamberlain as Prime Minister might have been all right in normal times; but unknown to him, England was about to face the strongest and most dangerous event in it history. Chamberlain was the wrong man in the wrong place at the wrong time.

His main mistake was in thinking you could do business with Hitler from a very weak position. You couldn't. Chamberlain found that out late, and almost too late for his country. He had a noble goal of maintaining peace, but he was dealing with a madman beyond his comprehension. Nevertheless, he was in control of English policy at this time, and events took their course.

Anthony Eden at this time was Foreign Secretary and had been active in the Baldwin government. He retained his post in Chamberlain's government. Chamberlain had his own strong views about foreign affairs; he began to encroach on Eden's office and act on his own in foreign affairs.

This produced a collision. By this time, Eden had become distrustful of Hitler and the entire appeasement policy. Eden was ready to take a stronger stand against Hitler, while Chamberlain's policy was just the opposite. A tense situation developed—each man believed firmly in his own ideas; in particular, Eden was for a stronger build-up of the military. During this period, Eden and Churchill began to draw closer together, which didn't make Chamberlain happy.

Once, Eden, having become alarmed over the slow rearmament of England, tried to express his concerns directly with Chamberlain, who told him to "go home and take an aspirin."

The increasing problem between Eden and Chamberlain was causing dissension in the government. The final straw came when President Roosevelt wanted to convene the representatives of various governments in Washington in order to head off a new world war. Roosevelt was sticking his neck out. He waited for the British reply.

In effect, Chamberlain's reply was a brush-off. He intimated that England would handle the problems and didn't need any help—a rejection of Roosevelt's and America's help, very stupid and arrogant on Chamberlain's part. Eden, who was on vacation at the time, had not been consulted on this important development. When he returned to London and found out about it, he was furious. Eden wanted to get America's involvement in Europe; he felt a crisis coming on. England could use all the help it could get, especially from the United States.

Other events intervened at this time as well, such as relations with Italy and also the Austrian situation. Finally, the gulf between Eden and Chamberlain was so large and contentious that one of them had to go. As Chamberlain was Prime Minister, it was Eden who went.

Eden resigned on February 20, 1938, and was replaced by Chamberlain's friend, Lord Halifax, another appeaser, and another big mistake by Chamberlain. Churchill received a phone call on that night at his home in Chartwell, informing him that Eden had resigned.

As we all know, Churchill was a very strong man, particularly in adversity. However, when he heard the news about Eden, he said his heart sank and dark waters of despair overwhelmed him. He said that in a long life he had had many ups and downs and had been able to cope with them and could sleep well knowing that in the morning he would grapple with the challenge. But on the night of February 29, 1938, he could not sleep. He lay awake all night, consumed by emotions of fear and sorrow. Eden, the one strong young figure standing up against the tides of drift and surrender, was out of the government. To Churchill, Eden represented the best of the British race, and now he was gone. Only bad things could follow.

Churchill felt that now, without Eden, things would go from bad to the worst—and they did.

Munich

In Munich on September 29, 1938, Neville Chamberlain along with the Premier of France, Eduoard Daladier, made an historic visit to meet with the Chancellor of Germany, Adolph Hitler. Hitler was accompanied by his ally Benito Mussolini, who had arranged the meeting. After devouring Austria, Germany was on the verge of attacking Czechoslovakia in a dispute over the Sudetenland. The Sudetenland was a province of Czechoslovakia inhabited mostly by Germans. Hitler's goal just as it was in annexing Austria, was to unite all Germans into one state—Germany. This he was determined to do one way or the other, politically or militarily. Indeed, plans for and movement of forces had already begun to invade Czechoslovakia when Chamberlain arrived at Munich. Much of the world expected war to break out in the next few days. The Royal Navy was put on alert.

Neville Chamberlain has been much discredited and even reviled for his decisions at Munich. However, it is useful to understand his position and the position of England at the time.

The great majority of the English people did not want war. For instance, in 1933 the students at Oxford had passed a resolution "that they refused to fight for King and country." I'm sure that years later they regretted this, but at the time it made a strong negative impression of England on Hitler and Mussolini. Britain's remembrance of World War I was too close at hand. The ghastly losses at Ypres, Passchendaele, and other forlorn places in France—losses that affected nearly every home in England—made the thought of a similar blood-letting too much to contemplate, particularly considering that these losses would be, as Chamberlain said, "in a land Czechoslovakia that is far from us and people unknown to us." It simply wasn't worth a world war to Chamberlain and the English people.

In particular, the hand that Chamberlain was playing at this time must be remembered. In 1938, the British army was one of the smallest in the world. While its navy was strong, the navy could have no effect on a great land battle in Europe. The air force was still small, although growing with the addition of Hurricanes and Spitfires—still not a formidable force at the time in 1938. The poor condition of the armed forces can be laid to Chamberlain and his predecessor, Stanley Baldwin, who refused to recognize the growing and menacing strength of Hitler's Germany. Chamberlain had put himself and his country in a perilous condition by his own and Baldwin's failures. Churchill had warned them, but they would not listen to him.

Incredibly, the victors of the First War were going to Munich as supplicants to the enemy they had defeated—Germany. It was as if the war had not even happened. By his fear tactics, Hitler won an amazing victory—he had wiped out the results of the last war without firing a shot. The suffering and deaths of millions had been in vain.

Thus, Chamberlain arrived at Munich with a very weak hand, in fact, almost no hand at all. The English people did not want war, and his armed force was weak, especially the army, which was almost non-existent.

The fact is that Great Britain, while thought of as a great power, was no longer a great power. The enormous effort and losses of the previous war had been too much. Great Britain was a great power in name only. It was trying to play the part but did not have the resources to back it up. Thus, for Chamberlain, to guarantee the protection of Czechoslovakia by England would be meaningless. He had no way to back it up (witness Poland in 1939).

The French were supposed to have the best army in Europe (augmented by the Maginot Line). However, the French, from their experience in the previous war, knew that they could not defeat the more numerous Germans by themselves. They knew they had to have an ally as in World War I, i.e., the British. The French were aware that England at that time could not provide them with any substantial assistance but hoped that over time, England would be able to, as in the previous war. Therefore, the French at Munich were led in their decisions by the views of Great Britain. Too much so.

It must be remembered that in the First World War, England had played a tremendous part in the struggle. British and Empire troops had defeated Turkey. They were a substantial part of the Allied forces at Salonica that had knocked Bulgaria out of the war; the domino theory did actually occur in World War I.

There were British troops on the Italian Front to bolster Italy. In France, 55 British and Empire divisions were in place. In fact, the decisive battles in the latter part of 1918 were not won by the French and Americans, but by the British army under Haig. Indeed, Great Britain at the end of the war was the greatest and most extensive power on the globe.

Following the war, rapid demobilization occurred and the power of 1918 was never to return. As mentioned, the enormous losses had sapped the Empire; they had expended their all to defeat Germany. The men that were lost over the world were not there to father the children to fight the next one. To some extent, after 1918, except for its navy, Great Britain was an empire in name only—the shell and reputation alone remained.

Thus, the options that Chamberlain had at Munich are boiled down to two. One was to go to war, which the majority of his people opposed, and with an armed force which, compared to Germany's, was appallingly weak. Also, Chamberlain's personal opinion of the French was one of disdain. The other option was to continue the appeasement policy. So far, that policy had been able to avoid world war, which Chamberlain believed would be disastrous for England.

Of the two options, Chamberlain chose the latter. Under the circumstances, he almost had no choice. Chamberlain reflected the will and thinking of the English people at that time. He had two options, both bad. He took the one he felt was the least terrible of the two. It is well also to remember that Chamberlain himself was a pacifist. To go against his own and his people's thinking was pretty much impossible. On a personal level, Chamberlain and Hitler lived in two different worlds. Chamberlain had no idea that he was dealing with someone who was close to being a madman. He had never met the likes of Hitler and was totally out of his league in dealing with an unscrupulous person such as Hitler. A naive British gentlemen had no place to be in Munich; he was a lamb dealing with wolves.

The French at Munich were of the same mind as Chamberlain with respect to appeasing Hitler. In fact, they were desperately trying to find a way out—which Chamberlain and Hitler gave them. Daladier knew the French people were appalled at the thought of another war with Germany—one was entirely enough. Thus, the French played a secondary role at Munich and were content to do so. When Daladier returned by air to Paris, there was a large crowd in the airport. He was afraid they were going to do him some physical harm for his part in Munich—instead, they were cheering him for averting a war.

Daladier's chief advisors for the Munich conference were 1) Georges Bonnet, his Foreign Secretary, the most ardent appeaser in the Allied camp. He believed in giving Hitler whatever he wanted even before he asked for it. 2) General Maurice Gamelin, the head of the French Army—he wouldn't fight for the Rhineland, he wouldn't fight over Austria, now he did not want to fight for Czechoslovakia. General Gamelin at least was consistent, in fact, when the war actually started he still did not want to fight. 3) General Joseph Vuillemin, the air force commander, who told Daladier that if a war started, the French Air Force would be wiped out in two weeks. No wonder the poor Daladier was irresolute at Munich. The mantle of Clemenceau, Joffre and Foch had fallen into the worst hands possible. France deserved better.

The French ambassador to Moscow, Coulondre, realized the extent of the French defeat at Munich. He wrote:

"Munich tolled the bell for a certain France, 'la grande France' of former times and even of 1914...the tolling bells do not kill a sick man; they announce his death. The accord of Munich did not provoke the fall of France. It registered it."

Hitler himself, it is said, was angry that Chamberlain had prevented his attack on Czechoslovakia. After meeting Chamberlain and Daladier, he was disdainful and contemptuous of them, and thus the countries they represented. It is obvious that Hitler, by nature, was a violent and aggressive person. While at Munich, he achieved his immediate goal, the annexation of the Sudetenland, he was frustrated that his invasion plan of the whole of Czechoslovakia was, for the moment, thwarted. The German General Staff was very relieved that there had been no war, as they felt the German Army was in no way prepared for a major war at this time. It is said that some of the generals were ready to remove Hitler if he started a war—the fact that he achieved his goals so easily disconcerted them and put them even more under his control.

If Hitler had stopped at this point—after gaining back the Rhineland, annexing Austria and securing the Sudetenland—he would have accomplished a great deal for Germany. Of course, we know he didn't and probably couldn't stop and took Germany down to almost utter destruction. The apparent victory for Hitler at Munich would turn into disaster for Germany. Munich was the road to World War II.

It is interesting to note the position of Poland, Hitler's next victim, in regard to the crisis at Munich. Poland's life was on the line at Munich even though they did not seem aware of it. Churchill once said of the Poles "The bravest of the brave too often led by the vilest of the vile." While Colonel Josef Beck, Poland's foreign secretary was not a vile man he was certainly stupid. Colonel Beck was inclined to be pro-German and anti-French, a fatal and irrational attitude which proved disastrous. Hitler's clock was already ticking for Poland and they played right into his hands.

France asked Poland that, in the event of a German attack on Czechoslovakia, if Poland would join in an armed response against Germany. The combination of the Polish and Czech armies would put well over a million troops on Hitler's eastern border. Even though they had an alliance with France, Poland vehemently denied any help would be given to France from them. In fact, later, when Hitler devoured nearly all of Czechoslovakia, Poland, in collaboration with him, took over a slice for herself (Teschen). Poland would find out the hard way that what goes around comes around. The Poles did not realize it but Munich and its aftermath would be a disaster for them as well.

With Czechoslovakia occupied, Hitler had brilliantly set-up Poland as his next target. The Poles were now surrounded on three sides—north, west and now their vulnerable southern border with the former Czechoslovakia. They had to extend their defensive perimeter and thinned out their forces to cover all these areas, which made them weaker everywhere. Munich and the occupation of Czechoslovakia by Germany, which Poland conspired in, made defeat inevitable for Poland. One could say they had gained Teschen and lost Poland.

What about the other players, or should we say non-players, who had a great interest in this consequence? Stalin was not there; no one invited him. In fact, the Soviet Union was the most powerful country in Europe, next to Germany. However, the Soviet Union was viewed as a pariah nation by all concerned, particularly by Chamberlain, who was more afraid of the Soviets than he was of Germany. After all, Germany still bore some resemblance to a capitalistic system, whereas the Soviet Union was totally Communist, an anathema to England.

Of the European countries that may have stood up to Hitler, Stalin was the most belligerent towards Germany. However, he was not going to do it alone. A combination of the Soviet Union, Great Britain, and France could possibly have prevented World War II. This combination at the time of Munich could have actually won a military victory against Germany. The Nazis were not nearly as strong in 1938 as they later became. Churchill in power would have done something to make an alliance to stop Germany. Chamberlain did not. Churchill would never have agreed to selling out a small ally—Chamberlain did. Chamberlain was making one huge mistake after another with catastrophic consequences. The sands of time were running out on Hitler's opponents as they squandered their chances away. What Hitler had won by bluff and daring would, in the future, be backed up by the mailed fist of the strongest, most efficient army and air force in the world.

Stalin was well aware of Germany's rapidly increasing power. He was aware, alarmed and frightened. He realized the survival of the Soviet Union could be at stake. Stalin had been hoping to join an alliance with the British and French to oppose Hitler. He had seen how cleverly Hitler was picking off one country at a time—and at some time in the future, Hitler may decide it's the Soviets' turn. Stalin regarded Hitler as a very dangerous enemy, and he did not want to face him alone. After the British and French caved in at Munich, Stalin became dubious of their worth as allies. The seeds of sort of arrangement with Hitler were planted.

Stalin

Joseph Stalin was born Iosif Djugashvili on December 21, 1879, in Gori, a town near Tiflis in Georgia. He was an only child (just as Roosevelt) whose mother doted on him. The family was very poor. Josef, as we shall call him, was cruelly beaten at times by his father, Vissarion, who was an alcoholic. Mercifully for Josef, Vissarion was stabbed to death in a barroom brawl when Josef was eleven. Thus, at an early age Stalin was no stranger to cruelty and brutality. Perhaps he inherited the trait of cruelty from Vissarion.

His mother, Ekaterina, though impoverished, had high ambitions for her son, particularly involving his education. His mother's devoted attention helped Josef's self-confidence and belief in himself. He was enrolled in a church elementary school in Gori, where he excelled. He was considered not only the best student in his class, but also the best student in the whole school. He graduated in July 1894 with a special certificate of honor and received a scholarship to the theological seminary in Tiflis to study for the priesthood. His mother wanted him to become a priest.

Stalin did not like the regimented life of the seminary. In an interview much later in life, Stalin commented on his discontent at the authoritarian structure there: "In protest against the outrageous regime and Jesuitical methods that prevailed, I was ready to become and actually did become a revolutionary, a believer in Marxism as a really revolutionary teaching." This from a man who would later control the most regimented country in the world. Compared to the oppression of the Stalinist state, the rules of the seminary were like a children's tea party.

While at the school, Stalin acquired a taste for reading, particularly the works of Thackeray and Victor Hugo. Contrary to later opinion that Stalin was almost illiterate, he was, in fact, a reasonably well read man. He also immersed himself in Marxist writings and philosophy, especially in the work of Lenin, who became his hero.

In his fifth year at the seminary, in 1899, he was expelled for his Marxist activities; Stalin became an ardent Communist and joined a revolutionary group. In 1902, Stalin was jailed for his revolutionary work and sent to Siberia. He escaped in 1904 and allied himself with the Bolshevik wing (Lenin) of the Communist Party. Stalin first met Lenin at Tammorfors in 1905—Lenin's view of Stalin was that he was a forceful and incisive young follower who was well worth watching. Lenin became Stalin's mentor and supported his ascent in the Party. For the next twelve years Stalin was in and out of prison until he was released in 1917. In that year he took over the editorship of *Pravda*, the party newspaper. At this point, the revolution in leadership in Russia occurred.

On March 15, 1917, beset by opposition from all sides, the Czar abdicated. The Russian Parliament, "the Duma," formed a provisional government and Alexander Kerensky emerged as its foremost leader. It seemed at last democracy was about to come to Russia. However, the provisional government and Kerensky made a fatal mistake. With the war becoming steadily more unpopular and desertions increasing, Kerensky and the government decided to vigorously prosecute the war. At the same time, the Bolsheviks were agitating for peace. After making several offensive attacks with high casualties, the Russian army collapsed. The soldiers had finally had enough. Chaos reigned, encouraged by the Bolsheviks. Support for Kerensky and the government vanished overnight.

Seeing the opportunity, Lenin and Trotsky rushed to fill the vacuum. The Bolsheviks, with little opposition, took over Petrograd and Moscow. Kerensky fled. A small, organized and dedicated group of plotters had taken over one of the largest countries in the world. Lenin was now absolute dictator of the Soviet Union. The poor Russian people had gone from bad to worse. Little did they know what lay ahead.

Stalin was not at the forefront of action as the Bolsheviks, led by Lenin and Trotsky, took over Russia. In spite of this, Lenin and the Party recognized Stalin's worth, and Stalin was elected to the Central Committee. He received the third highest number of votes behind only Lenin and Zinoviev. This was a portent of things to come and should have alerted Stalin's enemies, but did not. They would pay dearly for their shortsightedness. Beneath his rather ordinary exterior, Stalin was about as sinister a person as one would ever come across, as many of his colleagues would later find out.

During the civil war that followed the Revolution, Stalin participated in military activities. In May 1918 he was assigned to Tsaritsyn on the lower Volga. Through no direct involvement of Stalin, the Red Army won a victory at Tsaritsyn and Stalin was quick to claim credit for it, enhancing his standing with Lenin and the Party. In 1925, the name of Tsaritsyn was changed to Stalingrad. Stalin also distinguished himself in a crisis at Petrograd. All this time, Stalin was growing closer to Lenin and the ultimate seat of power. Simply put, Stalin's goal was to build himself up and to tear down his main rival Trotsky—and he was succeeding. Trotsky would prove no match for the shrewd Stalin who was the master power politician. One important person who sided with Stalin was Dzerzhinsky, the head of the secret police—a very valuable ally for Stalin.

Stalin continued to bring in more and more of his followers into the government, Molotov and Voroshilov in particular. In 1922, Stalin became one of the five members of the Politburo, the governing body of the Communist Party. Following that, he was elected General Secretary of the Central Committee, a post which Stalin turned into a very powerful office. The momentum Stalin was achieving made it all but certain that, when the time came, he would succeed Lenin.

On December 16, 1922, Lenin suffered a debilitating stroke which greatly curtailed his activities. As time passed, his health worsened. About this time, Lenin was beginning to mistrust Stalin. After Stalin had a heated argument with Krupskaya, Lenin's wife, Lenin's hostility towards Stalin increased. In a series of notes on what has become known as "Lenin's Testament," he comments on his negative feelings about Stalin: "Comrade Stalin, having become General

Secretary, has concentrated limitless power in his hands, and I am not certain that he will always be careful enough in the use of this power. . . . Stalin is too rough."

Thus, Lenin, who was not above using terror to meet his own needs, thought Stalin was too crude and extreme. Lenin indicated that Stalin should be removed from the post of General Secretary. Unfortunately, Lenin died on January 21, 1924, before he could act on his intentions. Lenin's death undoubtedly saved Stalin's career.

Over the next five years, Stalin continued to increase his power and outmaneuver Trotsky. Stalin's strength and force of personality prevailed. In 1929, Stalin assumed full command of the Soviet State—the era of Stalin had begun.

Stalin is a difficult person to understand because cruelty is difficult to understand. Stalin's personality had many other facets; he was highly intelligent, he had a sense of humor on occasion, he could be patient if necessary, and he had charm at times. These positive traits were usually reserved for foreign dignitaries such as Churchill and Roosevelt, who were very impressed by Stalin. Even the German Foreign Secretary, von Ribbentrop, was favorably impressed.

However, in the everyday world, the two words that best describe Stalin are—tough and ruthless.

Stalin had no friends; all of the people around him were afraid of him and subservient to him. Several years after Stalin's death, Krushchev, who had worked closely with him, felt safe enough to state his candid view of Stalin. Krushchev spoke of "Stalin's intolerance of criticism and dissenting views, his willingness to inflict suffering or death upon any person whom he came to regard as an 'enemy,' his intense distrust and suspiciousness and his thirst for praise and glory." Clearly, those around Stalin had every right to be afraid of him.

After Stalin's obtaining full power in 1929, many old-time Communists disappeared or were executed, particularly those who had opposed him in the past. Stalin had his rival Leon Trotsky, exiled to Mexico. Later, Trotsky was brutally murdered. There was no doubt about who was responsible.

Stalin pushed further communization of the country, particularly in agriculture. He eliminated private farms, the resistance of which meant the death of untold thousands of people. He forced a great industrialization of the country especially heavy industry, which was tremendously helpful to his country later when war broke out.

He increased the power of the secret police. Millions of people were either executed or sent to labor camps; fear was his governing technique. Everyone was afraid of everyone else, but mostly they were afraid of Stalin.

There was no question that Stalin was a tyrant and probably on the same scale as Hitler, if that is possible. It could be that during World War II only a man such as Stalin could have held the Soviet Union together under the heavy attack of Germany. Although a tyrant, Stalin was a very tough, brilliant man—very resourceful. In battling for his own survival and the survival of the Soviet Union, he performed extremely well. Interestingly, at one point early in the war, Stalin was asked what the Pope's reaction to a certain event would be. Stalin said, "And how may divisions does the Pope have?" The author finds this reply ironic, in that approximately 50 years later, Pope John Paul II was probably the main reason the whole Soviet Union disintegrated. Divisions are not everything.

Roosevelt—United States

Across the Atlantic Ocean, Franklin D. Roosevelt, President of the United States, looked on at Munich with considerable interest. After the Great War, the United States rejected the League of Nations, which its leader, Woodrow Wilson, had set in motion. The whole idea of the League was to avoid another huge war. With its rejection by the United States, the League became merely a forum. By turning its back on Europe, America was saying it did not want any part of any more European wars. The feeling grew in the U.S. that they had been cleverly drawn into the First War by the British and French. Though they had not suffered nearly as many casualties as the British or the French, there were enough to give America second thoughts about the wisdom of entering the war in the first place. The isolationist wing of the Republican party took over the Presidency and Congress. The dream of Woodrow Wilson had, for the time being, come to naught.

With the Great Depression, which Hoover was unable to stop, the Democrats regained power in 1932 with Franklin D. Roosevelt as President. Roosevelt was an activist President who started many programs which did not wholly end the Depression but made it less severe. Roosevelt, by nature, was an internationalist who was leading a country that preferred isolation. He foresaw the menace of Hitler but was unable to act due to the public opinion of the country. The United States armed forces during the 1930s were in pitiful condition. The appropriations for the Army and Navy were as low as possible. Fortunately, some aircraft carriers were built which later came in very handy.

While the Army was small, it somehow held together a small cadre of officers who sensed that possibly sometime in the future their services may be needed. These men went for years with no promotions or appreciation at all. After twenty years in service, Eisenhower was still a major. Men such as Eisenhower, Marshall, MacArthur, Bradley, and Patton were still there when the call came. Very fortunate for America that it had men such as these. In particular, General George Marshall organized and built the Army from almost nothing when the crisis came.

In 1938, at the time of the Munich crisis, the United States was vastly unprepared for any conflict. It is hard to believe that such a great and large nation should be in such miserable shape militarily. Perhaps the feeling was if you have a small military, it would restrain America from getting into another war. Perhaps it was the thought that the country was protected by two large oceans. Perhaps (possibly because of the Depression), the country was just being cheap. If you burrow your head in the sand, nothing looks dangerous.

Roosevelt was way ahead of the country in seeing the menace of Germany, and also Japan. But he couldn't shake the country out of its lethargy. Two events were to take place to finally wake the country up and change public opinion. The first was the quick defeat of France in 1940; and then on December 7, 1941, Pearl Harbor was attacked by the Japanese.

Post-Munich

Chamberlain returned from Munich and received a hero's welcome. Crowds of people thanked God for him and cheered his name; he had averted another great war. He was acclaimed by all, all, that is, but a very few, including Churchill, former Foreign Secretary Anthony Eden, and Duff Cooper, who resigned his place in the cabinet in protest. A huge sigh of relief came over the country as a result of Munich. It was to be only temporary.

Churchill stood in the House of Commons and called the Munich Conference "an unmitigated defeat." He believed that Hitler was a man whose word was not to be trusted for a moment. He foresaw Germany picking off one country after another until all possible allies of England were gone and England would be alone. In particular, he believed the honor of England had been besmirched by its betrayal of Czechoslovakia. He considered the appeasement policy craven and dishonorable. His view was that at some point, England would have to stand up to Hitler, but in the meanwhile, it was losing time and throwing away allies. In particular, Czechoslovakia had an army of 35 divisions which was lost to the Allies.

As 1939 began, an uneasy peace settled over Europe. The English began to reflect that maybe Munich wasn't so great after all, that selling out a small neighbor was not something to be proud of after all. More money was appropriated for the military, but still not enough.

France was still glad that war had been averted. After all, if there was a war, it would be fought on French soil with untold casualties. They hoped for the best but did not prepare for the worst. Lonely voices such as Charles de Gaulle and Paul Reynaud spoke up but were ignored.

In contradiction of the Munich agreement, Hitler on March 15 marched into Czechoslovakia and occupied Prague. Czechoslovakia ceased to exist. A sudden conversion came over one man, Neville Chamberlain. He saw that Hitler was intent on taking over the countries of Europe one by one if possible. He looked on Hitler as an evil man and a threat to humanity. In short, he swung around to Churchill's view. Chamberlain had awakened to reality.

Chamberlain announced that Poland might be the next name on Hitler's list. He guaranteed that if Poland were attacked, it would create a state of war between England and Germany. In a few days, the situation had changed from peace to what seemed to be another inevitable world war.

◆ ◆ ◆

So finally it had come to this. The author can think of no one other than Winston Churchill to describe how England had arrived at this place. Churchill says:

In this sad tale of wrong judgments formed by well-meaning and capable people, we now reach our climax. That we should all have come to this pass makes those responsible, however honourable their motives, blameworthy before history. Look back and see what we had successively accepted or thrown away: a Germany disarmed by solemn treaty; a Germany re-armed in violation of a solemn treaty; air superiority or even air parity cast away; the Rhineland forcibly occupied and the Siegfried Line built or building; the Berlin-Rome Axis established; Austria devoured and digested by the Reich; Czechoslovakia deserted and ruined by the Munich Pact; its fortress line in German hands; its mighty arsenal of Skoda henceforth making munitions for the German armies; President Roosevelt's effort to stabilize or bring to a head the European situation by the intervention of the United States waved aside with one hand, and Soviet Russia's undoubted willingness to join the

Western Powers and go all lengths to save Czechoslovakia ignored by the other; the services of thirty-five Czech divisions against the still unpinned German Army cast away, when Great Britain could herself supply only two to strengthen the front in France—all gone with the wind.

And now with every one of these aids and advantages has been squandered and thrown away, Great Britain advances, leading France by the hand, to guarantee the integrity of Poland—of that very Poland which with hyena appetite had only six months before joined in the pillage and destruction of the Czechoslovak State. There was a sense in fighting for Czechoslovakia in 1938 when the German Army could scarcely put half a dozen trained divisions on the Western Front, when the French with nearly sixty or seventy divisions could most certainly have rolled forward across the Rhine and into the Ruhr. But this had been judged unreasonable, rash, below the level of modern intellectual thought and morality. Yet now at last the two Western Democracies declared themselves ready to stake their lives upon the territorial integrity of Poland. History, which we are told is mainly the record of crimes, follies, and miseries of mankind, may be scoured and ransacked to find parallel to this sudden and complete reversal of five or six years of easy-going placatory appeasement, and its transformation almost overnight to accept an obviously imminent war on far worse conditions and on the greatest scale.

Moreover, how could we protect Poland and make good our guarantee? Only by declaring war upon Germany and attacking a stronger Western Wall and a more powerful German Army than those from which we had re-coiled in September, 1938. Here is a line of milestones to disaster. Here is a catalogue of surrenders, at first when all was easy and later when things were harder, to the ever growing German power. But now at last was the end of British and French submission. Here was decision at last, taken at the worst possible moment and on the least satisfactory ground, which must surely lead to the slaughter of tens of millions of people. Here was the righteous cause deliberately and with a refinement of inverted artistry committed to mortal battle after its assets and advantages had been so improvidently squandered. Still, if you will not fight for the right when you can easily win without bloodshed; if you will not fight when your victory will be sure and not too costly; you may come to the moment when you will have to fight with all the odds against you and only a precarious chance of survival. There may even be a worse case. You may have to fight when there is no hope of victory, because it is better to perish than to live as slaves.

If you notice in the quotation from Churchill, he never mentions Chamberlain's name. It is not necessary, as it is Chamberlain and his predecessor, Baldwin, who have brought England to this point of no return. In May, 1940, when the bills have to be paid, the British turn away from Chamberlain at last and turn to Churchill—almost too late.

France, without enthusiasm, followed England. Again, it would be France and England against Germany. War preparation began in earnest, particularly in England. Aircraft production was increased, but still not enough.

The reason that Poland's turn would be next involved Danzig and the Polish Corridor leading to it. This territory had belonged to Germany, but at the Versailles Peace Conference, in order to give Poland a seaport, Danzig was declared a free city and Poland was given a narrow corridor through Prussia in order to reach it. This meant that the Germans living there were now not part of Germany. Hitler's plan that all Germans should be part of Germany meant that Danzig and the Corridor should revert back to Germany. What is strange and different about this situation is that Germany's claim actually had some merit to it.

Poland would not back down on this, and after Chamberlain's absolute guarantee to protect it, England and France could not possibly back down. A line in the sand had been drawn; step over it and war began.

It is interesting that the Soviet Union's initial reaction to England's and France's guarantee to Poland was to welcome it. They were much more afraid of Hitler than they were of England and France. With Hitler, their survival was at stake. It seemed a propitious time for an alliance among England, France, and the Soviet Union against Hitler.

There were two problems, however. In order to protect Poland, Soviet troops would have to advance into Poland. To the Poles, the Soviets advancing into Poland was as bad as the Germans advancing into Poland. The Poles were afraid that once the Soviet troops were in Poland, they would never leave. It was impossible for the Poles to allow Soviet troops into Poland, and rightly so, as future events were to tell.

The other problem with the tri-party alliance was Neville Chamberlain's deep-down distrust of the Soviet Union. To him, the Soviet Union was as bad as Germany. To Chamberlain, the Soviet Union was "an evil empire." He could not bring himself to put his heart into an alliance with the Soviets. Together with the feelings of the Poles, this killed the English, French and Soviet alliance. With this, any hope for peace was over.

The English and French still made a half-hearted attempt at an alliance in the summer of 1939. After some weeks of dilly-dallying, Stalin realized that the English and the French were not sincere in their efforts. He had to change his plans accordingly.

In the meanwhile, unperturbed, Hitler made his plans. Indeed, Poland was next on the list as Chamberlain had foreseen. Danzig and the Polish Corridor were important to Hitler, but in the meantime he had decided to use that as a pretext to attack and occupy all of Poland. Hitler was a greedy man. His contempt for the English and French was complete. Chamberlain and Daldier were particularly repugnant to him. "Worms" he called them.

Still, his memory of his experience in the trenches of France and the savage fighting gave him pause. In particular, he did not want to fight a two-front war as Germany had in the First War. With the Soviet Union at his back, Hitler was uneasy. The British and French had a mission in Moscow talking about an alliance. In attacking Poland, forces could be unleashed that would put Germany in exactly the position he wanted to avoid, a two-front war.

As plans for the attack on Poland were completed and forces put in place for the attack, Hitler studied his predicament. An accommodation with England and France at this stage was out of the question. That left the Soviet Union.

As mentioned, Stalin was aware that negotiations with England and France were going nowhere. He realized that Germany was going to attack Poland. It is possible that Stalin realized (perhaps subconsciously) that war with Germany at some point was inevitable. Why not buy some time and space? In the meanwhile, perhaps the Allies and Germany would fight themselves into a stalemate, such as occurred in the First War. In this case, the Soviets had all to gain and nothing to lose. If the Allies and Germany fought for years to a bloody standstill, it would weaken them all and leave the Soviet Union as the pre-eminent power in Europe. In any event, it was even barely possible that Germany and the Soviets could coexist in peace, perhaps even as allies.

For all the considerations, Stalin was ripe for a deal with Hitler. In fact, he would welcome it. Hitler was arriving at the same conclusion. A deal with the Soviets would clear his Eastern Front while he smashed the Allies.

Hitler instructed his foreign secretary, von Ribbentrop, to approach Soviet Foreign Minister Molotov to test the waters. Indeed, the outcome was more than he expected. Von Ribbentrop was invited to Moscow. The pact between Germany and the Soviet Union was signed. One of the secret provisions was that shortly after Hitler attacked Poland, the Soviets would advance from the east and occupy a large part of Poland. Thus, two of Stalin's main objectives were secured—more space between the heart of the Soviet Union and Germany. Space meant time, so Stalin achieved what he wanted—space and time.

This pact, indeed, was exactly fitted to the needs of both parties. The world was shocked by the announcement of this agreement. With the signing of it, the Second World War was bound to start in the next few days. The die was cast.

◆ ◆ ◆

To a great extent, the events leading up to World War II were inevitable. The moment Hitler became Chancellor of Germany in 1933, it was just a matter of time before war broke out. From that time on, Hitler, bent on avenging the late war and expanding Germany, used all his cunning to confuse, divide and bully his adversaries who were petrified at the thought of another war. They would go to any length to avoid conflict, which only encouraged Hitler. Hitler wanted a war, the Western Allies did not, but they would get one anyway.

To sum up the weak and timorous attitude of the Allied leadership during the 1930's, there is this conversation in October 1936 between Colonel Charles de Gaulle and the new Premier of France, Leon Blum. Blum had invited de Gaulle, the one bright star in the French army, to come and see him. In the conversation de Gaulle outlined, considering current French defensive policy, what would happen if Hitler marched on Vienna, Prague and Warsaw.

It's very simple, I pointed out. According to circumstances, we shall have a limited call-up or a full mobilization. Then, peering between the battlements of our fortifications, we shall watch the enslavement of Europe.

There was only one way—one person—who could have stopped Hitler and prevented the tragedy of World War II, and that man was Winston Churchill. Churchill in power in the 1930's would have re-armed England, made an alliance between Britain, France, and Russia and stopped Hitler in his tracks. Churchill had the vision; unfortunately, the British leaders and people did not. Hoping for Hitler's good will was not enough. The British would pay a great price, indeed, the world would pay a great price, for ignoring Churchill. Churchill was a brilliant man whose time had not yet come.

There was no possibility in the 1930's of a man such as Churchill coming to power, as the British people did not want the risk of another war. The British were trying to avoid a confrontation with Hitler and chose Chamberlain. Thus, the policy of Chamberlain was inevitable as it accurately reflected the thinking at the time. Hitler was not bound by such constraints. By his tremendous oratorical skills, Hitler had the German people solidly behind him, and he could pursue his aggressive strategy—picking off countries one by one. Each success made him move further along.

Only when their backs were against the wall did the British and French stand up to Hitler. It was that or go under. By this time in September 1939, all the odds were in Hitler's favor and he was ready to begin his assault on Europe. Hitler had succeeded brilliantly. The Western Allies haplessly and hopelessly stood by waiting to be hit. When they were going down for the third time, they reached out for Churchill. Thank God he was there.

World War II Begins

"If we lose this war, then God have mercy on us!"
—Hermann Goering, September 3, 1939.

On September 1, 1939, Germany attacked Poland from three directions in an all-out effort. It was called "Blitzkrieg"—lightning war. A new kind of war waged with deadly efficiency by the German generals. A combination of armored divisions and air attack moving quickly. It resulted in chaos for the enemy.

The attack on Poland was in a few days followed by the declaration of war by Great Britain and France against Germany. World War II began—the greatest conflict in the history of the world.

At this time, it is well to judge the situations of Churchill, Roosevelt, Stalin, and Adolph Hitler. Churchill's situation was changed immediately. From being considered a doddering war monger, he was now called a man of vision whose voice should have been listened to. Many compare Churchill to Chamberlain, with Chamberlain not coming out favorably.

Pressure to put Churchill in the War Cabinet came from all sides. Although Chamberlain was not fond of Churchill personally (he said talking to Churchill was like talking to a brass band), he nevertheless did put Churchill in the War Cabinet as First Lord of the Admiralty—a post Winston had held at the start of the First War. Churchill was delighted to be back in the thick of things after so many years of isolation. Many people regarded Churchill as a man of genius, but still at the same time too impulsive and reckless. The cloud of the Dardanelles still hung over him.

Churchill had a wide range of experience and a genuine love of the British Empire. He thought so much faster than his fellows that he left them behind sometimes. Churchill did have many ideas, some good and some not so good. As Lloyd George said, "Winston needed someone to sort them out and discard the bad ones." That is why there was always some opposition to his having supreme authority; some feared he would act out of control and irresponsibly.

So, at the beginning of the war, we find Churchill vindicated, his star on the upswing. Really, all he had to do was wait for events to propel him to the helm.

Roosevelt was in a different position. His country was not at war. The people saw another great confrontation starting and wanted to stay out of it. While their sympathy was with the British and French, that was as far as it went. They hoped to remain on the sidelines in this war.

Roosevelt knew that it was only a matter of time before America would have to join the war. In his rhetoric, he was openly on the side of the Allies. He regarded Hitler as a menace to the whole of civilization. With public opinion being what it was, it was very difficult for Roosevelt—people such as Charles Lindbergh spoke vigorously against any involvement. Getting additional appropriation for the military was still very difficult. All Roosevelt could do was to prepare as best he could and wait for events to happen. Unfortunately, he knew the events he had to wait for would be bad. Only a very bad, or even desperate, situation would get the country to exert its full influence in the world. Roosevelt could only watch and wait.

Stalin, having divided Poland with his new "friend," Hitler, was feeling pretty pleased with himself. Hitler's attention would be directed to the west. Stalin took this opportunity to gobble up Latvia, Estonia, Lithuania, and part of Romania. This, in addition, to what he had already gained in Poland. Hitler was not pleased with these developments, especially with the Soviet move into Romania, which put it close to the large oil field at Polesti. Indeed, Hitler was very angry, but there was nothing he could do about it at the time. He would deal with this later.

Stalin did beef up his armed forces at this time—but he actually become somewhat complacent due to his (so far) good fortune. Indeed, it may be possible to coexist with his new friend, Germany. Indeed, he was helping them with shipments of raw materials. They were allied to some extent. Churchill remembered this later with bitterness.

Hitler, in this period of 1939, was intent on finishing off the Poles. The Polish Army tried to protect the whole frontier of Poland, which was a big mistake. Thus, it was stretched thin across the whole front. The Germans attacked from three directions—north, west, and south. They here employed for the first time their Blitzkrieg attack—fast moving armored divisions supported by the air force. The Poles tried to fight back but were overwhelmed by the fast moving Germans. Warsaw bravely held out for several weeks but was crushed by artillery and air attacks. Warsaw surrendered on September 29, 1939. The German Blitzkrieg assault had worked perfectly; Hitler was ecstatic.

The British and French made no effort to help their ally for whom they had gone to war. The French army, supposedly the best in the world, sat behind its entrenchments. Other than send a few divisions to France, Britain did nothing. A hollow guarantee, indeed, for the poor Poles.

After declaring war, the British and French had no idea how to proceed. They had no plan whatsoever how to win. So they remained by default in a defensive position, waiting to be struck. They went to war reluctantly, and now it seems they were reluctant to fight. Of course, the English by their failure to re-arm did not have much to fight with. And without the Soviets, the scales had tilted against the Allies, pretty much as Churchill had predicted.

Hitler did have plans, and they were to attack. A number of times in the winter and early spring, he had plans to attack the French. All were canceled due to the weather, to the great relief of the German General Staff. So, as 1939 wore down, we found all four waiting for the spring and summer of 1940. Only Hitler had a plan—only Hitler had the audacity to act. Hitler was in the driver's seat.

In April, 1940, the first engagement of the West occurred, and also the first engagement between Hitler and Churchill. Needless to say, Churchill was not at the time in supreme authority in England. He was in charge at the Admiralty. Both Hitler and Churchill were eyeing Norway. Shipments of Swedish iron ore for German war use were coming through Narvik and southward by the sea to Germany. Churchill's idea was to stop or impede this flow of materials by mines, sea action, or by occupying Narvik itself. Plans were made along these lines.

Hitler could see that he was vulnerable to having his iron ore supply curtailed. He thought, and then (contrary to the British) he acted.

On April 9, 1940, German forces occupied Denmark without opposition. German forces also occupied Oslo and several ports along the Norwegian coast, including Narvik. It was a very daring and exceptionally well-executed attack. The British were totally surprised, even though they had plans for Norway also. By the time they recovered their wits, Norway was mostly controlled by the Nazis. The Germans were too fast and furious for the English, including Churchill, to comprehend. As First Lord of the Admiralty, Norway was in his sphere of operations. The British did make several landings in Norway but were completely defeated by the much better organized and equipped Germans, particularly in the air.

The British did achieve success at Narvik when ten German destroyers were sunk. Several other German cruisers were lost or damaged in the Norway attack. These losses were later to affect the action of the German Navy, particularly, in the contemplation of the invasion of England in 1940. (Without air and sea supremacy, the Germans had little to no chance of success.) The German Navy was somewhat crippled at this point. At this time, that seemed a small price to pay for the prize gained in Norway, one of which was a base for sea and air attacks on Britain and British shipping. Later in the war, the Germans' base in Norway would take a heavy toll of Allied ships supplying the Russians with war materiel.

In their first encounter with the Germans, the British had come off very badly. The speed and efficiency of Germany seemed to baffle the British, including Churchill. Surprisingly, Churchill received little criticism for the Norway fiasco. Instead, the criticisms were directed at the Prime Minister, Neville Chamberlain. Chamberlain had, in effect, left the Norwegian campaign in the hands of Churchill, but Chamberlain was blamed for the loss by public and press alike. Perhaps the British public realized at last that they had been led astray for years by Chamberlain, which reached its culmination in the failure in Norway. Churchill was considered the fighter, the man of vision who had tried to prevent the country from getting into the situation.

Besides, Chamberlain with his waistcoat, high collar, and umbrella did not fit the picture of a fighting war leader. His voice in particular was sad and uninspiring. Churchill, on the other hand, was a virtual John Bull, with pink, flushed cheeks and pugnacious in the extreme. His rhetoric was heroic and inspiring. The public believed he not only could talk a good war, but could also fight a good war. It would take a very strong and tough man to stand up to Hitler. Churchill filled that bill, and Chamberlain certainly did not. Also, Churchill was the optimistic type—he talked of sacrifice, but he also talked of victory. The type of man that could lead a nation.

At this time, it is good to remember that Churchill had a wealth of experience, much more than Chamberlain, who was the provincial type. Churchill had traveled all over the world in various capacities—as journalist, soldier, lecturer, and also just for the sake of knowledge and experience. At one time, he was an escaped prisoner of war in South Africa—another time a journalist dodging bullets in Cuba. Other times, he was a soldier on active duty in India and in the Sudan.

Winston Churchill had one of the fullest and most interesting and lives of anyone in history. He participated in the last great Cavalry charge of Omdurman in 1898. He was involved in the Boer War, World War I, and World War II. He saw the beginning of the Atomic Age and the Cold War. He was certainly an unusual and brilliant man with extraordinary vision.

◆ ◆ ◆

Thus, in comparing the man Churchill with the man Hitler, you have the following contrasts: Churchill was a very intelligent man of the world—he had a world view, and in particular, of the importance of the United States. Hitler, on the other hand, was a very intelligent man with, at most, a European view. He was a brutal, self-taught man who had lived by his wits. His formal education was almost nil.

In 1919, when Churchill was a Cabinet minister, Roosevelt was Assistant Secretary of the Navy and Stalin was moving into the higher ranks of the Communist Party, Adolph Hitler was still a lowly, unknown corporal in the defeated German army. He had a long way to go but with fanatical zeal and belief in himself, he would go a long way fast.

Recently discovered records show that Dr. Ferdinand Sauerbruch, Hitler's personal physician in 1937, had serious doubts about Hitler's mental state. Dr. Sauerbruch says that Hitler was showing signs of growing megalomania "and was a border case between genius and insanity." This combination of traits would cause the world terrible death and destruction. It is hard to understand how the German people could unquestionably follow this man.

Thus, we have two great leaders—Churchill with a broad world view, and Hitler with a limited view that was narrowly focused on Europe. In spite of large defects, Hitler was still a very gifted individual, particularly in his oratory, his strength to sway the entire German people, and his audacity. There was no self-doubt in Hitler, a formidable and ruthless adversary.

2

Hitler Strikes—Blitzkrieg!

On May 10, 1940, two momentous events occurred. The Germans attacked with ferocity Holland, Belgium, and France. The war had really begun.

On that same day, Neville Chamberlain was forced out of office as Prime Minister. The times and the man collided on May 10, 1940, and produced Winston Churchill as Prime Minister of England. Chamberlain had lost the confidence of his own party and also the confidence of the British people for his incompetence. The choice to replace Chamberlain had come down to Lord Halifax and Winston Churchill. Chamberlain preferred Halifax. Much to Chamberlain's displeasure, the Labor Party, whose support was vital, preferred Churchill.

Another factor was that Halifax did not really seem to want the job as Prime Minister. In a meeting with Chamberlain and Churchill, Lord Halifax said that as he was a member of the House of Lords, he felt that he would not be the appropriate choice. That left one man. The British had muddled through and came up with the best man England had. The British are an indomitable people and they got the man they deserved.

Thus, at this momentous and dangerous time, Winston had achieved the place his father aspired to but never reached. Churchill thought that his entire life had been a preparation for this day. He felt entirely confident.

Hitler's Greatest Triumph
The Fall of France

Although the attack on France came on May 10, 1940, the fate of France was actually sealed on February 17, 1940, in Berlin.

At a meeting with Hitler in Berlin, General von Manstein outlined his new plan for the attack on France. Up until that point, the plan for the attack had virtually followed that of the First War. That is, a great sweep through

Belgium on the northern part of the front. Hitler was very angry with this plan, even though it seemed to be the only one his generals could come up with.

Hitler also remembered that this attack in 1914 had been unsuccessful. To Hitler, it seemed an uninspired, obvious attack with no particular objectives. What Hitler wanted was a sudden, shattering knock-out blow.

General von Manstein was a rather low-level general officer who had come up with a new plan to attack the French. He won von Rundstedt's approval, but the General Staff including Halder turned it down. Hitler's adjutant, Colonel Schmundt, was on a tour of the front where he met Manstein, who outlined his plan. Colonel Schmundt immediately recognized this plan was very much in line with Hitler's overall approach. Colonel Schmundt arranged for Manstein to present his plan to Hitler on February 17 in Berlin. Manstein explained his plan to Hitler in detail.

The Manstein Plan

General von Manstein's plan was that, rather than put the main emphasis of the attack on the north, it should be moved to the center with von Rundstedt's army. The Maginot Line to the south would be bypassed.

The attack in the north under von Bock with 29 divisions should still be continued to pin down and put pressure on that front. However, the main attack would come out of the Ardennes in the center with von Rundstedt's 45 divisions. Von Rundstedt's army would include the bulk of the German armored forces, seven panzer divisions. These would be under General Guderian, Germany's foremost tank expert advocate of Blitzkrieg tactics.

Von Rundstedt's army would strike hard with full air support, head due west and cross the Meuse River as soon as possible. His next objective would be Amiens and then the English Channel. This would cut off the large Allied army north of the breakthrough. The German Army would finish off the northern wing of the trapped allied Army—then it would move directly south and crush the remainder of the French Army.

Hitler was enraptured with von Manstein's plan; this was exactly what he was looking for. He liked it so much that the next day he presented it to the General Staff as his own. This plan (von Manstein's) became the actual plan of the attack on May 10, 1940, and was followed to the letter.

You have to give Hitler credit. He disliked the original staff plan and seized on von Manstein's plan. He recognized its value and put his full authority behind it. It was a brilliant plan and took the Allies by complete surprise.

Von Manstein recalled when he was outlining his plan before Hitler and a group of his generals that he told them the advance would cross the Meuse on the fourth day. "And what happens then?" asked Hitler. Von Manstein recalled that Hitler was the only one to ask this very important question.

Allied Plans

Meanwhile, the Allied plan remained strictly defensive. The Maginot Line was a large part of its defense. Thirty French divisions, about one-third of their army, were tied up in the Maginot Line, which was never attacked. The Maginot Line ended at the Ardennes Forest in Luxembourg; there were no fixed defensive fortifications north of its terminus. In fact, on the Ardennes front the French posted several lower grade divisions, as they felt the Ardennes were impenetrable.

When the Germans attacked, the Allies initiated plan "D." This was for the British and French armies north of the Ardennes to move forward and occupy the Dyle River line. This plan played actually into Hitler's hands. Since he was attacking to the south of this line, the Allies were walking into a trap, which they did, to Hitler's delight. Things were starting out even better than the Germans had hoped.

In overall forces, the Allied armies—that is, French, British, Belgian, and Dutch—were about equal to the Germans, about 135 divisions each. The number of tanks was also about equal. The Germans had more planes and knew how to use them.

However, the Germans had a number of large advantages:

1. They were operating under one command structure, and they were all Germans. The Allied army was made up of four different armies with a very loose command structure nominally under the command of French General Gamelin. Indeed, the Dutch and Belgians had refused to consult or make any plans with General Gamelin until the attack actually occurred on May 10. Of course, by that time it was far too late.

2. The existence of the seven panzer divisions concentrated in one place gave the Germans a huge advantage. The French tanks, although equal in total number and better in quality, were spread out in small units along the entire front. Thus, at the point of the attack, the German tanks were in overwhelming superiority. The Germans' air superiority was devastating.

3. The German generals von Bock, Guderian, and Rommel, to name only a few, were outstanding—very aggressive, confident, and determined.

Their goal was to hit as hard and as fast as possible and keep moving—never giving the enemy a chance to stabilize the front.

4. The Germans were on the offensive and could strike at any point or points in the Allied defense. Thus, they could concentrate their forces at the point of attack and overwhelm the stretched-out defenders. The Blitzkrieg attack was perfect in this regard, as it hit so hard and fast. The battle was over before the defenders knew what hit them. By the time the defenders reacted, it was way too late—in fact, in many cases the Blitzkrieg attack penetrated so quickly that there was no reaction at all other than a rout. This was a new kind of warfare, and the Germans used it very effectively; together with the use of the Luftwaffe, it created chaos to their opponents. Basically, the shock of the attack was a key ingredient to its success.

In the meantime, on the French side, there were very mediocre officers commanding the French army. They were still fighting the battles of 1914-1918. They had no conception of the "new" war, that is, the combination of armored divisions striking hard and fast supported by crushing air attacks. The French had learned nothing at all from Hitler's success in Poland. They were hoping to fight a defensive battle and somehow hold on. They really had no plan to actually win the war, a war they didn't want.

Thus, when the attack began on May 10, 1940, the Allied Army was in no way prepared for what was going to hit it. Von Rundstedt's army crashed through the Ardennes and crossed the supposedly formidable Meuse River in four days. While the panzer divisions were the decisive factor in the campaign, it should be noted that the first troops across the Meuse were German infantry, not tanks. The French defending the river had been subjected to heavy aerial bombing and when they found Germans on the west bank, they assumed they were accompanied by tanks. With that, the French troops immediately fled in great disorder even though the frightening panzers were not even across the river.

General Guderian, as planned, struck west towards the Channel. The Luftwaffe was very effective, particularly the Stuka dive bomber, in this advance. The French Air Force was ineffective; however, with a limited number of squadrons, the R.A.F. was putting up a stiff fight. Its new Hurricane and Spitfire fighters achieved good results, but their obsolete bombers took severe losses, 41 in one raid alone.

With the breakthrough by von Rundstedt's army, the French were totally demoralized, particularly the General Staff. They had no conception that the Germans could move this fast—incredibly, they had no reserves to throw into the breach or counter the attacks. Some French units fought bravely but were overrun. Confusion and panic set in. Thousands of refugees clogged the roads—chaos. The German armored columns raced across Northern France in the debacle with very little to stop them. In addition to everything else that was wrong, French communications between the front lines and headquarters was virtually nonexistent.

Paul Reynaud, the Premier of France, phoned Churchill in London on May 15. His first words were: "The battle is lost." It seemed impossible to Churchill, who still had a high regard for the French army. Unfortunately, Reynaud was correct. The speed and ferocity of the first German blows proved to be a knockout punch.

On May 21, General Guderian's forces reached Abbeville and the sea. General Erwin Rommel had distinguished himself by his daring tactics in racing across Northern France. His troops were the first to cross the Meuse at Dinant. His armored division was creating havoc with the French. When Guderian reached the sea, the northern wing of the Allied Army, including the British Expeditionary Force (B.E.F.) was cut off and pressed against the Channel. At this point, the war in France was, in effect, over.

Holland had been overrun in five days and surrendered. Rotterdam had been smashed by air attack. The Belgian Army was in full retreat and in danger of collapsing. The British were retreating, but in good order, while everything around them was falling apart.

Churchill made several trips to Paris to assess the situation and to try to buck up the French. As General Alan Brooke would say in a few days to Churchill in regard to the French Army, "You can't give life to a corpse." The French Army was entirely unprepared for the ferocity of the German armored divisions supported by overwhelming air power. It was retreating across the entire Northern Front in disarray. Not only the French, but the whole world was in shock—the vaunted French Army was being crushed in a matter of days.

By the latter part of May it seemed the English Army would be destroyed, captured, or pushed into the sea. All around them their allies, the Belgians and the French, were falling back in confusion. On May 28, the Belgian Army surrendered. The B.E.F., by heroic effort and good leadership, remained fighting and intact. Lord Gort, the British commander, decided the only chance for his army was to retreat to the Channel and embark through the port of Dunkirk. The English rushed over every boat they could land their hands on, even small private ones. Many civilian boat owners volunteered in the effort. In this crisis, the British rose to the occasion as they usually do.

It seemed at the time that Hitler had the power to destroy the English Army. Various explanations have been given for that failure. One was that he wanted to finish off the French army to the south. Another, more reasonable, explanation was that Air Marshall Goering told Hitler that the Luftwaffe alone could destroy the English. In any event, the B.E.F. miraculously escaped and lived to fight another day. The R.A.F. and the Royal Navy fought and worked splendidly through the operation to save the Army. In fact, the R.A.F. won the air battle over Dunkirk against the Luftwaffe, which had a great deal to do with the B.E.F. being able to escape.

Meanwhile, to the south on May 19, General Gamelin was replaced by General Weygand. By then, it was too late. Weygand tried to rally the remaining French army south of the Somme. The Germans attacked and, after a few days of fighting, broke through the French front and were racing south across France. The attack spread out in all directions as the French defense had virtually collapsed. The huge, expensive Maginot Line had been bypassed and played no part in the battle—thirty French divisions manning the Maginot Line were wasted. Paris fell on June 14, 1940—the swastika flew over the Eiffel Tower. Paris had been undefended, which proved to be a good thing for Paris. Berlin wasn't so fortunate five years later, thanks to Hitler.

Paul Reynaud was replaced by the aging Marshal Petain as Premier. With this, the war was over. Petain knew that France had lost and was ready to surrender. The French signed surrender terms on June 22 in the same railway car at Compiegne that the Germans were forced to surrender in on November 11, 1918.

While the British army had escaped, this was about the only flaw in German's conquest of France. The war, which began in 1914, lasted four years. This time, it was over in six weeks, with France prostrate. Hitler's brilliant plan had succeeded, even beyond his own dreams.

The reasons for the French defeat were many. In particular, they did not have the organized armored divisions to counter the panzer attack. The quick breakthrough in the center by von Rundstedt's seven armored divisions and crossing the Meuse in four days was the decisive moment in the campaign. The dam had broken, and the German Army powered through with little to stop it. The French command seemed paralyzed by the shock of the attack and the rout of their troops.

Incredibly, the French had no reserves. Once the front was broken by German armor, it was all over. The French had been defeated by surprise, concentration of attack, speed, and just about everything.

It must be said that the morale of the French Army in 1940 was not the same as that of 1914-1918. The elan of 1914 was no longer present. Its leadership in 1940 was also not to be compared with that of 1914-1918. There was no Joffre. There was no Foch. It is possible if General de Gaulle had been in supreme command of the French starting in 1939, the Germans would have had a much tougher time of it. Actually, the German Blitzkrieg tactics worked effectively against all of their early opponents, the Poles, French, Serbs, and initially the Russians.

In June, 1940, we find Hitler triumphant. He had eliminated one of his major opponents, France, from the war in a quick and brilliant campaign. England was on the ropes. Hitler's confidence in himself became ever greater; his plans had worked to perfection. He felt he could do anything with his superb army and air force. Hitler, as the saying goes, was on top of the world. However, there was a Frenchman who had not given up—Charles de Gaulle.

Charles de Gaulle

Among the few Frenchmen who did not surrender was General Charles de Gaulle. De Gaulle went to London on one of the last planes out of Paris.

Charles de Gaulle was an unusual person to say the least. He had fought in the First War and had a very fine record. Between the wars, de Gaulle had done his best to wake up the French army to the new techniques of warfare. In particular, armored warfare. Actually, de Gaulle was the first military man in Europe to propound the concept of elite armored divisions, striking hard and fast. In his book, *Towards a Professional Army*, he outlined his ideas on the army of the future. As is typical, his own countrymen ignored not only his book, but de Gaulle himself. However, the Germans took it seriously and adopted many of de Gaulle's ideas.

One of the French generals who was particularly disdainful of de Gaulle was the aging Marshall Petain. Petain was an exponent of the defense, and he regarded de Gaulle as an upstart. Petain's repudiation of de Gaulle had a great deal to do with de Gaulle and his prophecies being ignored.

Instead, France built the great Maginot Line, a marvel of defensive thinking. Millions upon millions of francs were poured into this venture. At the same time, Germany was beginning to form its first armored divisions. The only thing wrong about the Maginot Line, which began at the Swiss border, is that it did not extend to the North Sea. It ended in the north at the Ardennes Forest. This portion of France and also Belgium was not covered. A fact that was obvious to everyone, including the Germans.

Paul Reynaud believed in de Gaulle—but it was too late. With the invasion of the Low Countries and France on May 10, de Gaulle took an active part in the battle. He led several counterattacks which initially had some success, but did not have enough force to be really effective.

At the time of surrender, de Gaulle had gained a place in the government. He was against surrendering but wanted France to continue to fight from North Africa. Petain took control of the government and signed virtually complete surrender terms with the Germans. The French were left control of most of southern France and French North Africa. Hitler agreed to this in order to keep the French from continuing the war from North Africa. As southern France was completely defenseless, Hitler could walk in and take it at any time, which he did later. (Actually Petain had obtained rather good terms under terrible circumstances. As southern France was left under French control, the population there was spared for two years the occupation of German troops. Perhaps that is why many Frenchmen in 1940 viewed Petain as more of a savior than a traitor. Of course, after the war it was a different story).

General de Gaulle formed a provisional government in London and broadcast back to his homeland that France had lost a battle but had not lost the war. As the war went on, de Gaulle gathered support, and at the time of Normandy he was recognized as the new leader of France. His perseverance and strength of character had paid off.

Churchill had a sometimes stormy relationship with de Gaulle. Of course, without Churchill's support, de Gaulle was, in effect, powerless. Roosevelt also had strained relations with de Gaulle at times. Churchill at one time told de Gaulle that if he had to choose between France and the United States, it would always be the United States.

This did not perturb General de Gaulle one whit. He was a somewhat arrogant personality and was also a very proud man. He felt he represented France itself and expected to be treated like the leader of a proud and great country. Anything less than highly correct procedure towards him, he regarded as an insult not only to himself, but to France as well. Most people found it difficult to get along with de Gaulle; however, Eisenhower and de Gaulle had a good relationship throughout the war.

One cannot but admire General de Gaulle—Churchill certainly did. General de Gaulle represented the best of France—he would never be defeated by anyone or any circumstance. He had come a long way, starting with almost nothing.

As France became liberated, Frenchmen rallied to him and his cause. General de Gaulle became the leader of the whole country. France, again, was in the forefront of the powers of Europe, principally because of the personality of one man—Charles de Gaulle.

Hitler vs Churchill

Thus, in the first of two confrontations between Germany and Hitler versus Britain and Churchill—Hitler had by all counts come out the decisive winner. It is a fact that in the Norwegian campaign the British and Churchill had been completely outwitted by the Germans under Hitler.

However, we would do well to give a closer look to the campaign in France. Here, it could be said that the British gave a very good account of themselves and, in fact, were not defeated. With Allies crumbling all around them, the small British army of 10 divisions held together. Their line was never breached by the German forces. The German generals acknowledged that the British were tough soldiers—"tough as leather," said von Bock. The R.A.F. put up a fierce battle, although greatly outnumbered.

The only sustained counterattack of the campaign was made by the British armored vehicles. With very limited resources they attacked southward and achieved initial success. In fact, the Germans were thrown into some consternation. Recovering, they beat back the limited attack. However, for a few days they acted with more caution—days that were vital to the British later on.

The Dutch were defeated and surrendered. The Belgians were defeated and surrendered. The French were defeated and surrendered. The British were not defeated and did not surrender. They were forced to retreat due to crumbling Allies on both their flanks. The critical day came when the Belgian army on their north surrendered, leaving a gap between the British left flank and the English Channel. If this gap couldn't be closed at once, the B.E.F. could be cut off from the ports and annihilated. Corps commander General Alan Brooke ordered General Montgomery and his division to move to his left and close the gap. This Montgomery was able to do with an excellent maneuver of his troops. In some respects, the actions of the British army in Northern France at this time could be called "their finest hours."

With strong help from the Royal Navy and the R.A.F., almost the whole of the British army arrived back in England. The odds of this happening were long indeed. Three British generals who distinguished themselves in this battle went on to bigger things. General Alan Brooke became chief of the entire army. General Bernard Montgomery led the invasion of Normandy. General Harold Alexander commanded the Allied Army in the Mediterranean.

With the defeat of France, England faced an entirely new and dire situation. Alone in the world facing the might of Germany. A French general said that in three weeks, "England would have its neck wrung like a chicken." But Churchill and England, in effect, said what John Paul Jones had said many years earlier: "I have not begun to fight." Hitler had assumed the war was over, but Churchill and the British did not.

Operation Catapult
British Attack the French Fleet

The author encloses this account of the attack on the French Fleet by Churchill and Britain because I believe it shows the determination of Churchill and his country at a dreadful time.

With seemingly everything collapsing around them, the British show the fortitude they are noted for. With the signing of France's surrender at Compiegne on June 22, Churchill's thoughts are naturally turned to the survival of his country. England stands alone against the might of Hitler's Germany with only the English Channel between them.

Of course, the Royal Navy is still the strongest in the world—but what happens if the Germans acquire the French Fleet? The situation becomes even more perilous for England.

At the time of surrender, much of the French Fleet is in its base at Toulon. However, a large number of heavy warships are in different ports. Some are in England. Other large battleships and cruisers are at Alexandria and Dakar, and a large force at Mers-el-Kebir, near Oran. There are also large vessels at Casablanca. By the terms of the peace treaty, all these ships are to be demobilized. But what happens to England if, by some means, Hitler in his cunning gets control of these vessels?

Churchill makes a very hard decision. Churchill the man loves the French. As Prime Minister of England, he has to take a more detached outlook. Churchill cannot reach the fleet at Toulon, but the Royal Navy can make a difference in the other ports. Churchill decides at this critical time to take over and demobilize or destroy the French Fleet within his reach—which he does.

However, there is large trouble at Mers-el-Kebir. Admiral Somerville has sent the French Admiral Gensoul an ultimatum. Admiral Gensoul is evidently uncertain about what to do and delays answering the ultimatum. By the time he decides, it is too late. The British Fleet has opened fire. The bombardment lasts ten minutes. When the smoke has cleared, the battle cruiser Dunkirk and the battleships Provence and Bretagne are severely damaged, and 1,300 French seamen are killed. Several French ships that survive evade the blockade and make their way to Toulon. It was also necessary to attack the French ships at Casablanca.

Needless to say, this is a heartbreaking development between the two countries so recently allied. But Churchill has sent a message to Hitler and the world. England is not through and will take any measure to ensure its survival. They will not falter when the going gets tough; they are not afraid; Hitler is going to have a fight on his hands. The war is not over—it is just beginning. It is possible that this harsh action and attitude of the British gave Hitler something to contemplate in his thoughts about crossing the English Channel. In the next few months, the heroic bravery and fortitude of the R.A.F. would also give Hitler pause to think about the risks involved in crossing the Channel.

Under Churchill, the British were not going to give up. They were a tough bunch of people, and they were going to give it everything they had. Hitler knew that and in his own way admired and respected them for it— another thing for him to think about in considering crossing the Channel.

It is a curious fact about the British Islanders, who hate drill and have not been invaded for nearly a thousand years, that as danger comes nearer and grows, they become progressively less nervous. When it is imminent, they are fierce, when it is mortal, they are fearless. These habits have led them into some very narrow escapes.

—Winston Churchill.

The Battle of Britain

Hitler, with France defeated so quickly and easily, had no immediate plan on what to do next. He offered to make peace with England, which was rejected out of hand. Churchill's attitude was the same as that of the British people: they would fight as long as necessary, and they would never surrender.

Hitler pondered. He wanted to finish England off, but how? Goering believed he could destroy the R.A.F., which in turn would make an invasion of England possible. Hitler gave his assent. Thus began the Battle of Britain. The fate of England hung in the balance. It was in the hands of a relatively few young English pilots.

Actually, during the fighting over France, both the R.A.F. and the Luftwaffe had sustained serious losses. Even as early as May 15, the R.A.F. had lost 206 of their original 474 planes of all types.

The French, and in particular General Gamelin, were begging for more British fighters. On May 15 at a meeting of the War Cabinet, the question of how many more planes was the principal consideration. Churchill was sympathetic to the French and their plight and was anxious to keep them in the war. He wanted to send at least ten more fighter squadrons. The problem was that if the R.A.F. in France was heavily reinforced, there would be few fighters left in Britain. If France fell, Britain would be almost defenseless. The war could be lost.

The chief of the R.A.F. Fighter Command, Marshall Dowding, was particularly concerned. With Churchill leaning to sending more fighters to France, Dowding could stand it no longer. He drew from his pocket a graph of Hurricane losses during the last few days and approached Churchill. Tension was high. Some there were even afraid of a confrontation. Dowding showed the downward red line to Churchill and said, "This red line shows the wastage of Hurricanes in the last few days. If the line goes on at the same rate for the next ten days, there won't be a single Hurricane left in either France or England." This seemed to hit home with Churchill. The manner and sincerity of Dowding and what he had to say impressed him.

On May 16, the War Cabinet decided to send four more Hurricane squadrons to France. Dowding was deeply depressed. He needed a minimum of 52 fighter squadrons to defend England, and he was now down to 22, only 250 planes (Hurricanes and Spitfires).

In a bizarre turn of events, while Dowding told Churchill he needed 52 squadrons to defend England, Churchill's understanding that it was 25, not 52. When Dowding found this out later, he was shocked. He felt he had made himself absolutely clear to Churchill on this point.

Churchill flew to Paris on the 16th and arrived at the Quai d'Orsay at 5:30 p.m. There, he met Premier Paul Reynaud and General Maurice Gamelin, among others. Gamelin pleaded for more fighter squadrons, especially to stop enemy tanks. Churchill, as sympathetic as he was, pointed out that the rifle-caliber machine guns on the fighters had no effect on tanks.

Still thinking he needed 25 squadrons to protect England, Churchill wired the War Cabinet he wanted to send six more fighter squadrons to France. Fortunately, Dowding found this out and pointed out to the War Cabinet that the R.A.F. air bases in France were being overrun and there was no place to send the additional squadrons. Three squadrons were sent anyway. Dowding was slowly winning his battle with his superiors, particularly in regard to the rapid deterioration of the overall battle in France. France was approaching a state of collapse. On May 19, the Air Ministry decided to withdraw nearly all of the Hurricane squadrons from France.

After Dunkirk, Dowding had only 21 fighter squadrons left, about 330 planes in all types. At this time, Dowding got some good news for a change. Lord Beaverbrook had been appointed Minister of Aircraft Production. Immediately, production went up. In June, Beaverbrook produced 446 new fighters, and production was continuing to go up. Dowding and Beaverbrook became the best of friends.

Now that his stock of fighters was being replenished, Dowding's biggest problem was a shortage of pilots. The Battle of France had claimed 435. Dowding was 300 pilots short of his full complement of 1,450. Churchill instructed the Navy and also bomber and coastal commands to send every pilot possible. This helped a great deal to fill the gap. Also, there were pilots from various parts of the Empire. Canadians, Australians, New Zealanders, and South Africans—also Czech and Polish pilots. There was a squadron made up of all American volunteers, "the Eagle Squadron."

On June 11, Churchill again flew to France to meet with French leaders. By this time, the situation was a disaster for France. Again, the French pleaded for more British fighters. This time, Churchill refused. He realized that the war in France was over. He told the French he was saving his planes for the Battle of Britain.

On June 14, the Germans occupied Paris. The end was approaching for France. By June 22, it was all over.

On June 18, Churchill announced to the House of Commons that the Battle of Britain was about to begin. "The whole fury and might of the enemy must be turned upon us. Hitler knows that he will have to break us in this island or lose the war."

Immense efforts had been made to build up the fighter strength of the R.A.F., and by July 7, Dowding had 52 squadrons, roughly 700 planes. The Germans had over 2,000 including bombers and fighters. The German force was divided into three groups, two of them in Northern France and a smaller group in Norway. The British were at a further disadvantage in that they had to spread their defense out to protect nearly all of England. They had less than 500 fighters in the decisive southern sector nearest France.

One big advantage the English had was radar. That is, they had a number of radar stations near the coast. These stations gave warning of the approaching German air attacks. This gave the British squadrons information about where to intercept the attack. The Germans were aware of these radar stations but didn't seem to fully understand their significance.

The Germans had finally decided that they would invade England—Operation Sea Lion. They knew it was absolutely essential to gain air superiority. Without air supremacy, the invading German army would be destroyed by the R.A.F. and the Royal Navy in crossing the Channel. Without air cover, the Royal Navy would be decimated by the Luftwaffe. Hence, the air battle would be the battle that would decide the fate of England.

The German Luftwaffe began attacking shipping in the Channel during the month of July, hoping to draw the British fighters out. For the most part, the British refused the bait; however, there were a number of air battles at this time. According to William L. Shirer, the losses for this period were considerable: 296 German and 148 for the R.A.F.

Goering planned to begin an all-out air attack on August 13, Operation Eagle Day. The targets would be the radar stations and airfields—over 1,500 German planes were in the air. They would continue on this scale day after day with the objective of destroying the R.A.F. At the end of August 13, the Luftwaffe, while causing some damage, had lost 45 planes, compared to 13 for the R.A.F. Each side wildly exaggerated the losses of the other. Unfortunately for the Germans, they believed their own claims—that at this rate, they would destroy the R.A.F.

The weather was bad on August 14, so the next big attack was on the 15th. Included in the attack were air units from Norway. The group from Norway, lacking adequate fighter protection, was slaughtered. Thirty of the force of 130 were shot down. This was the last attack of any size from the Luftwaffe's bases in Norway. Overall, the German losses on August 15 were 75 planes, compared to the R.A.F.'s 34. Many of the German losses were the slow-flying Stuka dive bombers. On August 19, Goering withdrew all Stukas from the attack.

On that day, August 19th, Goering met with his air commanders and sternly lectured them. "We have entered the decisive phase of the Battle of Britain. Everything now depends on our beating the R.A.F." Perhaps a note of uncertainty had crept into the Field Marshal's mind by the events that had happened in the air on the preceding day.

Captain Peter Townsend, a Hurricane squadron leader, recounts his adventures of that day over Britain.

The squadron was flying well together as we entered cloud, at 10,000 feet heading straight toward 'a hundred plus.' We emerged from clouds somewhere over the Thames estuary and there advancing toward us was a massive column about a mile and a half high, stepped up wave upon wave. At the base were the bombers, then a layer of Me110s, and above 20,000 feet a swarm of Me109s.

As we closed in, the bombers turned away seaward. A dozen Me110s cut across us and immediately formed a defensive circle. 'In we go,' I called over the R/T and a moment later a Me110 had banked clumsily across my bows. In its vain attempt to escape, the machine I was bent on destroying suddenly looked pathetically human. It was an easy shot— too easy.

For a few more seconds we milled around with the Me110s. Then down came a little shower of Me109s. In the corner of my eye I saw one diving for me, pumping shells, a quick turn toward it shook it off, and it slid by below, then reared up in a wide left hand turn in front of me. It was a fatal move. My Hurricane climbed around easily inside its turn. When I fired, the Me109 flicked over and a sudden spurt of white vapor from its belly turned into flame. Down came another one. Again a steep turn and I was on its tail. He seemed to know I was there, but he did the wrong thing. He kept on turning. When I fired, bits flew off, the hood came away, and then the pilot bailed out. He looked incongruous hanging there, a wingless body in the midst of this duel of winged machines.

That day, August 18th, was a terrible defeat for the Luftwaffe as they lost seventy-one planes, twenty-eight of them Stukas. Thus the end of the Stuka dive bomber which had terrorized its enemy in France. No wonder the next day Goering was perplexed and worried. The R.A.F. which was supposed to be destroyed by now seemed to be getting stronger. An invasion of England was impossible without the destruction of the R.A.F.

There were not only heroes for Britain in the air but also on the ground. The entire British people were showing fortitude and courage under the German air attack. A sense of shared danger infused the spirit of the island people. The attacks appeared to make the British even more determined to resist the onslaught and drew them closer together.

Adolf Galland, the German air ace, who had fought many battles over England, had a lengthy talk with Hitler alone during this period. Galland expressed "his greatest admiration for the enemy across the water." Much to Galland's surprise, Hitler agreed with him. Hitler said he had the greatest respect for the English and he wished the Germans were not in this struggle with them. Hitler said all the inherent virtues of the English were now, in this critical moment of their history, showing up. Hitler knew he was in for a difficult battle with a very tough and courageous opponent.

Still, day after day, the Germans continued their attacks with ever mounting losses. But the R.A.F. was beginning to wear down also. Time seemed to be working for the more numerical Germans. The attacks on the radar stations and airfields were beginning to take their toll.

On August 24, by accident, some German bombs hit London. From small incidents, sometimes huge events evolve. This was the turning point in the Battle of Britain.

On August 25, in retaliation, the R.A.F. bombed Berlin. According to Shirer, who was a CBS correspondent there, the physical damage was slight. But the psychological effect on the Germans was immense. They thought the war was almost over. They had no conception that their own capital, Berlin, would ever be hit by bombs. The impossible had happened; Goering had promised that this would never happen. In short, the Germans were stunned (somewhat the same effect as when Tokyo was bombed in April, 1942). Needless to say, Goering's prestige began to drop precipitously, never to recover.

On August 28, the R.A.F. again bombed Berlin. Again on the 30th. Goebbels was in a fury. His propaganda campaign went into hysterics over "the cowardly British attacks." The British were "Air Pirates."

On September 4, Hitler addressed his people and threatened revenge for these attacks. He promised to raze British cities to the ground—to the cheers of his audience. Thus, the attacks by the Luftwaffe on the airfields and radar stations were to be switched to London and other urban targets. This at just the time the R.A.F. was staggering under the blows, running short of planes, pilots, and airfields. It was a critical moment for the R.A.F. By switching his attack to London, Hitler, along with the courageous actions of the R.A.F., had saved Britain.

On September 7, the first large attack hit London and caused huge fires and many civilian casualties. Goering was ecstatic. He would break the will of the English people while destroying the R.A.F. He continued to attack London daily, including night attacks.

In a huge raid on September 15 during the daylight hours, 57 German planes were shot down. Churchill called it a turning point in the Battle of Britain. On September 17, Hitler called off Operation Sea Lion. Without total control of the air, the invasion was impossible. Already, R.A.F. Bomber Command was attacking and causing serious damage to the invasion fleet in their ports.

The German Navy was too weak to protect the invasion fleet in the Channel. Any invasion without air control would be smashed by the British. Hitler faced that reality and called off any plans for a land invasion of England. In this crucial battle, England and Churchill had won—Germany and Hitler had lost. The war would go on.

Consider the effects on the war if Britain had *lost* the Battle of Britain and England had been occupied by the Germans. There were four main battles fought in Europe during the war—crucial to the outcome:

1. The Battle of Britain. England remains in the war.
2. The Battle of Moscow in late 1941. Russia stops the Germans and remains in the war.
3. Stalingrad. The turn of the tide in Russia.
4. The invasion of Normandy. The opening of the Western Front, which means defeat for Germany.

If Britain went down in the Battle of Britain, consider the effect on Russia. Russia would have faced the full force of Germany alone. There were 205 divisions in the German army. They attacked Russia with 150 divisions, only three-fourths of their force. Over 50 divisions were tied down in Western Europe and Norway. Almost one-third of their air force remained to protect Germany and Western Europe.

Consider how close the Germans came, despite Hitler's mistakes, in taking Moscow in late 1941. They reached a point only 20 miles away. If they had been able to use the bulk of their army and aircraft, what might have happened? It is true that Hitler overestimated the size of the British army in England. But if in his mind there were 40 divisions, then there were 40 divisions. Thus, he had to guard against any incursion on Europe from England.

Also consider the fact that Churchill sent units of his army to Greece in April, 1941. This brought about the attack by Hitler on the Balkans which then delayed his attack on Russia by five to six weeks. Crucial: Hitler later said this cost him the war in Russia.

By 1942, British and American supplies were beginning to arrive in Russia in considerable quantities. By 1943-44-45, there were tremendous amounts coming to Russia.

The German generals stated after the war that besides Hitler's mistakes, there were three things that cost them the war in Russia:

1. The bravery, size, and resilience of the Red Army.

2. The harsh weather and poor roads.

3. Supplies received by Russia from Britain and America. This, in addition to what the Russians produced themselves, was too much for the Germans.

The landing of British and American forces in Northwest Africa in November, 1942, led to a direct reduction of German forces in Russia, in particular aircraft. This at the height of the battle of Stalingrad. All of these developments because Britain had not been defeated. In effect, Hitler was fighting a two-front war when he attacked Russia in June, 1941.

Regarding the invasion of Normandy, of course this would have been impossible without using England as a base and using English army, air force, and naval units.

So, one might well say that England's winning the Battle of Britain had a very direct and favorable outcome on the winning of the entire war.

Churchill, the R.A.F., and the English people had earned the respect and gratitude of people for ages to come. They had met the challenge, and they had won. In regard to the men of the R.A.F., Churchill summed it up best: "Never in the field of human conflict was so much owed by so many to so few."

So, 1940 drew to an end. It had been a tumultuous year which ended with Germany in a very strong position on the European continent and France eliminated. Britain stood alone, but they were still standing. The hope of victory seemed very dim indeed for the British. But they should take heart—there was one man who would save them—Adolph Hitler.

1941

With France defeated and England alone and weak, Hitler considered his next move. Not one to be satisfied with what he had, Hitler was a man of action. With a splendid army and air force at his bidding, Hitler began to look eastward at his erstwhile ally, the Soviet Union. It must be remembered that during his assent to power, Hitler had a deep fear and revulsion for the Bolsheviks. The Communist Party in Germany in the 1920s and early 1930s was one of his strongest opponents. Hitler detested Bolshevism and considered Bolshevists his natural enemy. He had written as far back as *Mein Kampf* of the movement of Germany to the east and the dissolution of the Soviet Union. Stalin should have read it.

The signing of the Molotov-Ribbentrop Pact was an aberration done for expediency. The Soviets' actions in taking over Lithuania, Estonia, Latvia, and part of Romania while Hitler was engaged in the West infuriated Hitler. Besides, there was the question of Lebensraum—that is, open land for the extension of the German people. In addition, the Soviet Union possessed many natural resources which could be useful. By this time, Hitler had decided that Germany should be master of all Europe, including the Soviet Union.

The attack on the Soviet Union was the next natural move in achieving his goals. By conquering Russia, Hitler would also have eliminated the last large power on the continent. The odds of winning were much in Hitler's favor. For Hitler, the attack on Russia was not a mistake—it was the right thing for him to do—if he did it right.

In fact, Hitler had always considered that at some time he would have to fight the Soviets. With France gone and England virtually helpless on the sidelines, now was the right time—Hitler's credo—"one front at a time." In addition, Hitler considered the Russians to be an easily defeated opponent. "Just kick the front door in and the whole rotten structure will collapse." Hitler was not the only one to believe this—nearly everyone did.

He considered the fact that in 1940 the Soviets had attacked the very small country of Finland. In the first few months, the overwhelming Red Army was repulsed and defeated by the small Finnish forces. The Red Army seemed very ineffective, even against the smallest opponent. After several more months of bludgeoning the Finns with overwhelming numbers, the Red Army was finally successful, and a peace treaty was signed by the Finns. However, the damage done to the reputation of the Red Army and its organization was already done. The German army and air force was, in total, 50 times stronger than the Finns, with whom the Russians had so much trouble. Actually, the Russians had learned from their poor performance in Finland and had improved their armed forces.

A man of action, Hitler could not just do nothing. His next logical opponent was the Soviet Union. Hitler began planning Operation Barbarossa, the invasion of Russia. He said, "The world will catch its breath," and it did.

The Mediterranean Front

In June, 1940, as France was collapsing, Mussolini considered it safe to enter the war and share the spoils of victory (whatever the Germans had left over). He made a feeble attack on the weakened French which was easily repulsed.

Next, Mussolini's eyes turned to what he considered to be the dying British Empire. His considerable force in Libya crossed the Egyptian boundary and made a hesitant advance on Cairo and the Suez Canal.

British forces under General Wavell made a surprise attack featuring armor on the Italians. It was completely successful. The Italians were routed; over 130,000 prisoners were captured. The remnants of the Italians retreated back into Libya. To save his friend and ally, Mussolini, Hitler sent an armored corps, "the Afrika Korps" to Libya, commanded by General Erwin Rommel.

The British success in Egypt, combined with a very successful air attack on the Italian fleet at Taranto, gave the British new hope. They knew they had no hope of beating the Germans alone, but the Italians were a different matter. The Italian army had fought bravely in the First War, but in this war the Italian people did not have their hearts in it at all. It seems the only one in Italy that really wanted to be in this war was Mussolini. Hence, the morale of the Italian force was low. The only thing the Italian people wanted of the war was to be out of it. Mussolini had led his country into a war they did not want.

As far as Italy and the war is concerned, Hitler would have been much better off if Italy had remained neutral. The fact is that Italy was a large liability for Hitler. With Italy in the war, the whole of the Mediterranean, North Africa, and southern Europe was brought in to the picture. Over the years, these areas drained off over a million German troops and huge amounts of materiel, particularly aircraft. These troops and materiel could have made a major difference in the Russian and later Western fronts. The German invasion of the Balkans, in addition, set back Hitler's timetable in the vital attack on Russia.

With Italy neutral, Hitler could have concentrated his forces and efforts on the principal theatres of the war. Instead he was frittering away his most precious assets, his army and air force, on peripheral areas. This is just what the British wanted.

Actually, Hitler had no interest in Africa—there was nothing there he wanted. He allowed France to keep Northwest Africa because he had no interest in it. Hitler would have stayed out of Africa except for trying to bail out Mussolini. It cost him dearly.

Italy's being in the war opened up a new avenue for the Allies to attack. If Italy, and therefore Greece, had stayed neutral, huge areas would have been blocked off to the Allied advance. Indeed, Mussolini paid a very high price for his mistake. As a neutral, Italy and Mussolini could have come out of the war unscathed. In fact, in better shape than even the winners in Europe. As it was, Italy was almost destroyed, and Mussolini was executed. But this is getting ahead of the story.

In early 1941, Mussolini, thwarted in North Africa, turned his eyes closer to home. He wanted to be considered a full partner in the Axis Alliance, and the only way to do so was to emulate the Germans, that is, to be victorious.

Mussolini decided to attack Greece, which he did on October 28, 1940. He did so without informing Hitler. Since Hitler advised him of nothing, Mussolini decided to do the same. After the attack was launched, there was nothing that Hitler could do but accept it. The only problem was that the Greeks didn't cooperate. They put up a strong, determined fight and sharply repulsed the Italians, even pushing them back.

Hitler, although annoyed, again was sympathetic to his friend, Mussolini. Hitler's attack on Russia was scheduled for May 15. In the meanwhile, he decided to help his friend and also to sew up the Balkans. Many Balkan countries, such as Hungary and Bulgaria, were already on his side.

Meanwhile, Churchill, who was desperate for allies, considered ways to help the Greeks. The Greeks were not sure whether they wanted to be helped by the British; they were doing quite well on their own. Also, a British army coming into Greece might entice the Germans into the war—a prospect the Greeks definitely did not relish.

Both Hitler and Churchill approached Yugoslavia. Anthony Eden, the foreign minister, acted in British behalf. However, the Yugoslavs signed a pact with Hitler. A few days later, the Serbian military overthrew the government and retracted the agreement. This made Hitler furious. In a move that may have affected the entire outcome of the war, Hitler decided to turn his Blitzkrieg on Yugoslavia and Greece as well.

At about this time, a small British army of 60,000 men began landing in Greece. The decision by Churchill to send troops to Greece was a controversial one. On the face of it, one of the most stupid decisions possible. If the Germans intervened, the small British army could do nothing to affect the outcome but be overrun.

Churchill decided that British honor was at stake. He would not abandon a small ally as Chamberlain had done. Besides, with the help of Yugoslavia and perhaps Turkey, it might just be possible to create a Balkan Front. This was a very illusory hope on his part. It must be remembered that England had been on the ropes at the end of 1940. The victory in Egypt had helped the British morale and restored some of their confidence. Churchill was ready to try anything to get England back in the war with a fighting chance, even if it was extremely risky. In sending part of the English army that was victorious in Africa, he also weakened it just as the Germans were coming into North Africa. No matter it was time to stand with the Greeks.

Hitler attacked Yugoslavia on April 6, 1941 in a Blitzkrieg war and overran the country in a few weeks. He then continued on to Greece, where he defeated the Greeks and British. The British had to make another embarkation and saved most of their small army. The Greeks were left to be enslaved under Hitler. Hitler had won another battle rather easily. Another part of the European continent had become his.

Looking back, it was a victory that was very costly, some say immensely costly, to the Germans. The German attack on Russia had to be pushed back by five to six weeks to June 22 in order for the forces used in the Balkan attack to be refitted. Those five or six weeks were precious time that would be remembered in the snows of Russia later in 1941. Some say it cost Germany the war in Russia. Hitler thought it did, later.

Besides this, Yugoslavia and Greece became a hotbed of guerrilla activity. So much so that 20 German divisions were tied up throughout the war, divisions that could have made a difference in the other theatres of war.

Hitler—Frame of Mind—June 21, 1941

On the eve of his greatest venture, the attack on the Soviet Union, Hitler could look back on his past ten years with considerable satisfaction. As the saying goes, at least from his standpoint everything he touched had turned to gold.

Considering the events that occurred during the period, Hitler had every right to feel pleased with himself. The events that occurred were:

- His assumption of complete power over Germany in 1933
- The successful occupation of the Rhineland in 1935
- The annexation of Austria in 1938
- The taking over of the Sudetenland after the Munich Conference in 1938
-The non-aggression pact with the Soviet Union in 1939

On September 1, 1939, the war started with the Blitzkrieg conquest of Poland in less than a month—the occupation of Denmark and Norway in 1940 completely outwitting the British; and the brilliant campaign starting on May 10, 1940, which resulted in the defeat of Holland, Belgium, and France in less than six weeks. In April, 1941, he had invaded and conquered Yugoslavia and Greece—most of continental Europe except for Russia was under his command.

It is interesting, when you think about how good Hitler was feeling about all this, that his victories had come against relatively weak opponents.

The one defeat he had sustained was against a tough opponent, Churchill and the R.A.F. Hitler lost this battle, as the other side was just as skilled, tough, and determined as he was.

In any event, as he prepared for his Russian attack, Hitler's confidence in himself and his army and air force was unlimited. He felt the power of Germany could not be stopped by anyone. The only thing that had stopped him was the English Channel. There was no English Channel between Germany and Russia.

Hitler's string of victories against inferior opponents had given him a false sense of infallibility in regard to himself and a sense that his army and air force were invincible. Indeed, a great deal of the world did believe that his army was invincible—Hitler was not alone in believing this. The world was very much in awe and fear of Germany. It seemed to have a highly efficient, unstoppable military machine. Actually, without Hitler in command, the German Army *was* invincible.

Hitler believed his attack on Russia would follow the pattern of his recent quick, smashing victories. In fact, he was already planning what to do with the vast land mass of the Soviet Union, once the short campaign was over. So Hitler entered his biggest assault with complete confidence in himself—in fact, he was overconfident, as events would show. In taking into account his frame of mind at the beginning of the campaign, it helps to explain some of the decisions he made—his belief of supreme confidence in himself and the Wehrmact, and his contempt for his enemies.

In the meanwhile, Churchill welcomed Hitler's attack on Russia. At this point, Churchill's and Britain's fortunes were at low ebb, to say the least. Up to now, Churchill's main hope had been the United States. Now, Hitler had given him a new and possibly vital ally—the Soviet Union.

Churchill was a student of history and knew that in the past Russia had proved a quagmire for many invaders, including Napoleon. Churchill had always supported the alliance of Britain, France and Russia and had pleaded with Chamberlain in vain to form this alliance. Now, Hitler on his own had come through on this for Churchill. If Russia fell under the German onslaught, Churchill had nothing to lose—if Russia created and held the Eastern Front, Churchill had all to gain, perhaps winning the war. No wonder Churchill welcomed Hitler's attack on the Soviets—it could be a God-send for England.

Thus, Hitler was creating an alliance between Britain and Russia and potentially the United States. I wonder if Hitler had fully thought this through. Everything now depended on a quick victory over Russia. If it did not succeed and America entered the war—it was all over for Germany. It was as simple as that. I'm sure Churchill understood this, but Hitler in his overconfidence did not consider the sequence of events and its consequences—perhaps he should have.

Barbarossa—June 22, 1941

A little after midnight on June 21, 1941, the Moscow-Berlin express train chugged westward through the German lines on the Bug River. Stalin was fulfilling his commitments to Hitler of raw materials to bolster the German war machine. Little did Stalin know that at this time German artillery was already zeroed in on its targets east of the river. Stalin was continuing his bribe to Hitler and hoped he would keep his attention turned to England in the West.

On June 22, 1941, at 4:00 a.m., with immense strength, the German army and air force attacked Russia. The whole world was shocked. The person that was shocked the most was Joseph Stalin. Incredulously, he believed that he was Hitler's friend and ally. Perhaps he was hoping that he was Hitler's friend and ally. Hitler had no friends.

Stalin was in such a state of shock that he retreated into his villa and saw no one for ten days. It is a wonder that Stalin should have been so surprised, as his top agent, Richard Sorge, who operated in Japan, had on June 15 forwarded to Moscow the exact date of the German attack. Also, Churchill had warned Moscow of the impending attack—this information was dismissed by the Russians as an attempt by Churchill to draw them into the war.

After ten days at his villa, Stalin recovered and returned to the leadership of taking over the war against Germany, which, to say the least, at this time was not going too well. The Red Army and air force had been totally surprised by the sudden German attack; much of the air force was caught on the ground and destroyed. Red Army commanders were in a state of shocked confusion.

The German army was everywhere successful. Even though many Russians were fighting hard, many thousands, in fact hundreds of thousands, were surrounded and forced to surrender. Again, the speed and ferocity of the German attack had produced chaos and disruption on most of the front, somewhat similar to the Polish and French campaigns. Many bridges were taken intact by the speed of the attack, which made things only worse for the Russians. Still, at some points, the Russians were fighting bravely and inflicting casualties on the rushing Germans.

In London, Winston Churchill declared his support for the Soviet Union—he declared that, "Any state who fights Nazism will have our aid." Basically, he was saying the enemy of my enemy is my friend. There is actually not much in the short run that Britain or America could do for Russia. It all depended on the Soviets holding out until the Russian winter set in. At this point, the war hung on what Stalin and the Red Army could do in a fight to the death against Hitler and the Germans. Most military experts and statesmen around the world believed that Hitler would crush the Soviet Union in a short time, just as he had done in other previous campaigns. The German army appeared invincible.

Hitler's three-pronged attack was directed against Leningrad in the north under General von Leeb, Moscow in the center under General von Bock, and the Ukraine in the south under General von Rundstedt. The bulk of the Panzer divisions, nine, were concentrated on the central front, directed to Moscow.

The advances on the north and central fronts were even faster than the Germans had hoped. In the south, where Stalin had concentrated his forces, the going was slower. One thing that the Germans had run into that caused them surprise and concern were the heavy Russian tanks, the T-34 and the KV-1. Those tanks were heavier, better armored, and with a 76.2 mm gun were more than a match for the lighter German tanks. The German shells bounced harmlessly off the sides of the strong Russian tanks.

Another thing the Russians were doing right amid all the chaos was that the day after the war started, they began moving their war making plants and machinery far to the east, away from the fast-moving Germans. Looking back, this is probably what saved the Soviet Union.

In planning the attack on Russia, Hitler had assembled his generals and told them to conduct the war against Russia in a different manner than in all previous wars. He said: "This struggle is one of ideologies and racial differences and will have to be conducted with unprecedented, unmerciful and unrelenting harshness. In particular, the Commissars will be liquidated. The Hague conventions on war should be ignored." Hitler had no mercy for Russian civilians—if they got in the way or caused any kind of trouble, just shoot them. In the long run, this inhuman treatment of the Russians backfired on Hitler, as it made the Russians determined to fight even harder and to meet fire with fire.

Meanwhile, the German attack was succeeding and even seemed to be gaining speed, particularly on the central front. General von Bock had surrounded and captured hundreds of thousands of Russian soldiers in a Panzer attack near Minsk. One point, the city of Dvinsk, 185 miles inside the Soviet border, had been captured by June 26, five days after the beginning of the invasion. The Germans seized both bridges across the Dvina River intact—a remarkable feat.

General Halder, chief of Staff, thought the war had been won in the first two weeks, and Halder was a conservative man. The Russians were on the run; some were collapsing.

Von Bock's army on the central front was the main threat to the Russians. His attack was in the direction of Moscow, the hub of the entire country—transportation, communications, and munitions factories. If Moscow were taken, it was conceivable that the war would be over, regardless of actions on the other fronts. In three weeks, von Bock had reached the vicinity of Smolensk, 450 miles from his starting point and only 200 miles to Moscow. Things looked very bad for the Russians, although in many places they were putting up a brave battle. If Moscow was to be taken, it had to be done before winter set in, but at the rate von Bock's army was going, this didn't seem a problem.

There was only one person who could stop the attack on Moscow. Stalin couldn't, but Hitler did. Astonished?

For some weeks in July and August, Hitler had slowed the advance while he decided which attack to pursue (Stonewall Jackson would not have approved). As mentioned, the south wing under von Rundstedt in the Ukraine was not progressing as fast as the other wings. Hitler believed that switching a large part of the central army southward toward the Ukraine, together with an attack north by von Rundstedt, would create a huge pocket in which a large part of the Red Army would be surrounded and captured. The Ukraine would be his and the Red Army broken.

In spite of vigorous protests from all his generals, including Halder, von Bock, and Guderian, Hitler ordered a large part of the central army to attack south. This was in early August. The drive on Moscow was stopped. This decision was crucial to the whole war. Russia had two places that were indispensable to her continuing the war—Moscow and the Caucasus oil fields. They could not lose either of them and expect to survive. The war would effectively be over. At this time, Hitler, with a strong effort, had Moscow in the palm of his hand. His generals realized this, but Hitler was only looking south at a big tactical victory.

General Halder called Hitler's decision "the greatest strategic blunder of the Eastern Campaign." The German generals felt that Moscow was the driving hub of the Soviet Union and that its capture and the destruction of the Red Army defending it would bring victory in the east—and they were right.

Hitler's tactical plan worked. A huge pocket was created in the Ukraine, and hundreds of thousands of Russian troops surrendered. It was another resounding victory. But at what cost? By the time the central force under

Guderian could be switched back from the south to the Moscow front, it was October. The dreaded Russian winter was approaching.

What should the Germans do now? Should they make an attempt on Moscow, or should they bunker down for the winter and try again in the spring of 1942? The decision was made to attack Moscow at this time. This was late, but it was the correct decision. Von Bock and Guderian started out, hoping for the best despite the loss of almost two months of precious time.

Shortly after the attack began, another huge pocket was created by German Panzers at Vyazma, and hundreds of thousands of Russians were captured. The attack had started very well, and the advance was making good progress until the rains came. Russia's primitive roads, which were already poor, became almost impassable. Mud, not the Red Army, was the obstacle. The German mechanized forces became mired down in the mud. It was too much even for the Germans.

However, a few weeks later, the Germans received something of a break; the cold weather set in and the roads became harder and thus passable. The attack resumed in November. During this period, the Russians had time to bring up reserves, particularly from Siberia. Stalin also appointed his best general, Marshal Zhukov, commander of the Moscow front. Stalin and the Russian government did not leave Moscow, despite the closeness of the Germans. It was do or die. For Germany, it was a race against time, the weather, and the Red Army. Possibly the war hung in the balance.

The German advance approached Moscow against stiff resistance. The closer they got to Moscow, the harder the Russians fought. Then, the weather again changed. The temperature dropped to 20 degrees below zero. Snow fell in abundance. The German army was not prepared for winter; they had supposed the campaign would be over before winter. They had no warm clothing; the oil in their tanks and trucks froze up. Even the rifles froze up. Thousands of German soldiers were suffering from frostbite—still, they kept on.

By December 2, a battalion of the 258th Infantry Division had reached as far as Khimiki, a suburb of Moscow within sight of the spires of the Kremlin. It was the Germans' first and last glimpse of the Kremlin. Finally, with their strength stretched to the breaking point by the terrible weather and the fierce Russian resistance, the Germans stopped their attack. Moscow and Russia were saved. By his mistakes, Hitler had failed. His attack on Moscow had come too late. The critical Battle of Moscow had been lost—if started in August, it could have been won.

Guderian expressed the feeling of the Germans in retrospect:

The icy cold, the lack of shelter, the shortage of clothing, the wretched state of our fuel supplies—all this makes the duties of a commander a misery. Only he who saw the endless expanse of Russian snow during the winter of our misery and felt the icy wind that blew across it, burying in snow every object in its path; who drove for hour after hour through no man's land only at last to find too thin shelter with insufficiently clothed, half-starved men; and who also saw by contrast the well-fed, warmly clad and fresh Siberians, fully equipped for winter fighting can truly judge the events which occurred.

On December 6, 1941, General Zhukov began a strong counterattack all along the central front. The Germans were astonished and alarmed—they couldn't believe the Russians had this much strength left. The General Staff, almost in a panic, counseled Hitler to retreat. Hitler refused. He believed that under the circumstances a retreat would become a rout, and in the process the German army would be destroyed, similar to Napoleon's fate.

He ordered all units to hold their ground—no retreat. In doing this, Hitler was correct and was also able to stop the Russian attack. He probably saved the German army. But Moscow was not taken. The end of 1941 showed the Germans deeply into the country. They had won many battles, "Lost Victories" as von Manstein would say. They had captured millions of Russian troops—Leningrad was surrounded. But the end of 1941 showed Russia still in the war, fighting back hard. Moscow was still theirs. The Germans' hope for victory in Russia in 1941 was over.

Stalin, after his initial mistakes, proved to be a hard man to beat. He was ruthless, but in his situation that was probably an asset. Hitler had run up against a man as tough and as ruthless as himself.

Stalin's appointment of Zhukov, his best general, first at Leningrad and then at Moscow was a very wise choice. Stalin's movement of Russian heavy industry from the west to the Urals was almost a miracle. Although the Germans had overrun most of the industrial heartland of the country, Stalin's war making machine was mostly intact.

It also must be said that the individual Red Army soldier was a tough opponent; many fought to the death. Stalin had a great deal of help from his brave soldiers. Hitler had gravely underestimated the Red Army.

As mentioned earlier, the six weeks lost in the beginning of the campaign due to the Balkan war plus Hitler's swerve to the south away from Moscow played a large part in Germany's not having won in 1941. Eventually, not winning in 1941 had a huge effect on the outcome of the entire war, possibly decisive.

Hitler did not make a mistake in attacking Russia—his critical mistake was not defeating Russia in 1941, which he could have done. If he had just left his generals alone, they would have won the war for him in Russia.

Roosevelt—1941

With the fall of France in June, 1940, the American people began to wake up to their danger. To some, it seemed that Hitler was out to conquer the world, or if Hitler only conquered all of Europe, the world would become a much more dangerous place for the United States. Americans began to realize that Hitler was not only a threat to Europe, but possibly to themselves as well. There seemed to be no limits to his drive for power.

Roosevelt was able to get more appropriations for the Army and the Navy. The draft was instituted. So, as 1941 began, America was beginning to prepare itself for whatever lay ahead. With the German attack on Russia in June, concern again increased.

Roosevelt's main objective, other than increasing his Army, Navy, and industry, was to help England in every way possible. He believed that the existence of England, both as a partner and as a base, was indispensable in winning the war. Besides, Roosevelt liked and admired England. England's values were much the same as America's—he did not want to see the English go down under Hitler's boot. He found a way to send 50 older destroyers to England. Also, he began shipping them as much war materials as he could spare from his own forces. In short, Roosevelt tied America's fate in with the fate of England.

Roosevelt knew that at some point America had to get into the war against Germany. However, in 1941, his armed forces were still weak. The American people still did not want to get into another war, even though subconsciously they knew there was probably no way out of it. People such as Charles A. Lindbergh formed groups to denounce Roosevelt's helping the British and said that America should stay out of the war at all costs. There was considerable support from the public for these positions.

With conditions getting worse in Europe and Asia, Roosevelt strengthened his Cabinet by adding two strong Republicans. Frank Knox was appointed as Secretary of the Navy and Henry L. Stimson was made Secretry of War. To some extent, this was the American version of a coalition government on the eve of a crisis. Another great appointment was that of General George

C. Marshall as Chief of Staff of the Army. Roosevelt was battening down the hatches preparing for the war that was coming. "This generation has a rendezvous with destiny," Roosevelt had said, and he was getting ready to meet the challenge.

On December 29, 1940, Roosevelt gave a nationwide radio address to alert the American people to the crisis that lay ahead.

> Never before since Jamestown and Plymouth Rock has our American civilization been in such danger as now. . . . The Nazi masters of Germany have made it clear that they intend not only to dominate all life and thought in their own country but also to enslave the whole of Europe, and then to use the resources of Europe to dominate the rest of the world.

Roosevelt was also increasingly concerned about the Japanese, particularly their continuing attack on China. The atrocities committed by the Japanese in China stirred up American wrath. The belligerent leaders of Japan seemed to be intent on further attacks and expansion of the Japanese Empire— relations between America and Japan became very strained. Actually, the Japanese attack on China was a very stupid move on their part. What had they to gain? It turned into a quagmire for them. The more they advanced into China, the worse off they were.

In July, 1941, Japan moved into French Indo-China. Of course, the French could offer no resistance. It looked as if Japan intended to use it for future expansion to attack Malaya, the Dutch East Indies, and possibly the Philippines. The Japanese move into Indo-China was a very serious matter. The fall of France and Holland plus the weakening of Britain had created a vacuum in Southeast Asia, and Japan determined to fill it.

Washington was alarmed; shipments of aviation fuel and scrap metal to Japan from the U.S. were stopped.

Japan was an island nation with few natural resources. Its military machine was entirely dependent on imports, particularly oil. Without oil, its large modern navy would be immobilized. Japan feared that America would stop all oil from going to Japan. Their move to French Indo-China indicated that they might attempt to seize these natural resources by force. Japan's aggressive tendencies were pushing themselves into a corner.

Negotiations began between Washington and the Japanese to try to ease the situation. At the same time, Japanese military leaders, especially the navy, began plans to strike, in particular, at Pearl Harbor, the base of the American

Pacific Fleet. The American fleet was the main obstacle to any advance by the Japanese.

Negotiations through the fall of 1941 struggled on. The key demand from America was for Japan to get out of China. This demand the Japanese could never accept; it would humiliate them. They could not and would not lose face. Thus, with a large army bogged down in China and another army facing the Soviets in Manchuria, the Japanese were now planning on fighting America and Britain—they were doing what Hitler did—trying to do too much with too little. The result would be the same.

Since the negotiations, although continuing, showed no hope of success, Japan decided to put its military plan into action. The aggressive militarists were now in control of Japan; the Emperor gave tacit approval. (Hirohito's role in this decision remains somewhat obscure, probably by design on his part, and that turned out to be wise. He certainly made no effort to stop the attack and post-war accounts indicate that Hirohito had a quiet but active part in the war. Hirohito proved to be a survivor even though several millions of his subjects did not.)

On December 1, 1941, Tojo said, "At the moment our Empire stands at the threshold of glory or oblivion." It seems to the author like a very big risk to gain an abstraction "glory" at the possible cost of millions of deaths and terrible destruction. Tojo was buying a ticket in the lottery with the fate of Japan at stake. Admiral Yamamoto was somewhat reluctant to attack America, as he had spent some time there and was aware of its potential. He said for the first six months Japan would run wild in the Pacific, but after that, America would be a formidable enemy.

Japan attacked Pearl Harbor on December 7, 1941. The attack caught America by surprise and was a huge success; most of America's battleships were sunk. However, the American aircraft carriers were not in the harbor, and they survived. Thus, it was a victory, but not a complete victory. There was no turning back for Japan. It was victory or a humiliating defeat with untold consequences. Japan should have looked a little deeper before it leapt. The Japanese were somewhat like Hitler—they overestimated themselves and underestimated their enemies. Their early successes would be like a fiery comet that flashes quickly across the sky and then disappears into the abyss.

I think it is safe to say that December 7, 1941, was the day that the Japanese lost the war with the United States. The Japanese celebrated their victory at the end of the day on December 7th—what they did not realize was that their situation had just become hopeless.

3

The War Comes to America

Pearl Harbor

On November 26, 1941, the Japanese fleet which was assembled at Hikotappu Bay set sail. Its objective was to destroy the American fleet based at Pearl Harbor in a surprise attack. Admiral Nagumo was in command of this large force, which included six carriers. With the American fleet destroyed, Japan would have a free hand in the whole Pacific.

Once before, the Japanese had launched a war with a surprise attack. This was in 1904 against the Russian fleet at Tsushima, and it was entirely successful. The Americans should have considered this earlier attack in their assessment of Japanese intentions. Unfortunately, the Americans in 1941 did not have a realistic appreciation of the Japanese. They vastly underestimated the ability and resourcefulness of the Japanese military. That they were taken by surprise by their efficiency for the Pearl Harbor attack is no surprise.

Although American Intelligence services had detected naval movements by the Japanese, they believed the Japanese were headed south to attack Malaya and the Dutch East Indies. They couldn't conceive fully that the Japanese would start a war with the United States.

In the days before Pearl Harbor, as mentioned, tensions between the United States and Japan had greatly increased. An impasse had developed in the negotiations in Washington. The American leadership was uneasy with the situation. Alert signals were sent to all bases in the Pacific that a tense situation existed. One specific warning by General Marshall to Pearl Harbor on December 6 got lost in the bureaucracy of the cable system using antiquated equipment.

Pearl Harbor was commanded by Admiral Husband Kimmel for the Navy and General Walter Short for the Army and Army Air Force. While taking precautions, Pearl Harbor was not on an immediate general alert. Indeed, you would think that even in the normal course of events, long range patrol planes and submarines would be sent on patrol westward. They were not. You would think that the Army Air Force fighters and bombers would be on alert. They were not. In fact, they were gathered closely together on the open airfields—this on the order of General Short to prevent sabotage. Sabotage should have been the least of his worries, as events would prove.

In short, the base at Pearl Harbor was in no way prepared for the attack that was about to hit them. Simply put, the Americans didn't really believe that the Japanese would make this kind of attack. Besides, America and Japan were at peace—no self-respecting nation would make such a dastardly attack. They were to find out that protocol meant nothing to the Japanese. Victory was the name of the game, and if by a smashing surprise attack, so much the better—the same tactics as Hitler's.

Sadly to say, there were some indications to the Americans just before the attack that something was amiss. At 6:45 a.m., the destroyer Ward, on routine patrol duty, sank a Japanese midget submarine. This information was not passed along to a higher command. Shortly after 7:00 a.m., two U.S. privates watching their mobile radar screen noticed many blips. It indicated a large force of aircraft coming from the northwest approximately 140 miles away. The men immediately phoned the lieutenant in charge. At this time, the Americans were expecting a flight of B-17s coming from the mainland. The lieutenant thought this was the cause of the activity on the radar screen. He ignored the obvious fact that the swarm of unidentified planes was coming from the northwest, while the small flight of B-17s was coming from the east. In any event, the inexperience of the lieutenant on this day was very costly, even disastrous to the Americans. If he had notified his superiors, which he didn't, at least the Americans would have had a fighting chance.

Over 180 planes took off from the six carriers in the early dawn of Sunday, December 7, 1941, torpedo bombers, dive bombers, and their fighter escort. They arrived with complete surprise at 8:00 a.m. over Hawaii and began their attack. A second wave of 170 Japanese planes arrived at Pearl Harbor at 8:40 a.m. The Americans were trying to fight back as best they could, although they were unprepared for the attack.

The Japanese planes operated with tremendous efficiency. The pilots had been thoroughly trained for their assignments. The American battleships were lined up in a row along piers at Ford Island—they were sitting ducks for the Japanese attack. One bomb went down an open compartment of the Arizona, and it evidently hit the magazine. The Arizona exploded violently; nearly all of its crew were killed.

The Japanese attacked not only the U.S. fleet, but also the air fields; success was gained there as well on the parked American planes. Pearl Harbor was turned into a flaming hell by the Japanese attack, which was brilliantly carried out against an unprepared foe.

Four battleships were sunk and four damaged. In all, eighteen ships were either sunk or damaged; 164 Navy and Army aircraft were destroyed and 124 damaged. Twenty-nine Japanese planes were lost. The Americans reported 2,403 killed and 1,178 wounded, mostly naval personnel. The Arizona accounted for many of these casualties.

Fortunately, the Americans had one break among the carnage; its aircraft carriers were not in the harbor. Probably the main objective of the Japanese attack had come through unscathed. Thus, it was not a total Japanese victory. These carriers would play their part in avenging Pearl Harbor, and even more so. Most of the battleships that were sunk or damaged were raised and repaired. They played their full active part in the war. The seemingly immediate disaster for the Americans was not as bad as it appeared to be.

As mentioned, tactically, Pearl Harbor was a great Japanese victory. Strategically, it was a disaster which was to cost them the war.

On December 6, 1941, Americans were not totally agreed on the war which was taking place. The majority of Americans wanted to stay out of the war; there were some groups adamantly opposed to it. Indeed, some didn't even want to prepare for war. The vote in the House of Representatives on the extension of the draft earlier in 1941 was 203 for and 202 against. Only General Marshall's personal plea saved the day on this vital issue.

However, by the end of the day on December 7, 1941, there was no longer any division among the American people. They were united 100 percent in their fury at the Japanese. What Roosevelt couldn't accomplish by his exhortations had been accomplished by the Japanese Navy in a few short hours at Pearl Harbor.

The shocking films and pictures of the wrecked ships and planes at Pearl Harbor also enflamed the hearts of the American people in a strict resolve not to let this act of treachery go unpunished. The Japanese were to pay in full measure for their temporary "victory." Yamamoto, Nagumo, and Tojo included. The fury of America and all its resources were turned into a mighty war effort like the world had never seen before. The Japanese had awakened a sleeping tiger—not a good idea. "They asked for it and they are going to get it," said Roosevelt.

This writer was 12 years old at the time of the attack on Pearl Harbor. I still remember my anger at the time—even now, over 50 years later, it still upsets me.

By their attack on Pearl Harbor, the Japanese had invited their own destruction. They had challenged the number one industrial nation in the world. A nation that with only 30 percent of its resources devoted to the Pacific area, would still overpower them. At the beginning of the war, it was conceivable that the Americans could occupy Japan, but it was inconceivable that Japan could occupy the United States—this should have told the Japanese militarists that they were starting something that they couldn't finish.

Pearl Harbor was just the first battle of the war which soon spread all across the Pacific. The war ended in Tokyo Bay on the Battleship Missouri on a much quieter day than December 7, 1941.

America and Hitler
After Pearl Harbor

While Japan had attacked America and Roosevelt had declared war on Japan, the Germans were curiously silent. Actually, Roosevelt considered Germany the main enemy and preferred to fight the Germans. But how?

Adolph Hitler gave him his chance. On December 11, 1941, Germany declared war on the United States. This was one of Hitler's greatest mistakes. The American people were enraged at the Japanese and wanted to make war on Japan. Revenge was a strong motive.

Hitler could have done nothing and escaped the war with America. Once he declared war against the United States, he had three great powers arranged against him: the Soviet Union, Great Britain, and the United States. As Churchill would say, at that time the war was won. It was a question of time and applying the right amount of force in the right place. It is fair to say that in a short time in early December, 1941, with his army stopped at Moscow and with the United States in the war against him, Hitler was doomed. His credo, "One front at a time," was about to be shot to ribbons.

Why did Hitler declare war on the United States? He said that because of America's naval actions in the Atlantic and the U.S. supplying England and Russia, he was already at war with America. This certainly not a sufficient reason to go to war with a great power. Even von Ribbentrop counseled caution. He pointed out that under the treaty with Japan, Germany was obligated to go to war only if Japan were attacked. Hitler brushed this aside.

The main reason Hitler went to war with the United States was his complete underestimation of the United States. He had no conception of and no knowledge of the United States of America. He actually believed some of his own propaganda that America was made up of so many diverse nationalities and races that it could never organize and fight on a large scale. It is pathetic that Hitler would make such a huge decision based on so little knowledge. Such stupidity deserves to lose. He was taking on what proved to be the number one power in the world while he was already fighting Britain and Russia—a combination of disaster for Germany.

As mentioned earlier, Hitler was basically an uneducated man. He knew virtually nothing of the world outside Europe. In declaring war on America, he didn't realize what he was getting into. Just as he underestimated the Soviet Union, he also underestimated the United States. He seemed to have forgotten completely that America was the deciding factor in the First War, that a large and growing American army had arrived in France and fought bravely and fiercely. Ludendorf and Hindenburg could have told him. It was the American Army and its potentially increasing growth that tipped the scales for Germany to surrender. Germany lost the First War because of America. Why repeat the same mistake?

Hitler didn't seem to have learned anything from that experience. It was as if the First War hadn't happened. Churchill knew about America, but Hitler didn't. Perhaps he was so convinced of his own and Germany's invincibility that nothing else mattered.

In summing up, when Hitler learned of the Japanese attack on the Americans at Pearl Harbor, he had three options:

Option 1—Do nothing. Sometimes the very best decision is the decision to do nothing. In this case, that would have been the right course to take for Hitler. By doing nothing, Hitler could have kept the United States out of the European war. There would have been no invasions of French North Africa, Sicily, or Italy. In particular, there would have been no invasion at Normandy in Northern France, which established a Western Front—which led to the defeat of Germany. Germany could not win a two-front war. This correct decision should have been a "no-brainer" for Hitler. It wasn't.

Option 2—Hitler could have made a deal with Japan that he would declare war on America and Japan would declare war on the Soviet Union— quid pro quo. The Allies, and particularly Russia, were lucky that this didn't happen. The Soviets were in a struggle for their lives, and they didn't need another combat area to divert their forces.

The Japanese were afraid that Hitler would make this request, which would put them in a huge predicament. They wanted Hitler's help in the war against America, but they didn't want to fight the Russians at the same time. The Japanese evidently couldn't see that in helping Hitler to win, they would be helping themselves—short-sighted. If Hitler lost, they were doomed.

Hitler's viewpoint should have been that the Japanese had a large army in Manchuria doing nothing, facing the Russians in Siberia. It would not be necessary for Japan to defeat the Russians, only to keep them engaged and tie up Russian troops. This would keep the Soviets from using these men on the Eastern Front. Remember, at this time, reserves of Soviet troops from Siberia were making a big difference on the front at Moscow. The Eastern Front was turning into a life or death struggle for Germany that could go either way. Tying up Soviet reserves could be decisive.

Option 3—Declare war on America outright with no proposal at all to Japan. This was the option Hitler chose—the worst of the three for him. Hitler would be doing an awful lot or Japan while not making any demands on them at all regarding the Soviet Union—a great deal for Japan. No one knows why Hitler didn't press Japan on this. It could have made a significant difference on the Eastern Front, which he needed.

There may have been a number of reasons for Hitler's decision to declare war on America—none good. Hitler thought so little of American power that in making this momentous decision he gave little thought to it or the consequences that would follow from this decision. The fact that American ships were firing on German U-boats brought out Hitler's combative nature and the urge to strike back. In addition, there was his hatred for Roosevelt and his contempt for Roosevelt and the United States.

Perhaps he was thinking that Japan would keep America occupied in the Pacific. Behind all of his thinking, as previously mentioned, was his complete underestimation and ignorance of the potential power of the United States.

This decision proved to be a huge mistake, as time would tell. One person who was delighted with Hitler's decision to declare war on the United States was Winston Churchill—a good reason for Hitler not to have done so. This mistaken decision, along with several others, resulted in the defeat and destruction of Germany and Hitler's own death. Perhaps he should have taken a little more time to think it through. Those who don't learn from history are condemned to repeat it.

In the late part of the 19th century, Bismarck said that the most important fact in the world was that England and the United States both spoke English. Bismarck evidently was the last German leader to even consider the effect of a combination of England and America.

Bismarck also believed in the necessity of a strong friendship between Germany and Russia—in fact, a pact was initiated by Bismarck between

Germany and Russia. Bismarck was afraid of a future war with France and did not want a two-front war.

Of course, we know the Kaiser got rid of Bismarck and let the Russo-German pact lapse. It seems Bismarck was a great deal smarter than his all-knowing successors, Wilhelm II and Adolph Hitler—both as to Russia, and also the affinity between England and the United States. The price of the Kaiser and Hitler learning these lessons was the loss of two world wars.

Allied Coalition Formed—By Hitler!

Hitler had brought about Bismarck's worst possible nightmare—the combination of Great Britain, America, and Russia all together at once against Germany. Needless to say, if Bismarck had been in charge, this would never have happened.

Hitler, having attacked Poland, knowingly brought Great Britain in against him. On June 22, 1941, he attacked the Soviet Union, which brought Great Britain and Russia together. Now, on December 11, 1941, he had declared war on the United States—this drew America, Great Britain, and the Soviets together for their own self-protection. Hitler had begun in 1935 cleverly picking off one country at a time. Now intoxicated by his victories, he was taking on three great powers at once.

Great Britain, the United States, and Russia were led by Churchill, Roosevelt, and Stalin. In picking out his opponents, Hitler could not have chosen three better men. Churchill, Roosevelt, and Stalin were each probably the best men possible to lead their countries. Each man was brilliant, tough, and resourceful.

In the normal course of events, men such as Churchill and Stalin would have had nothing to do with each other. They were complete opposites. Churchill came from a wealthy background in a democratic civilized country. He had strong moral values. Stalin, on the other hand, came from a remote village in Georgia of very poor parents. He came up through a chaotic period and became the leader of Russia. Stalin had no moral values—in fact, pretty much the opposite.

There was only one man that could bring Churchill and Stalin together—Adolph Hitler. Churchill and Stalin needed each other. They knew if they lost the war, England and Russia would cease to exist. They would become "protected provinces" of Germany with all its consequences. No wonder they became fast friends overnight on June 22, 1941. Wouldn't you?

With Roosevelt and the United States entering the war on December 11, 1941, the coalition of Churchill, Roosevelt, and Stalin was formed. Hitler seemed to be his own worst enemy. He did not know it, but his only chance of winning the war would be to defeat Russia in 1942 before America could exert its power in Europe. With his mistakes and defeat at Stalingrad, Hitler threw away his chance.

Now it was a question of Churchill, Roosevelt, and Stalin working together to crush Germany. These three men were just the people to do it. Churchill the fighter, Roosevelt the mobilizer, and Stalin the man of steel. From December 11, 1941, on, their coalition became stronger and stronger with each passing day. In particular, their communication with each other was excellent—sometimes, it seems, almost on a daily basis. Churchill stands out as the center in the communication area. The "Big Three" were able to coordinate their efforts, all coming from different directions, to corner and crush Germany.

Each of the three made an effort to "get along" with the others. They knew they needed each other—Hitler held them together. Churchill, Roosevelt, and Stalin were great men and leaders—Hitler had picked the wrong men and countries to fight.

Japan on a Rampage

Simultaneously with the attack on Pearl Harbor, the Japanese attacked the Philippines and Malaya. Again, the Americans were surprised, and most of their air force was destroyed on the ground at Clark Field in the Philippines.

Japan invaded the main island of Luzon in the Philippines and made rapid progress against scattered resistance. America and Filipino forces under Douglas MacArthur retreated into the Bataan Peninsula and the island of Corregidor. They courageously held out for over five months with little food, ammunition, or medicine. Finally, on May 6, 1942, they were forced to surrender. In the meanwhile, President Roosevelt had ordered MacArthur to leave the Philippines and go to Australia. Roosevelt wanted to save his best military man in the Pacific for later operations—a wise decision.

The Prince of Wales and the Repulse

The Royal Navy in 1941 was stretched to its limits. It had to defend the home island of England itself, the North Sea, the North Atlantic, and the Mediterranean. The Far East had no practical presence of the Royal Navy.

Of course, Great Britain had an obligation to defend Australia and New Zealand, as well as Malaya. When the Japanese threat to these areas became more imminent in the latter part of 1941, the Royal Navy reacted. It formed a task force of the battleship Prince of Wales, the battle cruiser Repulse, the aircraft carrier Indomitable, and four destroyers. It dispatched this group to Singapore.

Unfortunately, en route, the aircraft carrier Indomitable ran aground at Jamaica. This proved to be a catastrophic accident. Indomitable had to lay up for repairs. The Prince of Wales and the Repulse with the four destroyers proceeded on to Singapore, which they reached on December 2.

The commander of these ships was Admiral Sir Thomas Phillips. On December 8, with the Japanese making landings in Northern Malaya, Admiral Phillips made a fateful decision. He decided to proceed north and attack the landings of the Japanese. Admiral Phillips had received a somewhat vague assurance of air cover from the local R.A.F. Most of its obsolete planes had already been destroyed on the ground.

The decision to proceed north without adequate air cover could be considered a very controversial one indeed. Actually, if this had happened several years later, it would have been called a suicidal mission. In late 1941, however, it had not fully sunk in that air power was indispensable in fighting a naval war.

It is conceivable also that the Japanese effectiveness had been underestimated. It is very unfortunate that the crews of these two huge ships would pay the price for this lack of knowledge. Admiral Phillips may have felt that he had no choice but to resist the Japanese landing with the means at hand. The loss of the aircraft carrier Indomitable was crucial.

Admiral Phillips' small fleet found nothing to the north on December 8 and turned back south on the evening of December 9. He received a report of another landing at Kuantan, midway down the Malayan east coast. (This report later was found to be erroneous.) In any event, Admiral Phillips decided to make a dawn attack. Unfortunately, he had been spotted by a Japanese submarine near midnight on the ninth. The submarine reported its findings to the Japanese Naval Air Force at Saigon.

A large formation of planes was sent out mostly armed with torpedoes. They came upon the British ships at approximately noon and attacked. Quickly, both British ships were hit and in a short time went under. Of the crews, 840 were lost, a further 2,081 were rescued—many died in Japanese prison camps. Admiral Phillips went down with the ship.

It is not certain what would have happened if the Indomitable had been with them. Perhaps they would have still been sunk, including the Indomitable. On the other hand, the Indomitable with its planes could have given them a fighting chance. As it was, they had no chance at all.

With the loss of these ships and Singapore, the British power in Asia vanished. An empire that had taken two hundred years to build vanished in a few short months. The world had changed virtually overnight.

Another factor was that this occurrence marked the end of the battleship as the main backbone of any navy. Battleships were still invaluable in providing anti-aircraft fire to protect the carriers. Also, battleships were very helpful in bombarding sites of amphibious invasions, such as Normandy.

Air power, particularly naval air power, would decide the war in the Pacific.

To Lose an Empire
Malaya and Singapore

With no naval presence in the area and limited air power, the British had to make a decision whether to contest the Japanese advance into Malaya from the north, or to pull back its forces and protect and defend Singapore itself.

On Luzon in the Philippines, the Americans had elected not to fight for the whole island but to retreat into the Bataan Peninsula, which was a natural and smaller defensive position. They were able to withstand the Japanese attack for five months in this position. Almost out of ammunition, food, and medicine and with no hope of any relief on the way, they finally had to surrender.

In Malaya in December, the British had a similar situation as the Americans on Luzon. The British elected to fight the Japanese attack in Northern Malaya with most of their army. As it turned out, this proved to be a fatal mistake. One reason for this decision was a complete underestimation of the Japanese. Although the British, Indian, and Australian troops outnumbered the Japanese, they were pushed back from the very beginning.

The Japanese under General Yamashita waged a brilliant campaign. The British, while attempting to defend everywhere, were consistently bypassed, cut off, and almost surrounded in places. They were in a continuous retreat through the jungles—the Japanese made amphibious landings behind the British lines to further confuse the defense. British leadership seemed to be completely baffled by the Japanese tactics. In some places, their forces put up a gallant fight only to have to retreat to keep from being surrounded. The Japanese had seized the offensive, and all the British could do was react.

Finally, at the end of January, the British forces from Malaya retreated into the island of Singapore itself. They were in a pitiful and demoralized condition and had sustained many casualties.

Churchill, of course, was keeping up with keen interest and dismay with what was happening. To his utter surprise, he found out that while Singapore was supposed to be an impregnable island, it definitely was not. The heavy guns and defense were lined up to face an attack from the sea to the south. Evidently, no one had thought that an attack would be made from Malaya itself to the north. There were no defensive positions on the north side of Singapore; possibly, the British thought that no one would come down through the jungles of Malaya.

In any event, the heavy guns on the island's south side were useless now. Churchill, for once, was dumbfounded. He had no suspicion whatever that there was no defense line in the northern part of Singapore. In the meanwhile, Churchill, somewhat against his better judgment, had sent reinforcements to Singapore: considerable ground troops and some airplanes. Unfortunately, the airplanes were shot down in a short time by the superiority of the Japanese in the air.

At this point on the first of February, the British Empire forces on Singapore outnumbered the Japanese by a two to one margin. The only problem was the British were in complete confusion, not only the troops, but the leadership as well. In contrast, the American and Philippine troops were putting up a strong defense against the Japanese and causing them a great many problems. It is obvious that the American leadership was much better than that at Singapore.

There was no such confusion on the Japanese side. They were determined to take Singapore.

On February 9, they crossed the Johore Strait and attacked the defenders. The first assault was driven off, but the next wave succeeded in making a landing. From there on, it was all downhill for the British. In a chaotic situation on the British side, the Japanese advanced rapidly. With their water supply for the whole island in jeopardy and the threat of many civilian casualties from continual fighting, General Percival decided to surrender. The exact number that surrendered is unknown. It is placed between 70,000 and 90,000 men. Many of these men perished in deplorable Japanese prison camps. Some of the captured Indian troops were recruited by the Japanese and formed the Indian National Army, the INA. Almost 20,000 men were assembled. They fought on the Japanese side in the attack on India. This would tend to indicate that the morale of many of the Indian troops was low during the fight for Singapore, which may be one of the reasons it fell.

The fall of Singapore is considered the biggest disgrace in British military history—it marked the end of the British Empire.

The Japanese continued their advance to the south and east almost unopposed. In one fleet action, the relatively small Allied fleet was wiped out. The Dutch East Indies with its coveted oil fell. Burma to the west fell. It seemed the Japanese were invincible.

Wake Island
Bataan and Corregidor

This book was not intended to cover every action in this vast war. But certain battles achieved significance because of time and place. Also, there is the fact that there were courageous men involved, and their deeds and accomplishments cannot and should not be ignored. These men were heroes, and they should not ever be forgotten.

Wake Island

Wake Island was a lonely outpost about 2,000 miles west of Pearl Harbor. Next to Guam, it was the most forward outpost of the American defense and as such was the most vulnerable.

Its forces consisted of thirteen officers and 365 Marines under the command of Major James Devereux. They had six five-inch naval guns; they also had on the newly constructed airstrip twelve Marine Grumman Wildcat fighter planes.

The Japanese attacked by air from nearby Kwajalein for three days; seven of the Grumman planes were destroyed.

In the early hours of December 11, the Japanese invasion fleet approached Wake and bombarded it with little result. The defenders were quick to reply. The counter fire hit the light cruiser Yubari and drove her off badly damaged. The destroyer Hayate was sunk, and three other destroyers were damaged and forced to retire. The four surviving Wildcats also attacked, damaged another cruiser, and sank the destroyer Kisaragi. The garrison had done a magnificent job and were elated. They hoped reinforcements were on the way.

Indeed, Admiral Kimmel in Honolulu did send a task force of carriers westward to help the beleaguered but distant outpost. They were on their way when Admiral Kimmel was removed from command and replaced by Admiral Pyle, an interim appointment. Admiral Pyle was given the option to continue this relief operation or not. Admiral Pyle thought his first priority was to conserve the remaining aircraft carriers for future action and also to protect Hawaii. Considering this, he ordered the task force to turn back. Thus, Wake Island was written off. Admiral Pyle was probably correct in this decision, because if the American carriers were lost, Hawaii would be virtually undefended. This was no consolation for the gallant defenders of Wake.

The Japanese returned to Wake with much heavier forces than in the initial attack and pummeled the island with bombs and shells. By this time, all the defending planes were gone and the ground defense was being steadily worn down. At 2:35 a.m. on December 23, the Japanese landed in several places on the island. They were fiercely resisted and 800 of their men were killed. Finally, the pressure was too great, and Major Devereux surrendered in order to save the remaining men.

They had put up a wonderful fight and did all that could be possibly expected of them, and more. In addition, they helped the morale of the American people immensely. They had lost, but they had won.

Bataan-Corregidor

With the invasion of Luzon in the Philippines in early December, 1941, General MacArthur, without air or naval support, withdrew his forces into the Bataan Peninsula. Bataan was a good defensible position. MacArthur hoped to hold out until help arrived. Unfortunately, with most of the American fleet destroyed or damaged at Pearl Harbor, there was no way to get reinforcements or supplies to the Philippines. The Japanese controlled the water and the air; anything sent would have been sunk. Bataan and Corregidor didn't know it at the time, but they had no chance of receiving help.

Nevertheless, with diminishing supplies of ammunition, food, and medicine, the Americans and the Filipinos continued their fight. Disease and illness had great effect on both sides.

On March 12, MacArthur was ordered out of the Philippines and replaced by General Wainwright.

The Japanese reassessed their position at Bataan and reinforced their troops. On April 3, the Japanese attacked and smashed through the almost starving defenders. On April 9, General King, the commander, ordered his troops to surrender in this hopeless situation.

Unfortunately, after the surrender, the Japanese treated their prisoners in a brutal manner. They ordered the weakened men to march 65 miles to San Fernando. During the march, many were beaten, clubbed, or bayoneted. Anyone who fell out from exhaustion or wounds was killed. It is unknown how many men were lost, but it was substantial. It became known as "the Bataan Death March." It succeeded in making the Americans at home and everywhere even madder at the Japanese and more determined to avenge these savage acts. After the war, General Homma was executed for allowing this to happen.

After Bataan fell, the Japanese turned their full force on Corregidor. They bombarded it intensely and landed there on May 5. The presence of Japanese tanks hurt the defenders, as they had no defense to stop them. The garrison put up a stiff resistance but were so weakened by hunger, disease, and lack of equipment that they were forced to surrender.

Bataan and Corregidor had held out for five months while Japan was running wild in the rest of southwest Asia. In the normal course of events, holding out this long should have been enough to receive supplies and reinforcements. The men on Bataan and Corregidor had done their part and more. They had and would suffer more than one can imagine. Japanese prison camps were horrible—one out of four prisoners of the Japanese perished in captivity.

Unfortunately, Japan had control of the air and sea, and it was impossible at that time to render help. These men served as an inspiration to their fellow countrymen then, and they still do now. They were avenged.

Japanese Americans

There were many Americans of Japanese heritage living in Hawaii and California. In fact, over one-third of the inhabitants of Hawaii were of Japanese descent.

With the treacherous attack by Japan on Pearl Harbor on December 7, 1941, a form of rage almost amounting to hysteria gripped America. There were rumors that Japanese Americans living in Hawaii had helped Japan in the attack by giving the location of the American fleet.

There was even fear that Japan would attack the west coast of the United States. As weeks went by and Japan claimed victory after victory, Americans were very uneasy. Animosity towards Japanese Americans began to increase. They were judged as possible traitors. There was no foundation for these fears, but they existed nonetheless.

As the Japanese Americans were such a large part of the population of Hawaii, nothing was done there. However, on February 19, 1942, President Roosevelt signed an Executive Order empowering military authorities to relocate residents of military areas. General John DeWitt declared California, Oregon, and Washington as military areas, which meant relocating all the Japanese Americans from that area. Forced to settle their personal affairs immediately, more than 110,000 Japanese Americans had to abandon homes and businesses and move to ten relocation centers in remote areas. Many had spent a lifetime acquiring their homes and businesses, and overnight they were gone.

The camps in no way resembled those of Nazi Germany. There was no violence, no threats; the food was good; and there was minimum security. However, the Japanese Americans were stunned and hurt by these developments. They considered themselves Americans and had done nothing to deserve this treatment.

It is remarkable after this kind of treatment that many Japanese Americans volunteered and were accepted into the armed forces. Perhaps they were trying to show that the authorities were wrong about them. Many were sent to the Pacific area, where they worked in intelligence, particularly as they understood the Japanese language. Strange that you would imprison a people and then let some of them work in sensitive intelligence positions. You have to proceed on the theory that the whole matter was an irrational reaction to the attack on Pearl Harbor.

Japanese American soldiers formed a large part of the 442 Regimental Combat Team, which fought with great distinction in Italy. Their casualties were among the highest of any unit in action, and they received many commendations for valor, including a Congressional Medal of Honor.

The action of these men became known throughout the United States. Attitudes began to change, and people began to realize they had made a big mistake by interning innocent patriotic Americans. The Supreme Court in 1944 ruled the internment was unconstitutional, basically that sending people to prison camps when they had not done anything wrong, was wrong. The Japanese Americans were allowed to return home. As time went by, most Americans were ashamed that this event had even occurred.

It was primarily that Japanese American young men were fighting and dying for America that changed the whole attitude toward Japanese Americans. The internment is an event that nearly all Americans would like to forget, but History won't let them.

Americans Bomb Tokyo
The Doolittle Raid

With the Japanese triumphant everywhere in the Pacific, Roosevelt knew that it would take time to build up American forces to regain the offensive. In the meanwhile, the Americans needed something to help their morale under the constant victorious march of the Japanese.

The American Navy came up with an idea—a great idea. To bomb Tokyo itself! The question was—how to do it. The possibility of naval aircraft from American carriers was dismissed. The range of naval planes was not enough. The carrier would have no chance, as they would have to get close to Japan and getting away would be doubtful. Also, getting in that close, the Japanese would be forewarned and waiting for the air attack. Surprise would be lost.

However, the Americans came up with an idea to make this attack feasible. Use medium range Army bombers, specifically the twin engine B-25s. These would be launched off an aircraft carrier, the Hornet, which was commanded by Admiral William "Bull" Halsey. The aircraft would be under the command of General James Doolittle, a very experienced pilot.

The main problem was getting the bombers to take off on the short deck of the carrier. It seemed impossible. Maybe that's why the Japanese didn't even consider it in their defense of the home island. However, Doolittle and his selected crews practiced over and over on the ground until they thought it could be done—only experience would tell. The sixteen B-25s were loaded onto the Hornet and it set sail. Destination: Japan.

The original plan was to launch the planes 400 miles from Tokyo. However, when at 700 miles the Hornet came across several small Japanese patrol boats, Doolittle and Halsey were afraid that the small boats had radioed Japan of the occurrence, so the Americans decided to take off immediately. This was at 8:20 a.m. April 18, 1942.

All sixteen made if off the deck, although one came very close to hitting the water after takeoff—the pilot had forgotten to set his flaps. The sixteen proceeded towards Japan. The Japanese in Tokyo were about to get the surprise of their lives, somewhat like the Americans felt at Pearl Harbor.

By coincidence, on April 18th, Tokyo had held an air raid practice just before Doolittle's planes came in. The Japanese thought the raid somehow was connected with the air raid practice. They were completely surprised and put up almost no resistance. Several other Japanese cities besides Tokyo were hit as well: Kobe, Yokosuka, and Yokohama.

Certainly, the physical damage inflicted by the bombing was relatively slight, but the psychological impact was immense on both sides of the Pacific. Yamamoto was particularly concerned about possible damage to the Imperial Palace, something he viewed as catastrophic. It wasn't hit this time, but what about the future?

Doolittle's B-25s continued their flight westward to China, fighting a severe storm. Most of the planes either crash landed, or the crews bailed out over China. One plane landed in Vladivostok in Siberia. It was a very rough ordeal for the airmen. Of the 80 who had taken off, 71 eventually made it back to the United States. Eight of the men landed in Japanese occupied areas and were captured, three of whom were executed by the Japanese by way of reprisal. When the Americans heard of this, it made them even more determined to defeat Japan, no matter what it took. In addition, thousands of Chinese civilians were killed in Japanese retaliatory actions.

In any event, the Doolittle raid was a terrific boost in morale for all Americans. They were fighting back. The airmen who took part in the raid were regarded as heroes, which they certainly were. This one raid, Americans believed, was just a foretaste of what the Japanese could expect in the future, and on a much larger scale.

The Japanese military and civilians were in a state of shock. They couldn't believe it, even though they knew it had happened. They thought the Americans were on the ropes, and here they were, bombing Tokyo. It was a sobering experience, to say the least. Maybe the war would not be over as soon as their propaganda had led them to believe. And, the thought may have occurred to them that when the war was over, it might not be ending the way they thought it would be.

It occurs to the author what Hitler thought when he heard of the American raid on Tokyo. I would imagine that he was surprised as much as the Japanese. Did he perhaps have a slight twinge of thought that maybe he had acted a little hastily in declaring war on America? I doubt if Hitler ever admitted to making any mistakes, but who knows? One can only hope.

From an actual military standpoint, the raid had immense significance. Admiral Yamamoto and the government decided to attack again in the direction of Hawaii, this time to finish off the American fleet and prevent any more actions like the Doolittle raid.

The Coral Sea

In launching their war against the Americans, the Japanese were at least realistic enough to know they could not invade and occupy the continental United States. Their goal was to establish the Japanese Empire over the whole of Southeast Asia. The natural resources of this whole area would then be at their disposal—oil, rubber, tin—in short, everything they needed to maintain their Empire.

They planned to establish a defensive barrier in the Central and South Pacific to forestall the Americans by fortifying a chain of islands on their outermost perimeter and then having strong, mobile naval forces to destroy the attacking Americans. They felt that after defeating American attempts to counter-attack, the Americans would get tired and accept the status quo. Little did the Japanese realize what they had done by stirring up the Americans at Pearl Harbor. In fact, the Americans were enraged and would stop at nothing to crush the Japanese. The Japanese had unleashed American power by their sneak attack and were now going to have to pay for it.

The militarists running Japan decided to isolate and neutralize Australia. They would occupy New Guinea to the north of Australia, Port Moresby in particular, and the Solomon Islands to the northeast. This would stop the supply lines coming across the Pacific from America to Australia. In addition, they would occupy Midway Island in the Central Pacific as a forward eastern outpost and possibly as a base from which to attack Hawaii to the east, meanwhile destroying the remnants of the American fleet. Remember, to this point the Japanese had achieved overwhelming victories everywhere they went. They were on a roll—nothing could stop them. Their contempt for their enemies was complete, and their confidence in themselves was unlimited. The seeds of disaster had been sown.

Their first move was the occupation of Port Moresby in New Guinea and also to occupy Tulagi and Guadalcanal in the Solomon Islands. In particular, they planned to establish air bases at Tulagi and Guadalcanal to cover that part of the Pacific.

As mentioned earlier, the Americans had broken the Japanese naval code and were aware of their plans. They sent a task force, consisting of the carriers Lexington and Yorktown with their escorts, to the South Pacific under the command of Admiral Frank Fletcher. They established themselves south of the Solomons in the Coral Sea and awaited the Japanese.

The Japanese force consisted of two carriers, the Zuikaku and the Shokaku, plus escorts, under the command of Admiral Inouye. The operation was code-named Operation MO by Yamamoto. The Japanese began landing on Tulagi on May 3. On learning of the landing, Fletcher attacked by air. There were few results—however, the battle was now joined. It was to be the first naval battle carried out by naval air alone, and the first of many to come.

In the ensuing melee, mistakes were made by both sides. The results were a tactical victory for the Japanese. The Lexington was sunk, and the Yorktown was badly damaged. On the Japanese side, the Shoku, a light carrier that had joined the other two Japanese carriers, was sunk. Also, the Shokaku was damaged and retired to Japan for repairs.

Overall, however, it was a strategic victory for the Americans. The Japanese abandoned their hope of an occupation of Port Moresby from the sea. In fact, they never got to Port Moresby. For the first time in the war, the Japanese plans had been thwarted. In addition, they lost the services of the carrier Shokaku for the next encounter with the Americans, which would be at Midway Island in the Central Pacific. It would prove to be a critical loss in the most important battle of the Pacific War. While the Yorktown had been seriously damaged, Admiral Nimitz had it at Midway. The Shokaku was only moderately damaged and was not at Midway. On such things, great battles are won or lost.

Midway—The Turn of the Tide

After the Doolittle raid on Tokyo, Admiral Yamamoto was even more determined to strike the Americans a hard blow in the Central Pacific. The objective was Midway Island, about one thousand miles west of Hawaii. Yamamoto would occupy Midway and, using it as a threat to Pearl Harbor, lure the remaining American fleet out and destroy it. Thus, the Japanese would have established their defensive perimeter further east and destroyed the American fleet at the same time.

During this time, Yamamoto sent a small fleet to the Aleutian Islands, just west of Alaska, to occupy Attu and Kiska Islands. Just what good these remote outposts would do for the Japanese is not clearly understood. It was actually a mistake, as it diverted part of Yamamoto's fleet away from the main action at Midway. As mentioned, the Japanese had little respect for their opponent and made their plans accordingly.

The advance fleet of four carriers under Admiral Nagumo would strike Midway and disable it. A follow-up fleet would occupy the island. Admiral Yamamoto would follow behind with a huge fleet of battleships and cruisers and mop up what was left. Nagumo, with his carriers, was to be on the alert for American carriers and attack and destroy them as soon as they were located. Thus, Nagumo had two objectives: attacking and neutralizing Midway, and also eliminating the American carriers. They were trying to do two things at once—impossible. This was a fatal mistake. The Americans had only one objective: to destroy Nagumo's carriers. With the Japanese carriers gone, they would have defeated Yamamoto's whole fleet. Without air cover, Yamamoto's battleships and cruisers would be just as vulnerable as the Prince of Wales and the Repulse.

As mentioned, the Americans had broken the Japanese naval code and were aware of their intentions. The American code breakers noticed the Japanese referred to their target as "AF." They suspected AF was Midway but were not sure. They had Midway radio back to Hawaii that their fresh water was low and the distillation machinery was broken. Shortly thereafter, American intelligence picked up a message from a Japanese listening post to their superiors that, "AF was running low on fresh water." This confirmed that Midway was to be the point of attack.

Nimitz had two carriers available, the Enterprise and the Hornet. The Yorktown had just arrived at Pearl Harbor but was heavily damaged. In three days, Nimitz had the Yorktown patched together and sent it to sea with the workmen still working onboard. Admiral Bill Halsey was supposed to command, but he was ill in the hospital. Nimitz appointed Admiral Raymond Spruance to command the Enterprise and the Hornet. Spruance had never commanded naval air forces, but both Nimitz and Halsey thought he was the best man for the job. Admiral Fletcher was in charge of the Yorktown and was in nominal command of the whole fleet; however, Spruance was on his own to make his own decisions.

The Americans sailed from Pearl Harbor on May 28th and stationed themselves two hundred miles north of Midway, on the flank of the approaching Japanese. American patrol planes spotted the Japanese fleet on June 3rd. On the next day at dawn, Japanese planes in full force struck Midway. The Americans put up a spirited defense. Seventeen Marine planes were shot down. In the meanwhile, American planes from Midway were attacking the Japanese fleet. In spite of repeated and heroic attacks, the Americans caused almost no damage to the Japanese.

Admiral Nagumo had sent out search planes to look for the American carriers, with no results. When his planes returned from the Midway attack, Nagumo was advised that another attack on Midway would be necessary. He ordered his planes to be fitted with bombs suitable for this attack.

In the meanwhile, Admiral Spruance, aware of the Japanese attack on Midway, determined to attack the Japanese carriers as quickly as possible. Admiral Fletcher on the Yorktown did the same. American torpedo and dive bombers took off on the morning of June 4th for their attack. Shortly after this, a Japanese search plane belatedly found the American carriers and radioed the information to Nagumo. Nagumo was in the midst of arming his planes for the attack on Midway. He was caught in total surprise by the report of American carriers in the area. Undecided as to what to do, he finally gave orders to change the Japanese plans from an attack on Midway to an attack on the American carriers.

This meant a complete change of armaments for the planes on the carrier decks. Bombs for the land attack were being taken off the planes, and torpedoes were brought to the flight decks. There were bombs and torpedoes all over the decks of the four Japanese carriers. At this time, American carrier planes struck—the worst possible time for the Japanese.

The first planes to attack were several waves of torpedo planes. They met a hail of fire from the Japanese fleet and were set upon by the fast flying Zero fighter planes covering the Japanese ships. One squadron of fifteen torpedo planes from the Hornet, under Lieutenant Commander John Waldron, was completely destroyed with only one survivor, Ensign George Gay. Of the 45 torpedo planes that attacked, 35 were shot down. Unfortunately, they were unable to make any hits on the Japanese carriers, but their sacrifice was not in vain.

With the Japanese concentrating their defense on the low-flying torpedo planes, they were suddenly attacked from above by 36 dive bombers under the command of Lieutenant Commander Wade McClusky. This may have been the most decisive moment in the entire Pacific war. In quick order, three Japanese carriers were hit, the Akagi, the Soryu, and the Koga. With their own bombs scattered on their decks, the American bombs caused havoc. There were explosions everywhere.

Planes from the Enterprise and the Yorktown participated in the dive bombing attacks. In just a few minutes, three Japanese carriers had been knocked out and eventually sank. Only the Hiryu was left. It sent its plans aloft to attack the American fleet and gain some measure of revenge. The Hiryu planes attacked and seriously damaged the Yorktown. The crew made an heroic attempt to save the battered Yorktown, but it was sunk the following day by torpedoes from a Japanese submarine. This valiant ship went down, but not before accomplishing all of its crucial missions. It had played an indispensable part in the battle—it deserves our salute!

The last planes off the Yorktown, ten dive bombers along with McClusky's planes, attacked the Hiryu and scored four hits. The Hiryu was mortally damaged, and it, too, sank. Thus, all four Japanese carriers went beneath the waves. Not only were their four carriers sunk, but also hundreds of their most skilled and experienced air crews were killed. The Japanese first team was gone, never to be replaced.

When Yamamoto learned the news that all four of his carriers were sunk, he was stunned. This was not supposed to happen. He was incredulous of the news, but it was true. It was the worst calamity imaginable to him. With American carriers still in action, Yamamoto pondered that to do. He hoped to lure Spruance into close range of his battleships, but Spruance was too smart for that.

Since the Japanese battleships had no air cover, they would be sitting ducks for American air attacks. With his heart sinking, Yamamoto ordered the entire fleet to retreat to Japan. Japan's high point in the war was over—from now on it was the Americans on the offensive. The tide of the war in the Pacific had turned. Midway was the most decisive naval battle in the Pacific and one of the most decisive in history. A relative handful of courageous American naval airmen had changed the course of the war. In a few minutes, Japan had gone from winning the war to losing it. For Japan, the days of wine and roses were over.

At the time of the Midway battle, President Roosevelt was in the process of having a huge fleet of carriers built in the United States. While during the Midway battle the United States had only three carriers, in later years it would have over 20 in attacks. The Japanese would be completely overwhelmed. All told, during the war the United States would build 25 large carriers and over eighty escort carriers. Roosevelt had appointed the right men to lead the American naval attack in the Pacific, and now he was going to give them the means to be successful. Pearl Harbor had been avenged, and then some.

It should be remembered that at this time President Roosevelt was engaged in a full-scale war against Hitler on the other side of the world from the Pacific area. He was the only one of the four world leaders in the war fighting full-scale on both sides of the world. Simultaneously, Roosevelt was fighting two strong powers. He was completely optimistic that America and its allies would prevail. That optimism and confidence was infectious and boosted the morale of the American people, spurring them on to even greater efforts. Roosevelt would turn the full power and resources of the United States against its enemies. Japan and Germany had completely underestimated Roosevelt and America and would suffer the consequences. There are mistakes, and then there are mistakes. In war, these kinds of mistakes evolve into losing the war.

4

Europe and Africa, 1942

Shortly after Pearl Harbor, Roosevelt and Churchill met in Washington to plan their strategy. They agreed that the policy should be to defeat Germany first. Also, the war against the U-boats should be given the highest priority. Germany was the most dangerous enemy they faced and a great menace to the whole world. They knew that the Germans would be a formidable opponent and that it would take the bulk of the Allied men and resources to defeat them. Meanwhile, in the Pacific, they would do the best they could to maintain an offensive with minimal resources.

The other objective set out by Roosevelt and Churchill was to keep Russia in the war. If Russia were defeated, almost 200 German divisions would be free to turn in any direction. It was an absolute imperative to keep Russia as an active belligerent. At the present time, all the allies could do was to send as many supplies as possible and to bomb German cities. For the future, various offensive ideas were considered. The most radical was an almost suicidal landing on the northern French coast in 1942. The idea was to draw off German forces from Russia. Churchill shot this idea down—one Dunkirk was enough, and they might not be as lucky to get away this time. Churchill knew the Allies were nowhere near invading France successfully. He preferred to wait until more resources could be devoted to it and the chance of success was greater.

Naturally, Josef Stalin was pushing for a second front as soon as possible to take pressure off his front. He knew the Germans would attack in 1942 as soon as the weather permitted. There was a possibility that Russia could be knocked out of the war in 1942, and Stalin wanted and needed all the help the Allies could give. In fact, the American army was a long way from being able to conduct large-scale offensive operations; it was still in the process of organization. Roosevelt and Churchill knew that they had to take some offensive action against the Germans in 1942, if only to bolster Russian morale and keep her in the war.

In June, 1942, General George Marshall flew to London to discuss with Churchill and the British the options for offensive action. Churchill and General Alan Brooke completely rejected the American plan to strike at the French coast in 1942; they were not even too favorable for it in 1943. This infuriated the Americans, including Eisenhower. The British had a lot more respect for the Germans from actual experience with the German army. In addition, history reflected that the British always preferred peripheral action first. At one point in their discussions on invading France, General Brooke asked General Marshall why he was so intent on landing in Northern France so soon. Marshall replied that it was the quickest way to end the war. "Yes," Brooke replied, "But maybe not in the way we want it to end."

Without England's cooperation, there was no chance of invading Northern France. As Roosevelt and Churchill both wanted to take offensive action in 1942, they agreed to attack French North Africa in late 1942 with a much safer operation, called Operation Torch. It would be the beginning of the long road to Germany, but, as the saying goes, "Every journey begins with the first step." It was the first step, but it was an important one. I'm sure the Germans didn't like it. This operation was basically Churchill's plan.

Basic Strategy of England

Winston Churchill, General Alan Brooke, and, to some extent, Anthony Eden were the men who decided the basic strategy for England in World War II. Churchill was the driving force behind everything; his experience and wisdom were indispensable. All of these men had been in the thick of it in the First War. They had seen the hundreds of thousands of casualties inflicted on the English by the Germans on the Western Front. They knew that their relatively small country couldn't stand another blood letting on this scale. For four years (1914-1918), the Allies had attacked against the tough German defense. The arrival of the Americans tilted the scale in favor of the Allies.

Now, in 1942, with England's ally in the west gone, an entirely new situation presented itself. Indeed, no longer having the French army to count on, the English had no foothold on the European continent at all. While they did have a strong navy and air force, their army was still relatively small. Churchill and his colleagues realized in 1942 that their army was no match for the German army in France. Though the bulk of the German army was fighting in Russia, they still left a substantial number of divisions in the West.

America's entry into the war changed the picture to a great extent. In the long run, it was decisive, but for the immediate situation, it didn't amount to a whole lot. As it was in World War I, many months passed before America was actually participating with any significant strength. Her army was still developing in 1942. We had gotten a late start but were working hard to catch up.

England's basic strategy was to wait until the American army would be in Europe in real strength which might take one or two years. This was somewhat like Petain's thinking in 1917—do nothing and wait for the Americans. It worked in the First War. Churchill and General Brooke had a great deal of respect for the German army—they were in against the first team, and they had to have every advantage they could to win. Survival was at stake. Accordingly, while waiting for the build-up of the Americans, Churchill knew that some offensive action had to be taken to keep up the morale of England and America, and also to keep the Russians happy. Thus, striking at the periphery was the only option possible. This strategy had defeated Napoleon.

With the use of their superior naval power, England could strike at the weaker fringes of the Axis. One advantage of this was that it stretched out the German defense. This would help bring in some German forces from the east, relieving the pressure on the Russians. Moreover, being on the offensive made it easier to mount more men and materiel at the point of attack. Meanwhile, as time went by, the Russians were wearing down the Wehrmacht. German casualties on the Eastern Front were reaching terrible proportions. The Germans were being bled to death in Russia.

So, the basic war strategy of England and Churchill was:

1. Wait for the build-up of the American army in Europe.
2. Attack the periphery and stretch the German defense. Also, this would keep the initiative in Allied hands.
3. Let time and the Russians wear down the Germans.

When these conditions were met, the English were ready to cooperate in a full-scale assault on Northern France. This would be the decisive battle in the West, and the English wanted every advantage on their side when this battle began. While the English were not enthusiastic about the assault on Northern France, they knew it was necessary, and the Americans were insistent on it. Churchill felt that if the invasion were a failure, it would be a devastating defeat. Nevertheless, he agreed to proceed. If it were successful, it would end the war.

This is how the war actually went. Although Churchill and the English were the junior partners of the United States, it was English strategy that was in the forefront and led to a successful conclusion of the war. Churchill and his men did a brilliant job. The war followed exactly the pattern they had laid out.

Churchill's Chief Adviser—General Brooke

General Alan Brooke was the Chief of the Imperial General Staff (C.I.G.S.) during most of the war. He was born in Ulster in Ireland and attended Woolwich Military Academy. He fought in the First War, achieved distinction, and rose from lieutenant to lieutenant colonel. After the war, he advanced rapidly and became major general in 1935. He commanded a corps in France in 1940 and again distinguished himself. He was recognized as one of the key people who saved the B. E. F. from destruction. Shortly after returning home, he was promoted by Churchill to full general and given command of the British army to resist the threatened German invasion.

All this time, he was gaining Churchill's respect, and in December, 1941, Churchill appointed him C.I.G.S., that is, the head of the British Army. Brooke became Churchill's principal military adviser and was in almost daily contact with the Prime Minister.

Brooke was an outspoken person; if he disagreed with Churchill, he did not hesitate to tell him so, sometimes to Churchill's chagrin and ire. Brooke thought it was one of the most important facets of his job to keep Churchill's eye on the main projects and objectives. Churchill had been known to go off on tangents and pursue his own personal, sometimes outlandish, ideas. Brooke thought it was his job to knock these down, and he was very effective at doing so. In particular, Churchill wanted to attack and invade Norway, a desirable objective, but not one that would influence the outcome of the war. Brooke and the Americans were able to squelch that idea also.

In the main, however, Brooke and Churchill agreed on just about everything, including the peripheral strategy of attacking the Axis on their fringes and weaker sides, while at the same time building up strength for the main blow, the invasion of Northern France. Brooke was a member of the Combined Chiefs of Staff, comprising the foremost military men of the United States and Britain. This committee was set up to work out strategy and solve problems in the execution of the war, and then report their decisions to Churchill and Roosevelt. Brooke was the leader of the British team.

General Alan Brooke had a somewhat brusque personality and at times did not get along well with his American counterparts, particularly General

George Marshall. However, they were both excellent military men and put aside their personal differences to prosecute the war very effectively. General Brooke made excellent choices of his generals for the various war theaters. Among his men were General Harold Alexander, General Bernard Montgomery in Africa, and General Slim in Burma.

All in all, General Brooke built a great record during the war. He was Churchill's closest adviser and deserves credit for his large part in winning the war.

Anthony Eden—Foreign Secretary, Adviser to Churchill

Anthony Eden was appointed Churchill's foreign secretary in December, 1940. Eden was a rather unusual man. He fought in France in the First War, serving as the youngest brigade major in the British Army. Eden was a handsome, typical British aristocrat with a certain urbane charm. Politically astute, Eden worked hard and advanced into high office. In December, 1935, he became foreign secretary in Stanley Baldwin's government. Chamberlain succeeded Baldwin in 1937, and Eden remained as foreign secretary. He and Chamberlain did not get along well; however, Eden basically went along with Chamberlain's appeasement policy. In February, 1938, Eden had had enough of it and resigned.

At this point, Eden's standing in the Conservative Party was much higher than that of Churchill. Eden, it seemed, had a good chance of becoming prime minister, much better, in fact, than Churchill. To some extent at this time, Eden and Churchill became allied in opposition to Chamberlain's continued giving in to Hitler.

In May, 1940, as fate would have it, Churchill became prime minister. In his new government, he appointed Anthony Eden secretary of state for war and in December, as mentioned, appointed him foreign secretary, a post which Eden served throughout the war. It was assumed by everyone that if something happened to Churchill, Eden would succeed him as prime minister.

While Eden and Churchill were not close, Churchill had a high regard for Eden's ability. Eden was the main force behind Britain going into Greece in 1941. He also visited Stalin in Moscow and Roosevelt in Washington. His goal was to hold the alliance together and work out any problems that might exist. He did an excellent job. One thing about Eden: he didn't mind standing up to Stalin. He also was a champion of Charles de Gaulle and frequently argued with Churchill in de Gaulle's behalf. Eden was an asset to Churchill and performed his duties very well; in particular, he got along well with the Americans. Roosevelt especially liked him.

Churchill and Roosevelt

Early in October, 1939, the First Lord of the Admiralty received a letter from Franklin D. Roosevelt, President of the United States, asking Churchill to, "Keep in touch with me personally with anything you want me to know about." Thus began a relationship that lasted until Roosevelt's death in 1945. During this period, the two leaders exchanged 1,949 written messages or cablegrams. Churchill signed his "Former Naval Person."

Churchill and Roosevelt were slightly acquainted before the war. They had a great deal in common. Both came from wealthy families and had strong mothers. Both were active in naval affairs in the First War, Roosevelt as Assistant Secretary of the Navy and Churchill as First Lord of the Admiralty. Both had similar views of the world. Roosevelt liked England, and Churchill liked America, particularly since his mother was American. As a student of history, Churchill was especially interested in the American Civil War. He had visited some of its battlefields; he knew what a tough struggle it had been, requiring courageous actions on both sides. He had a great deal of respect for the fighting ability of the Americans.

Hitler had no such knowledge. His actual familiarity with America was zero. Thus, Hitler was basing his decisions in regard to the United States on his own stupid prejudices. Perhaps he should have consulted the Kaiser in this regard. Churchill, especially, believed that the United States was potentially a very powerful country that England needed to have on its side. In fact, he believed that America's participation would be the decisive factor in any conflict, and he based all his plans on that belief. This was in contrast to Hitler, who really did not give much thought to the United States. To say that Churchill had a much more realistic attitude than Hitler is putting it mildly. It made a huge difference in the outcome of the war.

When Churchill became prime minister in May, 1940, his contacts with Roosevelt increased. With the fall of France, Churchill turned to Roosevelt and the United States as his only hope of winning the war. Britain had no chance of overcoming mighty Germany by itself. Roosevelt began increasing the flow of war materials to Britain, including fifty older destroyers. The British gave the Americans the right to have naval bases in their few possessions in the Western Hemisphere. This was the Lend Lease Agreement. Roosevelt was using every way possible to help England, even though in 1940 America was still neutral. Roosevelt knew that if England fell, it was possible the whole continent of Europe would fall under Hitler. There could be no invasion of Western Europe without England as a base; and Russia would be isolated in Europe to face the entire German army and air force by itself.

So, Roosevelt felt that saving England was of the highest priority. However, since American public opinion in 1940 was to stay out of the war, Roosevelt was in a predicament. This was solved by the Japanese on December 7, 1941, with the attack on Pearl Harbor. Hitler hastened to help Roosevelt by declaring war on the United States on December 11, 1941. Thus, Churchill and Roosevelt were now in it, shoulder to shoulder, fighting together. The British didn't know it at the time, but the American Revolution was the best thing that ever happened to them.

Churchill and Roosevelt had a very good personal relationship based on mutual respect. Each liked and admired the other. Both were great politicians, orators, and inspirational leaders. On his visits to America, Churchill stayed at the White House or at Roosevelt's home in Hyde Park, but mostly at the White House. This increased their intimacy and friendship.

On one of Churchill's memorable visits to Roosevelt, they went to Shangri-La, Roosevelt's refuge in the Catoctin hills in Maryland. Driving by car, the occupants were Churchill, Roosevelt, Mrs. Roosevelt and Harry Hopkins. After two hours of driving they approached the town of Frederick of Civil War fame. Churchill made inquiries about Barbara Freitchie who, when Confederate troops occupied the town, refused to haul down her American flag. Churchill's inquiry moved Hopkins to quote the famous lines:

> Shoot if you must this old grey head
> But spare your country's flag she said.

When it was clear that no one else in the car would add to the quotation, Churchill related in full the complete poem to the awe of his fellow travelers. This incident reveals Churchill's intimate knowledge off all things American even at times more so that the Americans did themselves. This knowledge of America by Churchill not only drew the Allies closer together, but also increased his respect for that great country. He was, in fact, one of them by birthright and understanding. A man who spanned the ocean at a time when just such a man was needed.

Churchill and Roosevelt agreed on the one great concept of the war— the "Germany First" policy. They considered that Germany was a much greater threat than Japan. Hitler may be a madman, but he was exerting great power;

his army and air force were the strongest of any nation in the world. They also considered that an Eastern front was vital to defeat Germany—that it was of the utmost importance to keep Russia going in the war against Germany.

For Churchill and Roosevelt to devote most of their resources to fight Japan would have left Hitler free to knock Russia out of the war. Churchill and Roosevelt could not stand idly by and let this happen—it would be catastrophic to the Allied cause. They agreed it was paramount to stop and defeat Hitler and it would require most of their resources to do it. From a practical standpoint, as Russia and Japan were not at war, this left Germany as the enemy that all three allies could unite on and focus their combined efforts to crush. Churchill and Roosevelt felt with the defeat of Germany, Japan could not, by itself, last long.

For Hitler, this decision by Churchill and Roosevelt to concentrate their strength against him meant that he would lose the war—something he should have thought of a long time ago. By his appalling ignorance of America and Russia and his complete underestimation of their strength, Hitler had made a fatal mistake. As mentioned, his superficial and absurd preconception of America was particularly disastrous. With America's entry into the war, the power balance shifted against Germany. Now the Allies were going to apply that power and it would be coming from all directions against Hitler's spread out forces. Seemingly oblivious to the long range consequences of his actions, Hitler was like the engineer on a runaway express train headed toward hell and the German people were his passengers.

Churchill and Roosevelt would do all they could to expedite the trip. Besides their voluminous correspondence, they also met personally many times during the progress of the war. On November 7, 1942, with the invasion of French North Africa, they had seized the initiative in the war against Germany and Italy. Usually, their personal meetings were planned to decide on the next steps to take in the initiative. Churchill, in particular, liked meeting with Roosevelt in order to use his persuasive powers in person. Churchill felt that with all his experience he could guide allied strategy, which in many cases he was able to do. The fact that they had mutual admiration and respect for one another was a big plus for the allied effort. Over the course of the war, Roosevelt and the Americans became exasperated at times with Churchill. That is, in a general way, they came to believe that Churchill wanted to go off on tangents, "dispersal," as Roosevelt would call it. The Americans wanted to keep their eye on the main effort—the invasion of France. The British wanted to carry the war forward in the Mediterranean, while the Americans, particularly General Marshall, wanted to build up for the invasion of Northern France as soon as possible.

Churchill and General Brooke's argument carried the day. In 1942 and 1943, they felt there was no way the Allies could defeat the German army in Northern France, and they were right. Even General Eisenhower later acknowledged that fact. Churchill convinced Roosevelt that the thing to do offensively in 1942 was to land in French North Africa. This would catch Rommel in the back and also open up Southern Europe, including Italy, as a whole new front which Hitler would have to contend with. This would also help the Russians by drawing off German troops from Russia.

The fact is, in 1942 and 1943, the United States could do nothing in the European Theatre without the British. The Americans had to have a base, and England was that base. They also had to have strong naval and air forces in the region, and England had those. Because of this, England was indispensable in any attack on Northern France. If England didn't agree to it, then it couldn't be done.

Thus, Churchill and England were making the strategy in 1942-1943. However, they were in agreement with Roosevelt and the Americans to invade Northern France in 1944, when they felt the time was right. By mid-1944, America was supplying the majority of the ground force in Europe, so Roosevelt was now in reality the commanding officer of the Western Allies. Churchill had become the junior partner, and his influence was not as strong as before. However, the combination of Churchill and Roosevelt throughout the war was very effective. Both were highly intelligent; thus, you have the resources of two highly gifted men. It is difficult to think of any mistakes they made, while Hitler, during this same time, was making one right after another. Churchill and Roosevelt always looked at the big picture. Hitler, who operated by intuition and impulse, with little knowledge of the whole world, was not even aware there was a big picture.

I think one of the cornerstones of the relationship of Churchill and Roosevelt was Churchill's understanding of the United States. He recognized its potential power and managed to get it on his side, with the help of Japan and Hitler. Churchill and Roosevelt were truly great men. Along with Stalin, they made a combination that was too much for Hitler.

Russia 1942
The Turning Point on the Russian Front

Churchill flew to Moscow to tell Stalin there would be no second front in 1942. Stalin naturally was very upset. Churchill explained that the Allies were going to attack French North Africa. This mollified Stalin somewhat, but he was still angry at the Allies. He needed help now, and he accused the British of being afraid to fight the Germans. Of course, this didn't make Churchill too happy—Churchill didn't remind Stalin that for two years the British had fought the Germans while Stalin had helped them. Churchill tried to explain to Stalin that there was already, to some extent, a second front in the West now. The Germans had tied down over 40 divisions plus air power there in occupation, and also as a defense against a British invasion. These divisions were not on the eastern front where they may have made a decisive difference. Stalin still wanted the real thing. Churchill was correct in his thinking in this matter. Churchill and Stalin had a fairly good relationship built on mutual need. In spite of himself, Churchill liked and admired Stalin, even though he had no illusions about him. He realized that Stalin was a dedicated Communist and a tyrant—but he was also putting up a great fight against Hitler.

In early 1942, Hitler was oblivious to the plans the Allies had for him. He was too busy thinking about what he was going to do to them, particularly to Russia. Hitler abandoned plans to attack Moscow, where the bulk of the Russian forces were located. He would attack in the south and drive then to Stalingrad, on the Volga River, and then to Astrakhan on the Caspian Sea, thus cutting off the Caucasus oil fields and securing them for German use. This would deprive the Red Army of oil and would probably end the war with Germany winning. This actually was a very good plan and, if successful, could be decisive. It all came down to how much fight was left in Stalin and the Red Army—and also to Hitler's acts.

The German drive in April began auspiciously. Russian forces were surprised, since they thought the Germans would attack in the Moscow area. The Germans under von Bock made rapid progress, even faster than anticipated; not fast enough, however, for Hitler, who fired von Bock. This was a big mistake, as von Bock was one of his best generals. Von Bock was sent home, where he spent the rest of the war, a huge waste of talent for the Germans. Ironically, von Bock was killed in an air raid two days before the end of the war.

In the meanwhile, another German army under von Manstein attacked the Crimea and Sevastopol. After a furious struggle, the Germans took Sevastopol and the Crimea. Thus, this army was free to conduct other operations. Here, Hitler made another big mistake. Instead of adding von Manstein's army to bolster his southern attack, he sent it north to the Leningrad area to aid in capturing Leningrad. This was to prove a disastrous mistake. What Hitler was thinking about is beyond this author's understanding. The decisive battle was going to be fought in Southern Russia, a vast area, and Hitler should have devoted every resource to it to ensure success. Leningrad was a peripheral area and of itself no consequence other than psychological. At this time in the war, when the tide could go either way, Germany could not afford to make these kinds of mistakes. Possibly Hitler was over-confident due to successes already achieved in his attack on Southern Russia; perhaps he thought Russia was collapsing. After his earlier victories in the war, Hitler's tendency was to underestimate his enemies and overestimate himself, a good way to lose.

To compound his mistake, he divided the German army in Southern Russia into two groups and changed the objectives. Army Group B under von Paulus was to continue eastward to Stalingrad and cut the Volga River. Army Group A under von Kleist was to attack the Caucasus directly. This plan was opposed by the General Staff as spreading his forces too thin over a vast area and that they should be concentrated on Stalingrad and the Volga. The Caucasus could be mopped up later.

Hitler, by now the Supreme Commander of the Army, ignored his general staff. His initial plan had been very good, but now he was deviating from it. It is not known whether if Hitler had stayed with his initial plan of concentrating on Stalingrad and the Volga would have won the war, but it had a much better chance than dividing up his forces as he did. Zhukov later said Hitler had made a huge mistake in doing so.

Obviously, overconfident by his success, Hitler was trying to do everything at once and finish Russia off. He believed, by the number of prisoners he had taken and those made casualties, that Russia was down to its very last thin line of reserves. The fact that Russia had twice the population of Germany and hence twice the available manpower seems to have passed Hitler by. It seems again, and yet again, that Hitler had underestimated Stalin and the Red Army. His belief in himself had overcome any other thought processes, especially from generals whose knowledge and ability he considered inferior to his own. The will was everything; if your will was as strong as his, you could overcome anything. General Halder, at this time, commented in his diary of Hitler that,

> The continual underestimation of enemy possibilities takes on grotesque forms and is becoming dangerous. Hitler's decisions had ceased to have anything in common with the principles of strategy and operations as they have been recognized for generations past. They were the product of a violent nature following to momentary impulses, which recognized no limits to possibility and made its wish-dreams the father of its acts.

Von Paulus did reach the suburbs of Stalingrad on August 22, 1942. However, here he was stopped. The Russians dug into the ruins of Stalingrad and fought for every building, every yard. They poured in reinforcements from across the Volga into Stalingrad. Again in a desperate situation, Stalin called in his ace, General Zhukov, to command the defense. Stalingrad became a maelstrom for both armies: perhaps a final clash to see who was the strongest and could hold out the longest; perhaps who was going to win and who was going to lose the war.

In the meanwhile, far to the south and west of Stalingrad, Army Group A pushed on and into the Caucasus. The Caucasus Mountains were an ideal defense position for the Russians, who were fighting fiercely. Needless to say, it was a critical situation for them. After initially making some good progress, the German army finally wore out in the mountains and snow and could go no further. The Russians held on to the oil fields and stopped the German offensive. For the Germans, there were too many objectives, too far apart, and not enough resources. If von Manstein's army had been there, it might have made the difference.

Churchill had been particularly concerned about the German attack on the Caucasus. If the Germans succeeded in taking the Caucasus, they could then proceed to move on the oil fields of Persia. If they occupied these oil fields, it would be a terrible blow to the British, as they were getting a large supply of their oil from that area. The British did not have enough forces in this area to stop a determined German attack. A German takeover of the Caucasus could have been a disaster for both Russia and Britain.

On the Stalingrad front, one day became as the next, with furious fighting and neither side willing to yield an inch. As time went on, it became obvious to the German General staff that time was working against them. The Russians refused to be defeated and another Russian winter was coming, the same scenario as at Moscow, only this time, worse.

Also, the General Staff considered that Stalingrad was the point of the furthest advance and that both flanks were extended for many miles. These flanks were protected not by German troops, but by Germany's allies, Italians, Rumanians, and Hungarians. These were not the same caliber as the German troops, not troops that would hold up in a crisis such as a Russian attack. General Halder pointed out to Hitler that Stalin still had a large reserve of forces, which made Hitler furious. Hitler refused to believe it. General Halder was dismissed; later, he was imprisoned at Dachau.

Halder and the General Staff (and even General Zeitzler, Halder's successor) had advised that under the circumstances it was best to retreat. Of course, they were right, but Hitler would have none of it. To retreat from Stalingrad would be to admit defeat. To admit defeat here would cast a doubt on the outcome of the war. At this point, Stalingrad became the critical battle that would decide the war on the Eastern Front. For Hitler, again it was a matter of wills, his against Stalin's. Surely the Russians had reached the end of their manpower; they could not produce divisions out of thin air. He who held on the longest and fought the hardest would win. No one could defeat the German army. Hitler probably sensed that this was the climactic battle of the war, a battle he could not afford to lose.

On November 19, Marshall Zhukov struck—not at the German army, but at the Italians and Rumanians on both sides of the salient. A rout ensued. These troops did not want to be in Russia in the first place, and who can blame them? Why suffer and die for Hitler and Germany in this desolate, remote area? Their only hope was to survive and somehow get out of this awful place. The Russians took account of the morale of these troops in making their attacks. Marshall Zhukov's objective was to trap the German army in Stalingrad and destroy it. The Russians from the north met the Russians attacking from the south, and the German army in Stalingrad was surrounded. Stalin had performed something close to a miracle in providing large numbers of men and materiel to the front. How he did it, considering the loss of a large part of his country and manpower, is almost beyond comprehension. No wonder Hitler was surprised!

The General Staff was in a panic. Von Paulus must attack westward and regain contact with other German forces, or he was doomed. Hitler refused to face the obvious fact. He could not admit defeat. He ordered a relief army led by General von Manstein, who had returned to the southern front, to fight its way from the south and join von Paulus. Von Manstein was probably Germany's best general, but he couldn't do it. He got within thirty miles of Stalingrad and urged von Paulus to break out westward, join him, and escape. Hitler rejected this plan, the only one that had any chance of saving von Paulus and his army. The German troops fighting and dying in Stalingrad were thus doomed by their Fuhrer for whom they had given everything. They were paying with their lives for his mistakes.

By this time, the Russian advance was posing a threat to cut off the entire German Group A in the Caucasus. By Herculean efforts, the Germans were able to save this army. In the meanwhile, the Stalingrad pocket was being reduced yard by yard, mile by mile. Von Paulus' army was running out of everything, food, fuel, ammunition, medicine. Goering's futile attempt at airlifting in supplies amounted to very little. Some wounded soldiers (the lucky ones) were flown out on the return trip. The Allied attack on North Africa was drawing away a large part of the Luftwaffe, including transports, at a critical time. The Stalingrad pocket was cut in two; further resistance was useless. Hitler made von Paulus a field marshal, hoping to encourage him to keep fighting—an empty gesture. At the end of January, 1943, what remained of Army Group B surrendered, possibly ninety thousand men. Very few were ever heard from again. Sometime after the battle, Charles de Gaulle was visiting Russia and made a trip to Stalingrad. Surveying the ruins and destruction, de Gaulle turned to an aide and said, "What a remarkable people." His aide said, "Yes, the Russians have fought a great battle." De Gaulle said, "I'm talking about the Germans—to have gotten this far!"

Von Paulus, instead of committing suicide as Hitler had hoped, became a prisoner of war. Later, he would become a member of the National Committee of Free Germany, a Soviet-inspired anti-Nazi propaganda organization, and made a number of broadcasts on their behalf. General Ewald von Kliest, the leader of the attack on the Caucasus, was not so fortunate. General von Kliest, contrary to Hiter's instructions, had a humane policy toward the people in his part of occupied Russia. After the war, Von Kliest was imprisoned in Russia for life and died in captivity there in 1954. His crime? He was charged with "having alienated through mildness and kindness the population of the Soviet Union." It seems Russia was a no-win situation for the Germans.

The Russian front was turning into the graveyard for the German army. After Stalingrad, it was the Russians who were on the offense everywhere; the Germans were retreating, stubbornly, but retreating.

Hitler's attack on Russia on June 22, 1941, which began so well, had turned into a nightmare. Stalin and the Red Army had stopped and then defeated the German army. Although an evil man himself, Stalin had done almost the impossible. Faced with staggering losses in men and materiel, he continued to produce both. In Stalin, Hitler had met his match and then some. On a personal basis, it was two scorpions in a bottle, and only one would come out.

Stalin—Man of Steel

Stalin the man at Stalingrad was not the same man as Stalin of June 22, 1941. With Hitler's surprise attack on that date, Stalin was in a state of shock. Even though there had been warnings of the attack, Stalin chose not to believe them. It was too awful to contemplate.

When his generals, Timoshenko and Zhukov, wanted to mobilize the army and put it on alert in mid-June, Stalin refused—he didn't want to alarm

Hitler. He didn't want to give Hitler any provocation to attack Russia. Indeed, Stalin thought he and Hitler were getting along quite well. At one point, he said the combination of Germany and Russia could be invincible. Hitler didn't share Stalin's outlook. In fact, he looked on Russia as just another victim to add to his list.

Ten days after the attack, Stalin regained his self-control. In fact, his thinking had undergone quite a transformation. In a speech to the Russian people on July 3, he called for an all-out effort to resist and defeat the Germans. In his speech, he did not mention Communism. He talked about Mother Russia. He was appealing to the essential patriotism of the Russian masses to resist the invader. Even by this time, word of German atrocities was beginning to spread. Stalin's speech galvanized the Russian people to fight as hard as possible, even to the death.

Stalin had two big advantages going for him against Hitler. First was the terrible winter weather, and second was that Hitler completely underestimated the size and strength of Russia and the Red Army. Where Hitler thought he had virtually wiped out the Red Army in August of 1942, there were still millions of Russian soldiers being thrown in against him. Hitler said if he had only known of all this strength, he would never have attacked in the first place. Too late!

While in 1941 Stalin had made many mistakes, particularly in not retreating soon enough, it was actually the speed and execution of the German attack which was destroying Russian armies. At one point in Dvinsk in northern Russia, the Germans had covered two hundred miles in four days. Hundreds of thousands of Russians were captured in the ensuing pocket on the central front.

One way to look at it is, if Stalin had retreated as much as he was urged to do, the Red Army would have wound up two hundred miles east of Moscow and out of the war. The war would have been over, with a German victory. He had to stand and fight somewhere or lose.

Another advantage he had was General Zhukov, his ace trouble shooter. First at Leningrad, then Moscow, and then Stalingrad, each time Zhukov was called on at almost the last moment and saved the day. You might say he saved Russia. It was Zhukov who planned the counter-attack at Stalingrad. Instead of using his reserves for the battle of Stalingrad itself, Zhukov took a daring gamble which Stalin approved. He left the forces already at Stalingrad to fight their own battle, while he built up forces on either side of the German extended flanks. His attack was completely successful and caught the Germans by surprise. Hitler thought the Red Army was practically wiped out and couldn't believe it when struck by strong new, large forces on his flanks. Hitler then and there lost the battle of Stalingrad, and in consequence the battle of Russia— and probably the war.

Zhukov was a great general, but Stalin had him in the right place at the right time. Also, Stalin had somehow managed, despite all the earlier disasters, to have a large reserve of men and materiel for Zhukov to use.

Hitler had not only underestimated Russia; he had also underestimated Stalin, which he admitted. Of course, some of the Red Army's tenacity was due to their fear of what Stalin would do to them if they didn't fight. Most of the Red Army was truly patriotic, but Stalin had no qualms about eliminating those who wouldn't fight. On the home front, his Security Police, under Beria, kept everyone in line. While Stalin had outwardly relaxed somewhat his overall approach, Russia was still a police state.

Stalin, the man of steel. During the war, he was the man of steel; and despite his excesses, he saved Russia. Possibly no other man in Russia could have done it. Hitler had taken on the wrong man in Stalin, and it cost him the war. One sometimes wonders why men such as Stalin are born and exist. Perhaps fate had put Stalin in the world at this place and time to stop Hitler.

El Alamein

Some have compared the battle of El Alamein in North Africa with Stalingrad. This really is not correct; however, in its own way, El Alamein was also a turning point in the war. The forces involved at El Alamein on both sides were small, compared to the huge forces of Germans and Russians at Stalingrad. Stalingrad was fought over a period of months, while El Alamein was over in days. Stalingrad was the biggest battle on the biggest front of the war. The result of its outcome meant that Germany was going to lose the war in Russia and, all things being equal, would therefore lose the war altogether. Still, El Alamein was the beginning of the Allied advance which culminated in meeting the Russians in the middle of Germany a little over two years later.

There was one man in particular who was vitally interested in El Alamein: Winston Churchill. Since the British were unable in 1941, 1942, and 1943 to face the German army on the European continent, the Middle East was the only place Britain could safely mount an offensive. During 1940, 1941, and part of 1942, the British and the German-Italian armies had chased each other back and forth across North Africa. Churchill devoted a great deal of his time and Britain's resources to the war in North Africa. The British desperately needed a victory somewhere, and this area was as good as any for them; in fact, it was the only one on land.

The British had the advantage until the arrival in 1941 of General Erwin Rommel and his Afrika Korps. Since that time, there had been a series of battles with Rommel mostly coming out on top. Although the British outnumbered him, they still usually lost. One of Rommel's favorite tactics was to lure the British armor out into the open and have it attack him. Of course, they would attack in a place that Rommel had properly prepared to receive them—tanks, mines, anti-tank guns, and artillery. The result would be a smashing repulse and almost destruction of the attacking British. Then Rommel would switch to the offensive and chase the reeling and fragmented British back to Egypt. This infuriated Churchill. He changed commanders, to no avail; whichever commander went against Rommel seemed no different: they lost.

The British command structure in the Middle East was to have one overall commander for the area who was stationed in Cairo. Another battlefront commander was with the Eighth Army in the desert. Of course, on the Axis side, Rommel was running the whole show. In 1942, the British commander in Cairo was Sir Claude Aucheinleck, and General Richie was in command of the Eighth Army.

On June 20, 1942, while conferring in Washington with President Roosevelt, Churchill was informed that Tobruk had fallen. Over 30,000 men had surrendered to Rommel's army. Churchill states that this was one of the heaviest blows he had received in the entire war. All his efforts in North Africa had come to this. It was, as he said, a bitter moment. He resolved to win at all costs in North Africa. Roosevelt and General Marshall rushed tanks and materiel to aid the British in North Africa, which Churchill greatly appreciated.

Churchill and General Brooke journeyed to Cairo in early August, 1942. At that time, General Aucheinleck himself had taken over command of the Eighth Army, and had managed to repulse Rommel's initial attack in the area of El Alamein. Aucheinleck appeared to be a good soldier but was not lucky in his appointment of battlefield commanders. Of course, Rommel had something to do with that. It is very possible that if Aucheinleck had been his own battlefield commander, he may have been successful. However, he did not appear to be the inspirational leader that Rommel was, or that the Eighth Army needed at this time.

Churchill had to consider if Rommel attacked and was successful against what seemed to be a disorganized Eighth Army, he could take the Suez Canal and move towards the oil fields of the Middle East. This was too awful for

Churchill to contemplate, but he had to. After talking with everyone, Churchill decided to make another complete change in the command structure of the Middle East. On General Brooke's advice, he appointed General Harold Alexander commander-in-chief and General Bernard Law Montgomery commander of the Eighth Army. General Brooke had known these men a long time, and, in particular, they had served under him in France in 1940. At that time, they all had done a great job under the worst of circumstances, which led to the embarkation at Dunkirk. Without Brooke, Alexander, and Montgomery, the B.E.F. probably would not have made it out. General Brooke admired Montgomery very much and was his chief supporter throughout the war—and Montgomery, because of his abrasive personality, would need a great deal of support.

The principal figure in all this change of command was General Montgomery. On him would rest victory or defeat. General Alexander, his nominal superior officer, left the actual operations in Montgomery's capable hands. Next to MacArthur, Montgomery was the most unusual personality in the entire war. He was very slight of build but had a large ego, which is not all bad for a military man. He had been severely wounded in the First War, to the point of death. Perhaps that is one reason for his efforts to hold down casualties by minute planning.

General Montgomery was an outstanding officer and leader of men. The men who fought under him had complete faith in his leadership. To say he was eccentric would be putting it mildly. Churchill once said that Montgomery was "insufferable, particularly in victory." Once, Montgomery was talking with Churchill and said, "I don't drink or smoke and I'm one hundred percent fit." Through the smoke of his cigar, Churchill replied, "Well, I smoke and drink and I'm two hundred percent fit." Even the congenial Eisenhower had great difficulty getting along with his unruly and outspoken subordinate. He was austere; he was rude at times; he spoke when should have been listening. He had complete confidence in himself and, like MacArthur, also liked publicity. Vain, eccentric, but a first-class military man, he became a hero to the British public at a time when they needed heroes.

Montgomery believed in the set piece battle; that is, he prepared everything meticulously before he launched his attack. He wanted overwhelming strength at the point of attack—men, tanks, artillery, and air. In short, he wanted to ensure victory. Also, he pulverized the enemy, which held down his own casualties. It has to be said that Montgomery was successful in all of his endeavors. And that was all Churchill was asking: to win.

When Montgomery took over the Eighth Army, it was in bad shape. Morale was at a low point—Rommel had thoroughly discouraged them. Montgomery began at once to change this attitude. He made visits and delivered optimistic speeches all over his command. His own self-assurance seemed to communicate itself to his men. Soon, a new spirit seemed to have lifted the Eighth Army. Montgomery had made believers out of them.

The British, meanwhile, had reinforced the Eighth Army; it now had three armored divisions and seven infantry divisions, vastly outnumbering Rommel. A brigade of the Free French under General Koenig was part of Montgomery's strong force. His brigade had distinguished itself at Bir Hakeim in June, 1942. The R.A.F. had command of the air with over twelve hundred planes. Montgomery had thoroughly prepared his forces for Rommel's expected attack; he posted a large part of his army in defensive positions at Alam El Halfa Ridge. This is where Rommel struck. He was hit hard and repulsed by the British defense. Round one for Montgomery. Rommel suffered heavy losses. Meanwhile, Rommel was not getting reinforcements or supplies due to interdiction by British air and sea forces based in Malta; in particular, he was short on fuel. Thus, he was in poor condition when Montgomery began his advance. Churchill was pushing Montgomery to attack, but Montgomery would not be pushed. He waited until he had everything he wanted and everything in place, his set piece battle. Overwhelming men, tanks, artillery, everything—nothing was left to chance.

At night on October 23, 1942, a thousand guns opened fire on the Axis army. The R.A.F. added to the bombardment. On October 26, the Australian Ninth Division struck north and broke through. Montgomery was quick to press his advantage and sent more troops through the gap, while also putting pressure on the whole German-Italian front. On October 27, Rommel counterattacked to stop the flow. He was repulsed with heavy losses. He tried again on the next day, with the same result. The R.A.F. played a major role in defeating these attacks. Rommel was now up against a strong opponent who, with General Montgomery in command, was very well led. In General Montgomery, Rommel had now met his equal.

Montgomery gathered his forces for the main attack, Operation Supercharge, which began on November 2. In fierce fighting, the enemy was pushed back. Hitler cabled Rommel not to retreat a step. "Victory or Death." However, the battle was out of Rommel's hands—the Eighth Army was about to overrun his entire army. It was retreat with what remnants he had left or have them totally destroyed. Montgomery was using his superior strength to pulverize the German and Italian armies. Rommel said Hitler's order "demanded the impossible—even the most devoted soldier could be killed by a bomb." After twelve days of continuous fighting, Montgomery had now broken the opposing army. He was now in pursuit which would end with the Axis army surrendering over 200,000 men in Tunisia after also being hit from French North Africa by Operation Torch under General Eisenhower.

Churchill had finally won, and all his efforts had finally paid off. North Africa was cleansed of the enemy. After Stalingrad and El Alamein, the Germans were constantly on the defensive. The tide had turned.

Dwight D. Eisenhower
Operation Torch
The Invasion of French North Africa

The man appointed to command the invasion was Dwight D. Eisenhower. This is quite remarkable, as Eisenhower had never seen action before. But Marshall had confidence in him, nevertheless.

Dwight D. Eisenhower was somewhat typical of the officers who had stayed in the army after the First War and made it a career. Eisenhower was a captain in 1919 and a major in 1939. Most people would have given up on this long ago, but Dwight loved the Army. His five brothers had been successful in law and business. In 1939, Dwight considered himself a failure compared to his brothers in a very competitive family. The American Army was so small that about the only way you could get promoted was for one of the senior officers to die.

Dwight was born on a stormy night in Dennison, Texas, on October 14, 1890, to very poor parents, David and Ida Eisenhower. The author mentions a stormy night, as the weather would play a significant part in Eisenhower's life, particularly in June, 1944. Interestingly, Dwight Eisenhower was of German heritage. (I wonder what Hitler thought of this.)

His family moved to the small town of Abilene, Kansas, when Dwight was two years old. His father took a job as a maintenance man at the local dairy. It is reported that his father was a dour, stern disciplinarian, while his mother was just the opposite, smiling and cheerful. It seems Dwight inherited more from his mother than from his father (thankfully). Dwight had a typical boyhood in a small Kansas town in the early 1900s. It is said he had a fiery temper, but over the years he learned to control it with the help of his mother. At an early age, he picked up the nickname "Ike," which seemed to suit him.

In 1911, it looked as though Dwight would be unable to go to college, as his family did not have the means to send him. Dwight's only chances were the Annapolis Naval Academy or West Point Military Academy. He applied for Annapolis but was considered too old. (He was twenty years old at the time.) He then applied to West Point and through some luck was accepted. A fellow classmate was Omar Bradley. Both became generals of the Army, a rank attained by only nine officers in American history.

Bradley was from Moberly, Missouri, and also had parents of very modest means. He, too, applied to West Point as his only chance of receiving a higher education. Bradley was not enthusiastic about going to West Point, but was talked into applying by a friend. Halfway through the test, Bradley came to questions pertaining to geometry, of which he knew very little. He decided to give up and went up to the front desk to turn in his incomplete paper. However, the instructor was asleep, and Bradley did not want to be rude and wake him up. So, he went back to his desk and made a stab at answering the questions. Three weeks later, he received a letter notifying him that he had been accepted. Big events sometimes hinge on small things.

Dwight's class of 1915 was an extraordinary class. Of the 164 graduates, 26 became brigadier generals, 23 major generals, seven lieutenant generals, and two full generals. It was called "the class the stars fell on."

Beginning his career at West Point, Dwight was particularly interested in athletics, especially football. He was a very good athlete, and he liked to compete. He was doing well in football until he injured his knee, ending his football career. He almost had to leave the Academy because of rules relating to injury, but was saved by a sympathetic instructor. Already a little on the rebellious side, with his athletic career over, Dwight did not fully apply himself to his role at the Academy. He did manage to graduate about midway in his class. His best subject was English.

Although at the time he didn't seem to particularly like going to West Point, later in his life, Eisenhower looked back on his days there with affection. Mark Clark, who visited him in the last days of his life, said that all Eisenhower talked about was West Point and his love and respect for that institution. Interestingly, it is said that in his last days, Douglas MacArthur also spoke mostly of West Point.

After Dwight's graduation, he was assigned with the rank of second lieutenant to San Antonio, Texas, where he met Mamie Doud, the daughter of a wealthy meat packer. After a time, they became engaged and were married on July 1, 1916. They came from completely different backgrounds and had different personalities, but they got along well. Mamie's family was particularly fond of Dwight. With his marriage, Dwight's attitude changed immediately. He decided to make himself the best officer possible. He buckled down and took his work very seriously. With the entry of America into the First World War, Dwight hoped to go overseas and make his mark. Instead, he was assigned to training command, much to his displeasure, for the entire war. He saw no action at all, while Douglas MacArthur and Dwight's friend, George S. Patton, were distinguishing themselves.

On September 28, 1917, Mamie gave birth to a son, David Dwight Eisenhower. His nickname was "Icky," and he was blond and blue-eyed like his father. He was the light of Dwight and Mamie's life. On December 23, 1920, little Icky became seriously ill; he died ten days later of scarlet fever. Dwight and Mamie said they never fully recovered from this tragedy.

After the war, the Army was drastically reduced. Eisenhower held a number of posts, one being an aide to Douglas MacArthur, who was Chief of Staff of the Army. When MacArthur went to the Philippines, he requested that Eisenhower come along as his assistant. Eisenhower spent several years in the Philippines, where, among other things, he learned how to fly.

At one point, he and MacArthur had a dispute. While minor, this dispute had a lasting effect on Eisenhower's feelings towards MacArthur. MacArthur had ordered a parade of ill-trained Filipino army units through Manila. When President Quezon found out about it, he was furious that he had not been informed and how costly the event would be. MacArthur told Quezon that he knew nothing about it, thus by inference fixing the blame on Eisenhower, who had only been carrying out MacArthur's order. Eisenhower was flabbergasted. He had been made out to be a liar and the goat of the affair. He confronted MacArthur and threatened to resign. MacArthur smoothed it over, but their relationship was never the same, although they did continue to correspond for many years. MacArthur's efficiency reports praised Eisenhower without reservation. He called Eisenhower "a brilliant officer."

MacArthur was known for his flamboyant, somewhat dramatic, personality. Eisenhower afterwards said he had spent three years under MacArthur learning theatrics. (At one point many years later, both Eisenhower and MacArthur were considered as presidential candidates. Eisenhower emerged successful because of his warm personality. MacArthur had come across as too egotistical and autocratic.)

After his stint in the Philippines, Dwight returned to the United States via Japan in 1940, still a major. As the war in Europe started to develop, America slowly began to increase the Army. Eisenhower became a lieutenant colonel in 1940.

One other important event occurred to Eisenhower in the years between the wars. He had been appointed to attend the Command and General Staff

School at Leavenworth, Kansas. This was an honor arranged by Eisenhower's long-time friend and mentor, General Fox Conner. This staff school was very tough and covered every aspect of the military. Eisenhower's class consisted of 245 officers, and studies began in August of 1925. After a very rigorous and stressful testing which lasted almost a year, on June 16, 1926, Eisenhower graduated number one in his class. He had come a long way from the somewhat rebellious cadet at West Point. This was considered by Eisenhower and his colleagues to be a turning point upwards in his career. He celebrated by throwing a large party at the Muehlback Hotel in Kansas City and invited all of his brothers, including Arthur, who had loaned him $150 to hold it. Everyone had a great time.

To those who, later in the war, suggested that Eisenhower was not all that smart, that he was just lucky: coming in first of 245 qualified men is not luck. As Pasteur said, "Chance favors the mind that is prepared."

In the spring of 1941, Eisenhower distinguished himself in large-scale maneuvers in Louisiana. He received several commendations from his superiors, notably General Krueger. The following is quoted from Merle Miller's book:

Eisenhower surely counted on promotion after the maneuvers, but his old friend Mark Clark, knowing that, decided to keep him in suspense for a while. Every officer who took part in the maneuvers was present for a final critique, and Eisenhower was in the front row. Clark, after going over what had happened in the maneuvers on a large map, was handed a list of officers who had been promoted, ten to major generals and ten to brigadiers. Clark said, 'I glanced at it quickly; Ike was number three on the list to be brigadier generals, but I read out the list—with one exception. I deliberately left out Ike's name. I tell you, you could hear a pin drop, and I didn't dare look at his face. I knew what must be going through his mind, and I knew his face had to be red, and that vein . . . had to be throbbing but I left out his name and I said, 'That's all, gentlemen. Congratulations.' People started getting up and then I banged the gavel and I said, 'Please be seated. I have an apology to make. I have made a grievous error, I neglected to mention the name of another officer to be a brigadier general; he is number three on the list.' I could hear Ike say, 'You sonofabitch, I'll get you.' He came up to the platform. 'I could kill you,' he said. I said, 'Ike, I couldn't resist the temptation.'

Some days, it was as if they were still at West Point. Clark and Eisenhower were later to lead the invasions of French North Africa and Italy. Each one had recommended the other for high command when America entered the war.

When Pearl Harbor was attacked, Eisenhower was on assignment in San Antonio. He received a call from General Bedell Smith in Washington that General George Marshall had requested that Eisenhower come to Washington immediately. The Philippines was under attack and they needed someone familiar with that area and Eisenhower filled the bill. Eisenhower took off from Randolph Field, but the plane encountered severe weather and had to land at Dallas. Meanwhile, Third Army Headquarters contacted the Kansas and Texas Railroad to ask that it hold the Blue Bonnet Express, which had pulled out of Dallas heading north a short while before. The train waited at Plano, Texas, until an Army car carrying Eisenhower arrived. Eisenhower was already becoming an important man, and the war was only a few days old.

A few days later, Eisenhower reported to General Marshall in Washington. He was given the task of doing anything he could to help the Philippines. By that time, the Philippines was surrounded by the Japanese. It was a desperate situation; after Pearl Harbor, the Navy was too weak to help the Philippines. Eisenhower did his best, but it was an impossible task. The Philippines could not be saved. Marshall, however, was impressed with Eisenhower's ability and put him in the war plans division. Eisenhower was upset because he wanted to be in the field and not stuck behind a desk. It looked like 1918 all over again.

General Marshall was a stern and remote taskmaster; he was very serious all the time. The officers under him knew that Marshall could make them or break them in a flash. He was reported to carry a little black book with him, and if your name got in it, your career was over.

One day, Marshall called Eisenhower in and was talking about promotions. Marshall said that in the last war most of the promotions had gone to officers on the staff and not to those in the field. In this war, Marshall said, the promotions were not going to staff officers, but to those in the field. He turned to Eisenhower and said that might be what would happen to him. Eisenhower's neck turned red. He told General Marshall, "I don't give a damn about your promotions; I'm here to do a duty the best I can, and if that means behind a desk, so be it." Eisenhower was startled at his own language in talking to the austere General Marshall. As he got up and left the office, he turned and saw that Marshall had a small smile on his face.

Eisenhower counted this conversation as the most important one of his life. A few days later, he was promoted to major general on the recommendation of General Marshall. In another week, he was sent to England by General Marshall to study the setup of the small Army contingent there. Reporting back to Marshall in Washington, he was told that he was to take over the American forces in England as commanding officer. It is very probable that his outburst of emotion to Marshall regarding promotion was what propelled Eisenhower to higher command. When the operation for the invasion of French North Africa was approved, Eisenhower was appointed as its commander. He was now a lieutenant general. Interestingly, Eisenhower was recommended for this post as commander of the invasion by Admiral Ernest King, Chief of Naval Operations. Eisenhower had thought that King disliked him; however, King told Marshall that Eisenhower was the best man for the job.

In just a little over one year, Eisenhower had gone from an obscure lieutenant colonel in Louisiana to lieutenant general in charge of the first Allied attack of the war. From a small town in Kansas to the top. Probably no one other than U. S. Grant had such a meteoric rise in the Army. Eisenhower bypassed hundreds of officers to reach this position. Marshall had seen something in Eisenhower that he liked. Eisenhower was a very capable professional soldier; he was a hard worker and, probably most of all, he got along well with everybody. Because of his optimistic and bubbly personality, everyone liked him. He was the perfect man for an operation that included the Allies. It is safe to say that Eisenhower did not let Marshall down; he succeeded at every task during the war.

The author goes into some length to talk about Eisenhower because he became Supreme Commander of the Allied Forces in the invasion of Northern France. He could possibly lose or win the war with one decision. Many say his decision to invade Normandy with the weather so threatening was one of the greatest military decisions of all times. He caught the Germans thoroughly unprepared, as they thought that with the bad weather, the invasion would be impossible. Eisenhower came out of the war an American hero. He later became the President of the United States.

Personal Notes on Eisenhower

The author at this writing is seventy years old. I began reading historical books, biographies, and autobiographies when I was about ten. My memory is that my interest in these kinds of books deepened when I visited my uncle's farm at the age of 16. He had a set of *Lee's Lieutenants* by Douglas Southall

Freeman. They were so interesting that it seemed I could hardly put them down. Since then, I have read many biographies and autobiographies of famous people, mostly military and political leaders. Through all this, I believe the most complex person I have ever come across is Dwight D. Eisenhower. The more I cannot quite figure him out, the more I read about him and still can't.

On the surface, Eisenhower seems to be a relatively simple person. Everyone says he was friendly, outgoing, cheerful, likable—an all-around nice guy. No one, as Mark Clark says, disliked him. Eisenhower was all these things and these traits did a great deal in getting him ahead. Yet, to the author, Eisenhower also was a tough, many-faceted person. Once he set a goal, he was determined to achieve it, no matter what, a trait most great leaders have in common.

Dwight came from a very competitive family in which he had five brothers. His greatest competitor was his older brother, Edgar, or Big Ike, as he was called. Edgar was a very good athlete, bigger and stronger than Dwight. He seemed to best Dwight at everything, which made Dwight furious. Particularly, Edgar could win at fighting. However, the boys were close. Once, when their stern father, David, was hitting Edgar with a strap, the young twelve year old Dwight grabbed his father and tried to pull him away, saying, "I don't think anyone should be whipped like that, not even a dog."

On another occasion, Dwight developed blood poisoning in his leg. It was quite serious. At times, he was unconscious. He made Edgar promise to stay by his bed and under no circumstances to let his leg be amputated. He would rather die. Edgar did just that and told the doctor in effect he would have to cut off Dwight's leg over his (Edgar's) dead body.

Dwight was tough as a youngster. He had the most celebrated fight between young teenagers in Abilene with a lad named Wes Merrifield. Wes was stronger than Dwight, but Dwight wouldn't quit fighting, even though he was being beaten almost senseless. Finally, after three hours, it was called a draw. Dwight was in bed for three days after the fight. In short, Dwight had a temper, was brought up in a very competitive environment and wanted to win. These traits showed up all through his life. However, it is said that he mostly learned to control his temper. So, here you have a friendly, bubbly, likable personality combined with a hidden toughness and competitiveness—and also a fierce determination. Perhaps it is this combination that led him to become Supreme commander of the Allied Invasion and also President of the United States.

Dwight Eisenhower had a rather curious relationship with his only living son, John. There was no doubt he loved his son, but John says his father was very strict. There seemed to be a certain gulf between them. They definitely had different personalities. It is possible that Dwight, being very smart, tough, and self-confident, did not see these same traits in his son to the extent that he had them. No doubt, outside of his wife Mamie, John was the closest person to Eisenhower in the world, yet there always seemed a sense of strain between them, some reservation, like the difference between a senior officer and a younger officer. One incident that may illustrate this is from Merle Miller's excellent book on Eisenhower. It was during the African Campaign, and Eisenhower had just received his promotion to four-star general. He had received congratulations from near and far, even from his brother, Edgar. But he had not heard from his son, John. This quote is from Miller's book:

Eisenhower had not received congratulations from his son and he did not take the matter philosophically. He was furious. On February 27th, John had written him that a friend was having trouble with West Point discipline, the latest promotion was not even mentioned. So Eisenhower began his reply on March 20, with a stern lecture, the type of lecture with which John had long been familiar. 'I know that, as they always have in the past, cadets jeer at the disciplinary standards the Technical Corps is always trying to instill in them. But I tell you this—if I could have in this entire force, today, the discipline of the United States Corps of Cadets, I could shorten this campaign immeasurably. Discipline wins battles. . . . Discipline makes a man salute—it also makes him hang on to his machine gun, firing it to the last round in the face of what appears to be an overwhelming attack.'

Then he got to the real point of the letter, his disappointment and anger not at what his son had said but at what he had not said. As always, he approached the matter sideways. He said he had 'chuckled over the fact that you did not even mention my promotion.' You can be sure that whatever he had done he had not chuckled. He went on, 'When I made B. G. (Brigadier General) you wrote a full page about it. When I was made a Major General, you asked me to defer all future promotions until you had gotten to be a Yearling. You congratulated me, at least feebly, on being a Lieutenant General; but you paid not the slightest attention to the fact that I finally got a fourth star.'

After that, trying ineptly to hide his hurt, he said, 'I do not mind confessing that I really got a laugh out of it because I have had so many messages of congratulations that I suppose I just naturally expected you to fall in line with the rest. As a matter of fact, you are the only one that had the sense to see it doesn't amount to a tinker's damn in the winning of this war—and that is all that concerns me.'

John saw through this camouflage, of course. He said, 'Regrettably, I never realized how much the promotion meant to my father.' This episode is a revealing insight to Eisenhower's personality and also his relationship with his son. The author believes that his father's great advancement made his son somewhat jealous; also, his father's overall attitude and strictness brought out a resentment in his son. These are only surmises; who knows what the problem was? John did say that he particularly enjoyed going on camping trips with his father in the Philippines.

As mentioned, Dwight Eisenhower was a many-faceted person. Probably his greatest strengths were:
1. Highly intelligent
2. Ability to get along with everyone
3. Winning personality
4. Strength, determination, and overall ability. Positive self-confident attitude.

His son, John, said that his father was a man who wanted to excel at whatever he did. It was good for America to have had such a man at this place and time. Was it that he was just lucky, as some suggest? To carry out one vital mission right after another successfully is not luck. It is planning, organization, decision making, and execution, putting up with difficult personalities and utilizing them to get the best out of them. Success in North Africa, Sicily, Italy, Normandy, and Germany is not luck. It is consummate ability.

Some say Eisenhower was just a "Chairman of the Board," while others actually performed the successful actions. Well, if he was just Chairman of the Board, which I dispute, he was the most successful one in military history. Results are all that count, and Eisenhower got results in every endeavor. Roosevelt and Marshall realized that, and that's why they had him there and backed him to the hilt. One might say that from mid-1942 to the end of the war, Eisenhower was the indispensable man. Who else could have accomplished everything that he did in the Allied Command?

Military—United States and Great Britain

In studying the military of the United States and Great Britain, it is interesting that overall, the United States produced better higher officers. This is only the author's opinion and is certainly open to argument. It is true, however, in World War II, that the British produced no Wellingtons or Nelsons. They had competent commanders such as Montgomery, Alexander, Brooke, Vian, and Slim. But on an overall basis, I believe the United States produced more and better commanders, particularly field commanders.

There are two reasons for this. One, the United States in 1942 was a much larger country than England. The population of the United States was approximately one hundred thirty million, while that of England was forty-five million. So, in the United States you had a much larger base from which to choose. The other reason is that England had a class system in regard to the military, while the United States did not. Thus, in America, anyone of the male population of the total of 130,000,000 people could go to West Point or Annapolis—rich, poor, in the middle, it made no difference. Young men such as Eisenhower, Bradley, and many others were definitely not rich. George S. Patton is the only one that comes to mind who came from a wealthy background.

With this huge pool of manpower to work with, West Point and Annapolis did try to bring in people who they thought would be successful. Local congressmen recommended up-and-coming young men. As time passed, the cream rose to the top—such men in the past as Robert E. Lee, Ulysses S. Grant, Stonewall Jackson, and William Sherman, among others. General Marshall graduated from the Virginia Military Institute, another great military school. West Point and Annapolis were also wonderful training schools. Nearly all who graduated looked back later in their lives and greatly appreciated these institutions. Many of these graduates went on to have outstanding careers in the Army and Navy and were of invaluable service. West Point and Annapolis were indispensable to the winning of the war.

On the other hand, in England there was more of a class distinction in the military. Generally, the higher officers came from the more affluent class; many had fathers and grandfathers who had served before them. Of course, some men did come up through the ranks, but it was difficult. Thus, with most of their higher officers coming from the upper class, and because its overall population was relatively small, the pool of candidates for higher officers was much more limited in England than in the United States. Certainly, this is in no way meant to deprecate the English military system, but it is only to say that the American system was better. The English Army in World War II put up a wonderful fight, just as it did in World War I.

Planning Operation Torch

While Roosevelt and Churchill agreed on invading French North Africa, there was disagreement on where the landings should take place. The Americans, particularly General Marshall, wanted the landings to take place at Casablanca and Oran. Indeed, they were not too happy about landing in Oran, since it was inside the Mediterranean Sea area. Casablanca and Oran were hundreds of miles from the probable scene of conflict with the Germans. Meanwhile, the British, led by Churchill, wanted the landings to take place not only at Casablanca and Oran, but also at Algiers on the Mediterranean. This would put the Allied army in closer contact with Montgomery's Eighth Army coming from the east, and thus trap Rommel's army.

Marshall was hesitant about going too far inside the Mediterranean. He thought it too risky, especially if Gibraltar were seized by either the Spanish or the Germans. As mentioned, the American plan of landing at Casablanca and Oran put their landing forces hundreds of miles from their main objective, Rommel's army, and thrusting the Axis out of North Africa.

It is very strange indeed that Marshall, who was ready to send only six divisions into the teeth of the German army in Northern France, now was so cautious about attacking the weakened French army in the fringe area of North West Africa. Possibly because he was opposed to the whole operation in the first place. Perhaps in this kind of war he was out of his element, which was the direct attack.

Indeed, Churchill and the British were entirely correct in wanting landings in the Mediterranean, principally Algiers. Not to land in Algiers was to automatically hand it to the Germans, along with Tunisia. With that much area, the Germans could put a prolonged fight for North Africa. It could be a year or more before any success could be gained there by the Allies. Thus, the whole war timetable could be delayed significantly. Churchill insisted that landings be made at Algiers and farther east if possible. As England was supplying major naval forces and bases for the attack, Churchill could not be ignored. Eisenhower, who was in command of the attack, was also in favor of landing at Algiers.

Roosevelt again overruled his military and sided with Churchill and Eisenhower. Landings were approved for Casablanca, Oran, and Algiers. Some light forces would be landed farther east at Bone, near the Tunisian border. Undoubtedly, this was the right decision. The British at this time were more experienced in the war and in Churchill and Brooke they had outstanding men in leadership positions. Sir John Dill, Britain's military liaison man stationed in Washington, also played an important role in this decision.

General Marshall had a great deal of respect for Field Marshall Dill, who at one time commanded the entire British army as C.I.G.S. Later, the two developed a close friendship. Sir John was buried in Arlington National Cemetery and a statue of him was placed on his grave. This was a very rare happening and was due primarily to General Marshall's admiration for General Dill. In fact, Sir John Dill is the only foreigner buried in Arlington National Cemetery.

French North Africa—1942-1943

On November 7, 1942, Allied troops under the command of General Eisenhower began landing in French North Africa, Casablanca, Oran, and Algiers. Some small units were even at the border of Tunisia far to the east. The Germans were taken completely by surprise and were somewhat shaken by this unforeseen event. Hitler, however, reacted quickly by occupying all of France and began sending troops into Tunisia. Already, he was having to begin moving forces from Russia, particularly transport aircraft, this while the Battle of Stalingrad was raging. Thus, Churchill and Roosevelt were accomplishing what they had promised Stalin—to try to relieve the strain on Russia on the Eastern Front.

Before the invasion, the Americans led by Mark Clark had traveled clandestinely to French North Africa in the hope of convincing the French generals there to offer no resistance to the invading troops, but rather to join with them in fighting the Germans. A few of the French military, such as General Mast and General Bethouart, were cooperative. Most were not. They felt they were under the command of Marshall Petain at Vichy and it was their duty to follow his orders.

The invading Allied troops were met with scattered resistance, and in some places with tough resistance. There were Allied casualties. The situation was somewhat chaotic. Fortunately, Admiral Darlan, the Vice-Premier of the Vichy French government, was in Algiers visiting his ill son. General Eisenhower was faced with a major problem. His objectives were to secure French North Africa and at the same time to push as rapidly as possible to the east to Tunisia to confront and expel the Germans who were landing there in force. With the unsettled situation with the French army, he was in a bind. The French generals indicated they would take orders from no one but General

Petain, but since Petain was now a virtual prisoner of the Germans, they would take orders from Admiral Darlan.

To Eisenhower, the obvious solution was to make some kind of arrangement with Darlan. The trouble was that Darlan was considered to be something of a collaborator with the Nazis, not active, but compliant. In short, he was regarded by the American and English people as an enemy. Eisenhower's interest at this time was military, not political. The German forces in Tunisia were increasing each day. He decided to make a deal with Darlan. Darlan ordered the French to cease all resistance and cooperate with the Allies, which they immediately did. To Eisenhower, problem solved.

However, a great controversy arose. Eisenhower was under heavy criticism for dealing with a man considered the enemy. Tacitly, Roosevelt and Churchill approved of Eisenhower's decision, but did not rush to defend him. Politically, that would have been unwise. Eisenhower was hurt by their seeming lack of support. In a short time, the furor died down. In a bizarre quirk of fate, Admiral Darlan was assassinated. By this time, he was no longer needed, so his passing from the scene was not an unwelcome development.

In the race for Tunisia, Eisenhower was at a disadvantage. German reinforcements could flow quickly from Italy and Sicily; Hitler moved fast to build up his forces. Eisenhower, whose base was at Algiers, was hundreds of miles away with only a few poor roads and a rickety rail line to move his forces. By the time he had gotten sufficient troops to the front to attack, heavy rains came, turning the whole area in to a mass of mud. Mobility of vehicles was practically impossible. Eisenhower, regrettably, postponed that attack for better weather.

In the meanwhile, Montgomery's Eighth Army had been pursuing the remnants of Rommel's army westward across Libya. Rommel's objective was to keep ahead of the pursuit and join the mounting German forces in Tunisia. It is interesting to consider if Hitler had poured the same amount of men and materiel that he was now giving to the Tunisian front—that if the amount of men and materiel had gone to Rommel's army one year earlier—Rommel would probably have taken Cairo and the Suez Canal. Too late—too late.

Hitler was anxious to forestall the Allies in Tunisia. If Tunisia fell, North Africa was lost. A whole new front would be open, i.e., the whole of southern Europe, and in particular his shaky ally, Italy. Hitler's forces, already stretched thin, would be stretched even further. To be strong everywhere is to be strong nowhere. Thus, his determination to stand and fight in Tunisia. Actually, I think Hitler at all times was trying to keep the Allied forces as far away from himself as possible.

Rommel's army, escaping Montgomery, did join up with the army of von Arnim in Tunisia. This made for a considerable force of over 150,000 men. Rommel decided to attack and unsettle the Allies. He attacked westward and defeated scattered elements of the American Army at the Kasserine Pass. With this limited objective achieved, he returned to the Tunisian redoubt. This was a blow to the Americans, but they gained valuable experience from this defeat. Eisenhower made a change in command, and shortly thereafter, his classmate at West Point, Omar Bradley, was installed as head of the American forces.

Now that Montgomery's army had reached Tunisia, a change in command was necessary. Although a majority of the forces were British, Eisenhower remained as commander-in-chief. General Harold Alexander was now in charge of all ground forces. General Tedder was Air Force commander, and Admiral Cunningham was in charge of naval forces. All operational commands were in British hands. Eisenhower, to some extent, had been kicked upstairs. However, this was an effective command setup with experienced and able men in charge. No doubt, the Germans didn't like it, which made it the right thing to do.

In the spring of 1943, the Allied forces, having achieved a considerable buildup, began their offensive. The Germans were hampered by the disruption of their supply chain across the Mediterranean Sea by attacks from air and sea, especially from Malta. The first plan to make the final attack appeared to exclude the American army. General Bradley protested to General Eisenhower directly. As a result, Eisenhower ordered Alexander to include the Americans in the northern area, and they performed very well. In particular, in their area was hill 609, which dominated the scene. The Germans had made it a stronghold, and it was the key to the whole battle. Bradley assigned the Thirty-Fourth Division to its capture. Aided by heavy artillery and tanks, the Thirty-Fourth took hill 609—the way was open to Bizerte.

By May 7, 1943, the German and Italian armies were compressed into a small area of Northeast Tunisia. In the final attack, the British captured Tunis and the Americans captured Bizerte. The Germans could not evacuate due to the Allied control of sea and air. They surrendered en masse. Over 200,000— this is a conservative estimate. All of North Africa was in Allied hands. The offensive now was in Allied hands. With their control of the sea, they could strike at many different points. It was a big problem for Hitler. Russia was on the offensive in the east, and now the Allies were on the offensive in the south. Potentially, there was a forthcoming attack on Northern France. The tide had definitely turned.

It was now not a question of German victory; it was a question of how long they could hold out. They had only two hopes. One was that the Allied coalition would somehow fall apart. The other hope was for smashing defeat of the Allied invasion force in Northern France. Time would tell. Perhaps Hitler's declaration of war on America was not turning out too well for him— and it would get worse. Option 3 wasn't the right one.

In regard to the African Campaign, as usual, Churchill summed it up best. In a speech to the United States House of Representatives on May 19, 1943, he said,

In North Africa, we builded better than we knew. The unexpected came to the aid of the design and multiplied the results. For this we have to thank the military intuition of Corporal Hitler. We may notice, as I predicted in the House of Commons three months ago, the touch of the master-hand. The same insensate obstinacy which condemned Field Marshall von Paulus and his army to destruction at Stalingrad has brought this new catastrophe upon our enemies in Tunisia.

The African excursions of the two Dictators have cost their countries in killed and captured 950,000 soldiers. . . There have also been lost to the enemy 6200 guns, 2550 tanks and 70,000 trucks. . . Arrived at this milestone in the war, we can say, 'One continent redeemed.

The War at Sea—Atlantic

At the beginning of the war in September, 1939, Hitler knew that his surface naval forces were no match for the Royal Navy. His only alternative was the U-boats, which were very effective in the First War. Hitler believed his submarines could cut off supplies to England from the outside world. This, combined with air attacks, would either force England to surrender or at the least keep her in reduced circumstances, unable to influence the outcome of the war.

It began on September 3, 1939, just twelve hours after the British declaration of war on Germany. The U-30, commanded by Lieutenant Fritz Lemp, sank the large passenger liner the SS Athenia with 1,417 people aboard. Fortunately, 1,305 persons were saved. Some of those killed were Americans. The sea war had begun on a frightening note. For Germany, it was no holds barred. Several other important naval engagements occurred in 1939. On September 16, U-boat 47, under Lieutenant Prein, entered the great base of

Scapa Flow in Scotland and sank the Royal Oak, a 29,000 ton battleship. It was a brilliant and daring operation.

At the outbreak of war, the Graf Spee, a new pocket battleship and the pride of the German navy, dashed into the South Atlantic to prey on Allied shipping. The Graf Spee was a formidable ship featuring six eleven inch guns and heavily armored. Her captain was Hans Langsdorff. After sinking a number of helpless Allied ships, on December 13 the Graf Spee was off the coast of Uruguay. At that point, it ran into three British cruisers which had been sent to find her, the Exeter, the Achilles, and the Ajax. A running battle commenced which lasted fourteen hours. The largest British cruiser, the Exeter, was hit a number of times and damaged so severely that it was put out of action. However, the Achilles and the Ajax continued the battle. Suffering some damage, Captain Langsdorff decided to seek neutral waters in the harbor of Montevideo nearby. The British cruisers stood off the coast and radioed for help. The Uruguayan government ordered the Graf Spee to leave or be interned. For five days, there was great uncertainty. What would the Graf Spee do: Try to escape and elude the gathering forces outside the seaport, or fight it out?

On Sunday, December 17, 1939, the question was answered. As 300,000 people watched, the Graf Spee weighed anchor and proceeded out of the harbor. Suddenly, it stopped. Smoke began to appear, followed by flames and large explosions. The flames spread quickly, and within a few minutes the Graf Spee sank to the bottom. The Graf Spee had been scuttled by its crew. Captain Langsdorff and the crew escaped. On December 20, Captain Langsdorff committed suicide by gunshot. He felt he had suffered a tremendous humiliation for the German navy. The order to sink the ship came from Hitler himself, who was devastated by the developments. One less major German warship that could have participated in the invasion of England in 1940.

The Bismarck

The Bismarck was a new super dreadnought which set out into the North Atlantic at the end of May, 1941, accompanied by the cruiser Prince Eugen. Its objective was to attack and destroy Allied shipping. The Bismarck was one of the best warships ever built, a very formidable fighting vessel. The commander of the group was Admiral Lutjens, and the captain of the Bismarck was Captain Lindemann.

The Bismarck presented a major problem for the Royal Navy. The first would be finding her in the vast expanse of the Atlantic Ocean. Also, it would require capital ships to engage the Bismarck with any chance of success. The

Germans were taking a gamble, as their two ships could be heavily outnumbered by the British fleet. Admiral Lutjens felt that since the Bismarck was so heavily armed and still fast, he could out-gun and then outrun the British. He also hoped that if the British found him, they would attack with ships they had at hand, and not their whole fleet.

The British ships were led by the H.M.S. Hood, a giant battle cruiser, along with the battleship Prince of Wales. The British found the Bismarck off the coast of Greenland, and the battle began. Shortly after the first shots were fired, the Hood received a direct hit on its magazine and exploded. After the smoke cleared, all that remained was small bits of wreckage. Only three men survived. It was a disaster; over fourteen hundred men were lost in an instant. The Prince of Wales was also hit but, along with other several cruisers, continued to dog the Bismarck. The British high command was calling in ships from all over the area to head off the Bismarck, which was trying to reach the French port of Brest. After the disaster of the Hood, the British were even more determined than ever not to let the Bismarck get away.

Two days after the battle, a Catalina patrol plane spotted the Bismarck, a fatal event for the Germans. The British aircraft carrier Ark Royal, coming from the Mediterranean, received the news and made plans to attack. On May 26, planes carrying torpedoes located the Bismarck and attacked. One torpedo hit at midship, and another hit the stern. Disastrously for the Germans, the torpedo that hit the stern crippled the steering gear; the giant ship could only go around in circles.

The Bismarck was doomed; the Germans frantically tried to repair the damage, but it was impossible. The next morning, the British closed in on the struggling Bismarck. The battleships King George V and Rodney poured shell after shell into the German ship. After a time, the Bismarck was a blazing wreck. The British cruiser Dorsetshire issued the coup-de-grace with a salvo of torpedoes. The Bismarck went down at 10:40 a.m. Only one hundred men were rescued, as the British had reports that German submarines were in the area. Over twenty-two hundred men were lost; among the casualties were Admiral Lutjens and Captain Lindemann.

It was a frightening experience for both sides. As one British admiral said, "One minute the Hood was there and the next minute it was gone." Fifty years later, one of the three survivors of the Hood was being interviewed. He said he didn't know how he made it. He then choked up at the thought of his fellow crewmen and couldn't continue the interview. The battle provided a huge lift for British morale, which was at a low point. It also showed that air power was more powerful than had been thought, that it was, in fact, supreme.

Hitler was furious at the loss of his mightiest ship. He lost confidence in Germany's surface fleet, and from then on devoted nearly all his efforts to submarines.

The U-Boat Menace

After the failure of the air attack on Britain in late 1940, Hitler decided to turn his U-boats loose and blockade England, cutting off supplies and munitions that would effectively put England out of the war. The construction of U-boats was pushed to the utmost. In 1942, the Germans had 101 submarines operational, and they took a huge toll on Allied shipping. In the first six months of 1942, they sank 585 Allied ships, a phenomenal score. In early 1943, they sank 96 ships in a period of 20 days. They were close to crippling the entire Allied war effort.

However, Britain and America were up to the challenge. Roosevelt and Churchill made the winning of this naval submarine war their number one priority. They devoted enormous resources to ships, planes, and men to defeat the U-boat By the end of 1943, the tide began to turn in favor of the Allies. Airplanes equipped with radar were a large factor in this success.

Admiral Doenitz, the German commander, realized the battle was going against the Germans by the sheer weight of resources turned on them, particularly by the Allied scientific detection devices. Towards the end of the war, the Allies were sinking more U-boats than the loss of their own merchant ships. Also, Allied air bombing was destroying U-boat construction and their bases. By the end of the war the Germans had lost 783 U-boats from Allied action and were practically driven from the sea.

Besides the tragic loss of lives of the Allied merchant seamen, there were also thousands of German submariners who perished beneath the waves. They sacrificed their lives following the command of one deranged man, Adolph Hitler, who lost not one wink of sleep over the fate of these brave men.

The winning of the war in the Atlantic had a great deal to do with winning the entire war. As in all the other theaters of the war, the Germans were being overwhelmed by the enormous resources of the Allied powers. Roosevelt, Churchill, and Stalin made sure of that.

Arctic Convoys—Aid to Russia

The primary goal of Churchill and Roosevelt during 1941-42-43 was to keep Russia in the war. They knew that the Soviets were under terrific pressure from the German armed forces and were bearing the brunt of the war. Almost two hundred German divisions were tied up in Russia. Without the Eastern Front, in fact, it would be very difficult or almost impossible for the United States and Britain to defeat Germany. Probably the best they could hope for would be a stalemate. (Of course, this is before the atomic bomb, which changed everything.)

Therefore, Churchill and Roosevelt were determined to do everything possible to maintain Russia in the war. However, they didn't have the forces to invade France and thus their primary goal was to forward military supplies to Russia. There were three routes for this: one across the Pacific to Vladivostock; the second the land route through Persia; and thirdly, the most direct and difficult route, across the Arctic to the northern Russian ports of Archangel and Murmansk. The difficulty lay in the fact that the Germans had air and naval bases in Norway directly on the flank of the convoy route. Airplanes, submarines, and heavy surface ships were based there. In effect, the convoys would have to run the gauntlet of all these opposing forces to reach their destination.

Stalin desperately needed help, and he looked on these convoys not only for the materials they brought, but also as a test of the Allied resolve to help him. Thus, it was not only militarily important, but politically important to push these convoys through.

Beginning with the first convoy which sailed from Scotland on August 21, 1941, the convoys continued until the end of the war. The loss rate on these convoys (ten percent) was greater than any other route in the war. Thousands of merchant seamen were killed. As the war progressed and it became obvious to the Germans that Russia was not going to be defeated quickly, they diverted more and more resources to Norway to stop the material coming in on the convoys.

The worst disaster for the Allies in this endeavor was convoy PQ 17, which sailed from Iceland on June 27, 1942. The Royal Navy had been advised by Ultra that the heavy battleship Tirpitz and the cruiser Hipper had left port to attack the convoy. The Royal Navy command ordered the merchant ships to scatter and to proceed to their destination on their own. The individual ships were pounced on at once by U-boats and aircraft, and of the 37 ships involved, 26 were sunk, carrying many merchant seamen to their deaths along with the loss of the precious cargoes. The frozen water of the Arctic allowed the seamen less than 20 minutes of exposure before their deaths.

As a result of this disaster, Churchill had to temporarily suspend convoys across the northern route of the Arctic. This made Stalin furious and led to a bitter exchange of telegrams between him and Churchill. However, Churchill was determined to build up his naval escort strength first before continuing the convoy, and also to eliminate the Tirpitz, which he was eventually able to do. The convoys were restarted in December, 1942. At this time, much of the German air strength had to be diverted to contain the Allied offensive operations in the Mediterranean. As time went on, fewer and fewer German resources could be used in Norway, which made it easier on the Arctic convoys, although they were still dangerous. The men who manned these merchant ships were courageous indeed and played a significant part in winning the war.

Over four million tons of materiel were shipped to Russia over the Arctic route, about one-fourth of the aid that reached Russia from all sources. In a battle that was so closely fought between Germany and Russia, this aid was of much importance. Psychologically, it was also important, in that it showed Stalin and the Russian people that they were not alone and that Churchill and Roosevelt were going all out to help them. The materiel shipped across the Arctic plus that coming through Vladivostok and Persia was used to good effect by the Russians. The sacrifices of the men that took part in these operations were not in vain.

The Casablanca Conference

On January 14, 1943, Churchill and Roosevelt met at Casablanca. Plans for the coming year were made. The most famous thing remembered from the Casablanca conference was that Roosevelt and Churchill called for the "unconditional surrender" of their enemies. Actually, Roosevelt unexpectedly proposed it, and Churchill agreed. Roosevelt said he remembered how Ulysses S. Grant had used the phrase *unconditional surrender* during the American Civil War—a phrase that showed the resolve of the Union forces. One reason that Roosevelt proposed this was to let the Russians know there would be no negotiated peace with their common enemy, thus strengthening the alliance among Britain, the United States, and the Soviet Union. Mainly, this proclamation was issued because of the circumstances surrounding the end of World War I.

One of Hitler's main topics in his rise to power was that Germany had not really been beaten in the First War, that the German army on November 11, 1918, was still on French and Belgian soil; although retreating, it was still intact. Hitler's contention was that the Germans surrendered too soon and that, in fact, they should not have surrendered at all. He claimed that the Jews and the Communists had stirred up such turmoil in Germany and that was the reason that Germany was defeated. They had "stabbed the army in the back." Hitler spoke of this many times, so much so that he convinced the German people that they had been duped and really hadn't lost the war—that the German army was invincible.

The truth was that in the first week of November, 1918, Germany was collapsing both internally and on the battlefront; the internal collapse was mostly caused by what was happening on the battlefront. Its ally, Turkey, had surrendered; its ally, Bulgaria, had surrendered. Austria-Hungary, its largest ally, had already asked for an armistice. Its whole southern front had collapsed. Since the German army was tied up on the Western Front, there was nothing to stop the Allies from walking into Germany from the south. The German fleet was ordered to attack the Royal Navy, and the men refused; it would be a suicide mission with the war drawing to a close. The Navy was in a state of mutiny.

On the Western Front, Ludendorff had been imploring the Kaiser for several months for an armistice. Each day, the situation worsened. The British, the French, and the American armies were all the while increasing their attacks to add to the pressure. German casualties and those surrendering (350,000 prisoners) were mounting; each day was one of retreat. Ludendorff knew it was just a mater of days before the German army either collapsed or was routed. The Kaiser fired Ludendorff; he retained Hindenburg, who shared Ludendorff's beliefs. With things continuing to go from bad to worse, the Kaiser was forced to abdicate; he went to Holland for refuge.

Finally, with the whole country in chaos, the German government asked for armistice. When in early November members of the new German government asked the new German army commander, General Groener, his views, Groener said Germany had lost the war, the Western Front would collapse in a few days, and that an armistice should be signed immediately before that happened. The Germans had no choice but to surrender. Indeed, some of the Allied commanders, such as General Pershing, wished the war would continue for about two weeks. Pershing felt the German army would then be completely routed and defeated without a doubt. Then it should surrender unconditionally. In any event, an armistice was signed on November 11, 1918. The armistice actually helped Germany, as it saved it from complete anarchy and kept the state intact.

Hitler's version of events was completely opposite the facts. Germany was decisively defeated; however, Hitler had convinced himself to the contrary, and unfortunately, the German people believed him. The basis of the Second World War.

Thus, at Casablanca, Roosevelt and Churchill were not going to let that happen again. Germany would be thoroughly defeated this time without any doubt. Unconditional surrender meant the utter and complete defeat of Germany. No peace conditions, no negotiations, just the admission of total defeat. Roosevelt and Churchill wanted to absolutely rule out any future German leader following the line Hitler had used. In this they were correct. Some have said the unconditional surrender policy lengthened the war by making the Germans fight harder and longer as there was no way out. Actually, I do not think this made any difference. Hitler was determined to fight to the end, and in any event, who would want to make a deal with Hitler? He was about as trustworthy as a rattlesnake. It was impossible for the Allies to make a deal with Hitler.

Another objective at Casablanca was to bring together the various French factions. This was a waste of time, as General de Gaulle was much smarter and more determined than all the others put together. He would emerge as the sole leader of the French. It was also decided at Casablanca that the next offensive action, once North Africa was cleared, was to attack Sicily. This would bring intense pressure on Italy and Mussolini. The war would be coming home to his doorstep, something Mussolini did not foresee when he attacked prostrate France in 1940. The tide of war had definitely changed.

Churchill and Roosevelt had planned well. They had achieved their objective with the relatively small forces on hand. Hitler now had to worry not only about the east, but also about the south and northwest as well. The German army, still a very powerful force, was being asked to do too much to cover thousands of miles of fronts and potential fronts. Hitler's one-front war was beginning to look like a three-front war. Even though the allies had not actually invaded Northern France, Hitler had to assign forces there to meet the threat which, as time went on, became increasingly imminent. Moreover, the air war over Germany was intensifying daily, and a large part of the Luftwaffe was needed to keep German cities from being blown to bits. The war was almost out of Hitler's hands. The most he could do was to react to Allied initiatives. The defeat in North Africa, together with Stalingrad, had changed the whole character of the war.

Overall Strategy—Middle of the War
The Four Players

The summer of 1943 found the situation much different from the summer of 1942. As you remember, at that time the Germans were on the offensive, both in Russia and in North Africa. In Russia, Hitler's troops were moving rapidly eastward with the Volga River and Stalingrad as its objective. In Africa, Rommel was also moving eastward towards Suez. At about this time, Hitler made the key mistake of splitting his forces and sending one part to Stalingrad and the other directly against the Caucasus oil fields. Each attack was thereby weakened, and neither objective was attained. As a result of the disasters at Stalingrad and in Tunisia, Hitler had lost the offensive, which was now held by the Allies.

At this stage of the war, it might be useful to examine each of the leaders' plans and objectives. Of course, the overall objective of the three allies, Great Britain, the United States, and Russia, was to crush Germany and eliminate Hitler. They would do this by attacks from three sides—east, south, and west.

Since Churchill and Roosevelt and their forces were working so closely together, we will consider them as one. Their objective was directed at the northern coast of France. With the invasion of France, the Western Front would be opened and the bulk of all of Britain's and America's power would be applied at that point. The Western Front, along with Italy, together with Russia coming in from the East, would crush Germany. The overwhelming resources of the Allies would overpower Hitler. Stalin's plan, now that he was on the offensive, was to pound and push the Germans out of Russia. He would continue eastward toward his objective—Berlin. In the meanwhile, he would have to run over Poland, Rumania, Hungary, and Bulgaria. Stalin believed it would be a good thing if those countries were "friendly" towards Moscow. In other words, he would set up Communist governments in those countries which would be subservient to Moscow.

Since the Red Army would occupy these countries, there was absolutely nothing that Churchill and Roosevelt could do about it except protest. Stalin didn't mind protests; he just ignored them. He knew the West would never start another whole new war over Eastern Europe. The American and the British public would never stand for it. Stalin could promise a lot to the Western leaders, but he intended to deliver on none of those promises. Churchill, in particular, was aware of this but could do nothing about it. He did manage to save Greece and Austria.

In the summer of 1943, if Hitler truly looked at the whole picture, he would realize that Germany's chances of winning the war were slim to none. Of course, Hitler didn't want to look at the whole picture: it was too bleak. Instead, he told the German people of the new miracle weapons which would change the war. He was talking about the V1 and V2 rockets and jet aircraft.

Indeed, if he had developed the weapons sooner, they might have had a direct positive influence for the Germans on the war.

For instance, the progress on the jet airplane was going well until Hitler decided to modify it from a fighter plane to a fighter bomber. Chalk up another huge mistake for Hitler. This would be ideal, except it set back production almost a year. The Messerschmitt 262 twin-engine planes appeared in small numbers in the air over Western Europe in late 1944 and early 1945. Indeed, with their speed, they were a formidable weapon, and the few that were used caused the Allied air forces serious problems. However, the war was over before they could participate in appreciable numbers, which was very fortunate for the Allies.

Consider what might have happened if on D-Day, June 6, 1944, 800 to 900 jet fighters had been operating over Normandy. The Germans probably would have achieved air superiority. This would have made the invasion a huge gamble, and possibly a losing gamble for the Allies. Indeed, if the V1 and V2 rockets had been deployed six months earlier than they were in 1944, they could have, in the spring, been aimed at the invasion ports in force and created havoc. And if they had had the eight hundred to nine hundred jet planes operating at this same time, a successful invasion would have been impossible.

Yes, Hitler had his miracle weapons, but they came too late. However, Hitler's propaganda in regard to these new weapons did encourage the Germans to keep fighting, which resulted in many more thousands of Germans and others dying needlessly. It is tragic that one miserable man, Hitler, caused so much death and devastation to so many millions of people. Hitler was going to lose the war, and he did not care how many people would die unnecessarily. His sole preoccupation was himself. If he was going to be destroyed, as far as he was concerned, Germany should also be destroyed as unworthy. It was for this man that the Germans were fighting.

The Pressure Mounts

There was no reason for Churchill and Roosevelt to contemplate the next move after expelling the Axis from Africa; plans were already underway for the invasion of Sicily. They realized that the invasion of Northern France in 1943 would be impossible. They moved the date back to May, 1944. In the meanwhile, they could not stand idle after their victory in Africa. The pressure on the Axis had to be maintained. They knew they had to do something to mollify the Russians since the invasion of Northern France had to be postponed. The next logical step was Sicily.

166

Although the Allies controlled the Mediterranean Sea, it was also necessary that wherever they made amphibious landings, they had to control the air as well. Since the range of fighter craft was limited, Sicily fit the bill in all respects. Also, the capture of Sicily would pose a direct threat to Italy. The command arrangement which had done so well in the last few months would be maintained. One addition was the tough and colorful General George S. Patton as commander of the American Seventh Army.

Before landing in Sicily, Eisenhower determined to take Panterlleria, a small island about midway between Sicily and Tunisia. Here, there was an airfield which the Allies could use to provide air cover for their landing in Sicily. After a naval and air bombardment, the eleven thousand Italian troops there surrendered without a fight, and there were no Allied casualties in seizing this important base.

The plan was for the Allies to land on the southern tip of Sicily near Syracuse, the British on the right and the Americans on the left. Sicily had a large garrison made up mostly of Italians. It was not known whether the Italians would put up a fight or not. The plan had to assume that they would, bolstered by German forces.

The largest amphibious force ever assembled assaulted Sicily on July 11, 1943; even though the weather was bad, Eisenhower made the decision to go ahead with the attack. The landings were relatively unopposed except in the American sector, where German troops attempted to drive them into the sea. Naval gunfire and hard fighting beat them off. American and British paratroopers were used on a large scale for the first time, with mixed results. Tragically, some air transports were mistakenly shot down by their own forces; but overall, the action was a success. Even though they were spread over a large area, the paratroopers caused confusion and disruption to the Axis troops. The Germans were fighting hard as usual, but the Italians were content in most cases to surrender.

The battle for Sicily lasted 38 days. The Allied objective was Messina, a town situated at the east end of the island directly across the straits from mainland Italy. If Messina could be captured quickly, the German troops would be cut off; however, the presence of Mount Etna slowed the Allied push, and the Germans were able to make a clean getaway. With his slow, methodical offensive up the east cost, Montgomery failed to cut off the German retreat. Patton, in the meanwhile, had dashed westward to take Palermo, which had no strategic purpose whatsoever. He then turned eastward but was too late to take Messina, although he beat the British there. Still, Sicily was in Allied hands by the end of August. Italy was under the gun so to speak.

There was some controversy in the Allied camp about what to do next. The British wanted to follow up the victory with an invasion of Italy and knock it out of the war. This action would threaten all of occupied Southern Europe. The Americans were afraid the British wanted to entangle them in the Mediterranean, thus delaying or even canceling the invasion of Northern France in 1944, something they were determined to do. They thought the most direct way to defeat Germany was to cross the plains of Northern France and into Germany itself.

Finally, a compromise was reached whereby the Allies would invade Italy, but only use the minimum necessary forces to do so. There would be no commitment to an all-out campaign replacing the Normandy invasion in 1944. Churchill was not too happy about the limits, but he realized that he was becoming a junior partner in the Alliance. In 1944, two-thirds of the troops involved would be Americans.

In the meanwhile, Italy was in a convulsion. The Italian people were never fond of the war and now it threatened to destroy their country. They had no liking for the Germans. Why die for Germany? On July 10, 1943, Rome was bombed. This hastened events that were already fermenting beneath the surface.

Mussolini, whose glitter had been greatly tarnished when he led his people into a desperate situation, returned to Rome from a meeting with his ally, Hitler. He was summoned to a meeting of the Grand Council, normally just a rubber stamp for whatever Mussolini wanted. However, this meeting was deadly serious. In a vote of the Council, Mussolini was thrown out of office. The meeting was endorsed by King Emmanuel, the nominal ruler of Italy, who assumed control. Mussolini was immediately arrested and imprisoned. The whole thing was probably a great shock for Mussolini, who had ruled Italy with absolute authority for almost twenty years. Now, he was nothing, somewhat like the Kaiser at the end of the First War.

Mussolini's actions during the fateful meeting with the Grand Council were strange indeed. Far from being his bombastic usual self, Mussolini's attitude was almost passive. It is said that for some time he had been physically and mentally exhausted, no doubt due to the deteriorating war situation. The members of the Council were taken aback by Mussolini's almost indifferent mood. When he was asked the crucial question as to whether he saw any chance of victory, Mussolini had no answer. This really shook up the Council members and brought about their decision to remove Mussolini and to try to make peace with the Allies. Even his own son-in-law, Count Ciano, voted against Mussolini.

Strangely, Mussolini made no objection to the Council's decision. He had his own armed guard but made no resistance to being arrested and meekly surrendered to his captors. Some have even suggested that Mussolini was actually relieved to have the crushing burden of a losing war removed from his shoulders. Whatever the reason, the once proud, strutting leader of Fascism had gone down with hardly a whimper. What he thought was a sure thing with France's collapse in 1940 now, because of him, had put Italy in a very perilous position.

The Italians, realizing that an invasion of Italy was imminent, wanted to spare their country from destruction. They wanted to surrender; in particular, they wanted the Allies to occupy their country before the Germans took it over. The Italians had greatly overestimated the size of the Allied forces. In surrender negotiations, the Allies could not disclose that they did not have the power to occupy all of Italy. Their plan was an invasion at Salerno, just below Naples, which was in range of their cover from fighter aircraft. A tentative plan was to send an airborne division to occupy Rome itself, a daring move. If this occurred and was successful, it would stop German reinforcements moving south and opposing the invasion of Salerno.

Hitler, in the meanwhile, was quick to grasp the implications of the whole situation. He was infuriated with the treachery of the Italians, particularly their treatment of Mussolini. In a brilliant operation, Mussolini was rescued by German special forces under General Otto Skorzeny. While negotiations were going on between the Allies and the desperate Italians, Hitler began quietly moving forces of considerable strength into Italy. The Italian Army was in a trance; they wanted out of the war but were terrified of the Germans. So they did nothing and became a non-factor in the proceedings. This was really too bad, because if the Italian Army had cooperated with the Allies and fought the Germans, Italy would have been liberated much more quickly and much destruction would have been avoided.

On September 3, 1943, formations of General Montgomery's Eighth Army crossed the Strait of Messina to land at Calabria on the toe of Italy. They were unopposed and moved northward in the direction of Naples. The invasion of Salerno occurred on September 9. Simultaneously, the Italians announced that they had surrendered to the Allies. The decision was made not to send the airborne division to Rome, which had been predicated on the assurances that the Italian Army would join in the fight in Rome. Since the Italian Army had thrown in the towel, the operation rightly was considered too dangerous.

The Italian Navy left ports in Northern Italy and sailed southward. The Germans attacked the fleet, probably just for spite, and sank the battleship

Roma, killing over fifteen hundred seamen. The rest of the fleet, 28 ships, reached Malta and safety.

The landing at Salerno was strongly opposed by the Germans. At one point, it seemed the relatively small Allied force would be thrown into the sea. Montgomery's forces came from the south relatively unopposed and moved north very slowly. They could have been a big help to the forces fighting at Salerno, but didn't arrive until the crisis had passed. No wonder the Americans became frustrated with Montgomery. Hard fighting, air attack, and naval gunfire, together with reinforcements, saved the day. The port of Naples was taken on October 1, 1943.

Churchill and Roosevelt had mainly stayed out of the proceedings, leaving it to the people on the spot. They were fully aware of the situation, but realized that with the limited forces available and the swiftly moving events, Eisenhower and his chiefs needed a free hand. With the capture of Naples, the Allies had secured a foothold on the European Continent, something I'm sure that Hitler and the Germans were not happy about. The net was starting to close in around them.

Anzio

With the departure of General Eisenhower to take over the Normandy Invasion, the command of the Allied Armies in Italy went to British General Harold Alexander. Since a majority of troops in Italy were British, they were in command in this theater. This gave Churchill a chance to exercise his strategic vision. One of his hopes was to completely defeat the German Army in Italy. His long-range goal was to somehow exert the Allied presence into the Balkans and Central Europe, particularly since the Red Army was approaching these objectives. The fact that geography, including the Alps, was against him didn't deter the redoubtable Churchill. Moreover, the fact that the Allied Army in Italy barely outnumbered the tough German Army in front of them was a serious challenge.

Churchill's plan was not to attack the German Army in front of them, but to go around them. Since the Allies controlled the sea, why not mount an amphibious operation and land behind them? With a simultaneous attack from the Allied Army to the south, it might be possible to give the German Army a decisive defeat.

There were two main problems with the operation. The first was a shortage of landing craft; the Normandy invasion build-up had first priority on these craft. This didn't stop Churchill. Begging here and borrowing there, he came up with enough landing ships to mount the invasion. The second problem, and ultimately the greatest mistake in the campaign, was that only two divisions were assigned to the initial attack: one American and one British. This was due to the shortage of available troops in Italy and the limited number of landing craft. Churchill was mounting what should be a major campaign on a shoestring. He definitely should have realized that the relatively small force could not achieve decisive results. His plan was strategically good but tactically bad. He was trying to do too much with too little. British resources were strained to the limit, and Churchill did not have the troops to attain his vision.

The commander of the expedition, American General John Lucas, did have doubts about the operation. For one thing, neither General Alexander nor General Mark Clark, his immediate superior, had given him clear-cut objectives. Indeed, General Clark urged Lucas to be cautious. Both Lucas and Clark had been in the Salerno operation, where shortly after the Allies landed, the Germans counterattacked and almost drove the Allied forces into the sea. For Churchill, the objective was to cut the roads from Rome heading south in the Anzio area, thus cutting off the retreat of a sizable portion of the German Army, hopefully capturing them. The town of Cisterna on Route 7 was a key objective. If this could be accomplished, Churchill felt the entire battle in Italy would be changed in favor of the Allies. General Lucas and his corps landed at Anzio on January 22, 1944. Anzio was just thirty-three miles south of Rome.

At the moment General Lucas landed, there was little to actually block him from going to Rome itself. The Germans had been completely caught by surprise, and with a stronger force, he might have attempted to strike out for Rome. In the next several days, he did push several miles inland, at one point reaching within four miles of Cisterna. However, General Lucas's main concern in the first days at Anzio was to prepare for a German counterattack. He didn't want his small force to be so spread out that it could not resist the attack which he felt was forthcoming.

While the Germans had been caught by surprise, they reacted quickly to what they saw could be a dangerous situation for them. Within several days after the landing, they had gathered a number of divisions to oppose it. Hitler ordered his commanders to thrust the Allied forces into the Mediterranean Sea. The Germans attacked and pushed the Allied forces back; the Germans commanded the high ground, which gave them an additional advantage. One American Ranger battalion was cut off and virtually destroyed.

On January 30, Allied reinforcements landed on the beachheads. With the aid of naval gunfire, they were able to stop the German advance. The Germans, just as at Salerno, had come close to pushing the invading Allied force into the sea. As it was, the Allied Army at Anzio was bottled up in a small area by a strong German defense.

General Lucas was replaced by General Truscott. In effect, the Allied small landing had failed. Churchill was furious, particularly at General Lucas, who he thought had been too timid. Controversy has gone on for many years as to what went wrong. Many have blamed Lucas; many have blamed Alexander and Clark; and many have blamed Churchill himself. In general, Lucas has been the main target (especially by Churchill). The author believes that General Lucas was not at fault at all. He was not given a clear objective; even if he had been, he was not given sufficient forces to carry it out, especially in the initial stages. If his small force had been pushed into the sea, Lucas could possibly be blamed. But as it was, the strong German attack was defeated; in fact, one could say rightfully, that Lucas had been successful.

Actually, if anyone is to be blamed, it would have to be Churchill. His plan was good, very good. He just did not have enough resources to carry it out—ships and men. One might say the British had reached the overall limit of their resources. They could not conduct a strong operations contingent with their own limited resources; this was proven later in the war by the defeats in the Dodecanese Islands. The British, urged on by Churchill, invaded and occupied several of these islands but were counter-attacked by the Germans and defeated with many casualties, most of them captured.

It seems at times that Churchill was determined to redeem past defeats—thus, his attempts in the Eastern Mediterranean in 1944 and his effort to bring Turkey into the war, thereby making up for the Dardanelles disaster in 1915. Also, his repeated attempts to convince his general staff to invade Norway in 1944—Operation Jupiter—possibly attempted to make up for the defeat in Norway in 1940. Churchill was a fighter, and his motto was, "Never give up. Never—never—never!"

With the Allies bottled up in Anzio and stopped further south on the main front, we will not go into further detail on the Italian Campaign. Suffice it to say that thousands of good men became casualties there. Theirs was a secondary but important front. It drew approximately 25 German divisions into Italy and away from Normandy and Russia. Its air bases were used to attack targets in Germany; supplies were sent to the guerrilla forces in Yugoslavia and Greece. The armies thus performed important work under miserable and dangerous conditions. They contributed to the final victory and will not be forgotten. At the end of the war, almost one million German soldiers in Italy surrendered. It is a tribute to the Allied soldiers fighting in Italy that they contained this many German troops from the Western and Eastern Fronts.

Russia—Westward Ho!

Hitler's attention was not only on the Mediterranean Front, but also on the reeling Russian Front. After the disaster at Stalingrad, the German Army was in disarray. Hitler and the German generals did an outstanding job of holding this long front together. The Army of the Caucasus barely escaped the fate of Stalingrad. While Hitler hated to give up ground, he did so grudgingly in order to shorten and strengthen his front. Some local counterattacks were successful in checking the Soviet rush. The German Army was hurt, but it could still fight, and fight effectively. Von Manstein, particularly, was successful at this time. It is interesting to speculate that if von Manstein and von Bock, Germany's best generals, had been used in the advance on Stalingrad, unhindered by Hitler, what would have been the result? Perhaps victory for the Germans.

With the front at last stabilized, some of Hitler's confidence returned. His nature was to attack. He realized that he did not have the resources to mount an all-out attack along the whole front. He looked for some point of weakness in his enemy, some point where he could deal a hard blow and a setback to the Red Army.

The most obvious point was the large salient at Kursk. By attacking from the north and south of the salient, he could pinch it off and destroy or capture large forces of the Red Army, just as he had done in previous years. The effort was called Operation Citadel. Hitler decided to wait for his new Tiger tanks to spearhead the offensive and then launch a full-scale assault. Perhaps this large defeat of the Russians might lead to stalemate on the Russian Front—a stalemate was better than the German Army being forced back into Germany.

Of course, the Kursk salient as a large target was not lost on Stalin and the Soviet generals. After two years of fighting Hitler, they were aware of his tactics. They had learned a lot the hard way and were not about to repeat the mistakes of the past. Stalin sent substantial forces into the salient, including large tank formations. In fact, Stalin hoped the Germans would attack at Kursk so that the Russians could give them a resounding defeat. The Germans were walking into a trap.

On July 5, 1943, Hitler attacked the Kursk salient from north and south. The Germans had assembled very strong forces: 40 divisions led by its Panzer divisions. In the old days, they would have been successful. But, with the Red Army dug in belts of defensive formations, the Germans made some progress but were stopped by the concentrated fire power of the Soviet defense. The

Germans gave it all they had but could not penetrate the Soviet defense; they incurred severe casualties. This was their last great attack on the Eastern Front. They had shot their bolt.

With the defeat of the German attack, the Soviets resumed their offensives without missing a beat. The Germans, outnumbered and outgunned, fell back. It would be interesting to speculate what the outcome on the Eastern Front might have been if the German divisions that were scattered all over Europe and North Africa had been added to the forces already in Russia. Hitler had squandered his most precious assets—his army and his air force—all over the map.

It is also intriguing to wonder what position he might have been in on the Eastern Front in 1943 if he had been able to finish off England in 1940. His dismissal of England and his underestimation of the United States and the Soviet Union had had placed him in the predicament he now found himself in. He was his own worst enemy. His army and air force were putting up a terrific battle, but their leader, Hitler, was not equal to their sacrifice—nor was the cause they fought and died for. Millions of German troops fought and died for Hitler—a man who in a normal country would be locked up in a mental institution.

Further speculation: What might have happened on June 22, 1941, if Hitler had turned the operations on the Eastern Front over to his very competent generals without his interference? It seems that after the fall of France, Hitler made one mistake after another, each one compounding itself. In his fight with Churchill, Roosevelt, and Stalin, he was going in against highly intelligent, strong and resourceful leaders. They may have made some mistakes along the way, but nothing compared to the mistakes made by Hitler. Most of the time in war, it is the one who makes the fewest mistakes that wins, and Hitler was making his full share of mistakes—most of them big and, once done, impossible to be undone. The tide of Hitler's mistakes would, in the end, become an avalanche which would bury him and Germany.

One of Hitler's problems was that he seemed to be unable to take advice from any of his very competent military leaders. He gave great credence only to his own intuitions and impulses. There was no one like Alan Brooke or George Marshall to whom he would listen. Being a corporal does not qualify one to be commander-in-chief of the German Army. Hitler's intuition and impulses, in the end, were no match for the combined political and military professionalism of the Allies. Hitler had generals with brains around him, but he failed to use them.

In many instances, his subordinates failed to speak up because they were afraid of him, and with good reason, as they were dealing with a violent and irrational man with unlimited power. Hitler was a one-man show, fighting opponents who used all the resources and brainpower they could command. It is true that Churchill also was a headstrong man, but his people were not afraid to speak up and tell him when they thought he was wrong—exasperated, maybe, but not afraid. Someone like General Alan Brooke would not have lasted a day with Hitler.

So, in 1943, on the Russian Front as the Red Army advanced, Hitler was reaping what he had sown. His resources were dwindling while his enemies were getting stronger. Despite incredible casualties, the Red Army was stronger than ever, something which must have and astonished and dismayed Hitler. His knowledge and respect for Stalin and Russia had come, as always, too late.

Teheran—November, 1943

An important event happened on November 28, 1943: the meeting of Stalin, Roosevelt, and Churchill at Teheran. This was the first meeting of Roosevelt and Stalin. This meeting showed off the strengths of all three: Roosevelt, the master politician and conciliator; Churchill somewhat verbose but always conscious of the future and expressing the feelings of the English people; and Stalin the taciturn, shrewd man of steel. He knew what he wanted and played every card he had. With the Red Army carrying the bulk of the fighting, Stalin had a strong hand to play. Meanwhile, as Russia and the United States grew in strength, Churchill's influence began to diminish. England now was the smallest of the three countries operating against Hitler. While Churchill could hold his own with anybody, he still recognized the reality of the situation.

Both Roosevelt and Churchill were very impressed with Stalin. He had not gone through all he had to become master of the Soviet Union without having considerable strength and ability; and he was waging a tremendous battle against Hitler. The biggest thing going for Stalin was the Red Army. The fact that the bulk of the German army was tied up on the Russian front was the dominant reality of the talks. The Eastern Front was indispensable to the defeat of Hitler.

The two main topics of the Teheran meeting were Poland and the opening of the front in Northern France. With the Red Army advancing on Poland, there was little Roosevelt and Churchill could do in regard to the future government of Poland. They tried their best and Stalin gave them answers that sounded good, but they couldn't pin him down. The United States and Great Britain were not going to war with Russia over Poland. What happened to Poland was in Stalin's hands, unfortunately, as well as most of eastern Europe.

One episode that somewhat marred the conference occurred at a banquet following the end of one day's working session. It showed vividly the contrast between the character and attitude of Stalin and that of Churchill and Roosevelt.

The banquet was relaxed—vodka and wine were flowing—everyone was in a good humor. At that point, someone brought up the fact that the German professional military caste system had brought on two world wars. The German officer corps was highly disciplined and very efficient. The subject turned as to what to do to prevent these military men from causing another war in the future.

Stalin spoke up that perhaps it would be best to shoot 50,000 of the German top officers. Churchill recoiled and with vigor replied that neither he nor the British people would stand for such a thing—they would have nothing to do with anything like that. Roosevelt, seeing the tension increasing, tried to make light of Stalin's remark. Roosevelt said that perhaps only 49,000 should be shot. He was trying to pass off Stalin's remark as a joke.

At this point, Churchill got up and stomped out of the room. To everyone's surprise, Stalin quickly got up and followed Churchill. In the hall Stalin tried to mollify Churchill that he was only joking. He finally was able to get Churchill back in the room and everyone changed the subject. The need for unity of the big three superseded all other considerations. The conferees at the conference put this behind them and proceeded on as though nothing had happened.

Churchill definitely didn't forget this episode, as he mentions it in his history of the war. I don't believe that Churchill thought Stalin was joking—if it was a joke, it was a bad one and bordered on what Stalin was really thinking. After the war it was discovered that in 1939 and 1940 after Russia had occupied eastern Poland, 15,000 Polish officers under Russian control had disappeared. Actually, the Russian NKVD (the Russian secret police similar to the Gestapo) were in control of these prisoners.

After the war, at Katyn in Poland, over 4,400 bodies of these men were discovered. Their hands were wired behind their backs and they had been shot in the back of the head. It is assumed that the rest of the 15,000 men were disposed of in like manner. Or course, Stalin's government denied any part in this, but later Russian officials (Yeltsin) turned over documents that the NKVD had executed these Polish officers under the direct orders of Stalin. So it is possible that Stalin's remark about executing 50,000 German officers was not a joke—he had already done something of that exact nature to the Polish officers.

At the time of the Teheran Conference, Churchill was not fully aware of the Katyn massacre, but he was surely right on vigorously opposing Stalin mentioning his way of disposing of German officers. Perhaps Churchill's reaction did prevent Stalin from actually carrying out his policy in eliminating the German officer corps under his control (although very few German officers captured at Stalingrad ever returned home). Although Churchill, Roosevelt and Stalin were all fighting the same enemy, other than being brilliant, Churchill and Roosevelt had very little in common with Stalin—particularly in regard to human values. As mentioned, after this episode the conference went back to its regular order of business.

Considering their differences, the three men seemed to get along well personally. It seems rather odd, but at times, Roosevelt would make small, pointed jokes at Churchill's expense when the three were together. Of course, this upset Churchill and Stalin enjoyed Churchill's discomforture. Roosevelt's objective, evidently, was to show Stalin that he and Churchill were not "ganging up" on Stalin. Perhaps Roosevelt was trying to ingratiate himself with Stalin and to improve their relationship. Roosevelt's objective may have been to establish an independent relationship between America and the Soviet Union— thus Roosevelt being the bridge between East and West. Roosevelt's motive was excellent but perhaps unrealistic—however, with the stakes involved it was worth trying.

On the second front, Stalin received assurances that the attack would be made in May, 1944, for sure. Stalin made a point of pinning Churchill down on this; also, Stalin wanted to know who the commander would be. It had been decided earlier between Churchill and Roosevelt that since the Americans would have more forces involved, an American would the commander. It was Roosevelt's choice.

When Stalin asked Roosevelt who the commander would be, Roosevelt had not made up his mind and told this to Stalin. Stalin was impatient and said he was not sure the invasion would be carried out as promised if a commander had not been appointed. Roosevelt replied that he would inform Stalin in two weeks.

On the voyage home, Roosevelt pondered his decision. His inclination was to go with the man he had the greatest respect for, General George Marshall. In fact, he asked Marshall his preference. Marshall preferred to leave the decision up to Roosevelt. Roosevelt felt confident having Marshall by his side in Washington, where they could direct the war over the entire globe. He didn't want to give up an arrangement that was working so well. Another factor was that placing Marshall in charge of the Normandy attack would constitute a demotion for Marshall.

Roosevelt decided to leave his team intact and appointed Eisenhower as Supreme Commander of the Allied Forces in England. A message was sent to Stalin accordingly. Thoughtfully, Marshall sent Eisenhower the handwritten message that Roosevelt had directed to Stalin. Frankly, Roosevelt made a good decision in assigning Eisenhower and not Marshall to lead the invasion. By this time, Eisenhower had a great deal more experience in this type of operation. Marshall had none. Moreover, Eisenhower knew all of the people involved, their strengths and weaknesses. In particular, he got along well with all of the British, including Churchill. Eisenhower was the ideal choice to lead the invasion, as time would tell.

5

1944: Year of Decision

Normandy

All eyes were on Northern France in the spring of 1944. Allied forces were assembling in England for the long awaited Second Front. As mentioned, Eisenhower had been appointed Supreme Commander. General Bernard Montgomery would initially lead the ground forces. Montgomery was a good choice for this job, as he was a master of the prepared battle. Despite his eccentricities, Montgomery was a first-class soldier.

Normandy had been chosen as the point of attack, with the port of Cherbourg the principle objective. This area was chosen because it could be covered by air power based in England. While Calais was much closer to England and the obvious choice for invasion, it was for that reason turned down. The Allies knew the Germans had concentrated their defenses there. Hitler's intuition was that the attack would be made at Normandy; however, for once he did not fully act on his impulse. He did move two more divisions there, which caused the Allies great trouble on June 6.

The attack had been scheduled for early May, but for a number of reasons, including a shortage of landing craft, it was rescheduled for June 5. Meanwhile, Eisenhower and Montgomery had insisted that more divisions were needed for the initial landing than had been proposed. They succeeded in increasing the strength of their forces from three to six divisions, as well as adding more follow-up troops. Eisenhower had also demanded control of all of the American and British air forces, including heavy bombers. He was opposed on this by the heavy bomber commanders of the air forces, but insisted and got his way.

As the date approached, weather became the foremost problem. The invasion could not succeed if the weather was too unfavorable. Specifically, air support would be practically nil. Without air support, the balance swung to the German side. At this time, about the only thing that could save Hitler would be a smashing defeat of the Allied invasion. Once defeated, how long would it be before another could be mounted, or would another attack be mounted at all? With the Allies defeated in the west, Hitler could then turn his attention back to the east. While it would be virtually impossible for him to defeat and occupy the Soviet Union, Hitler could probably stop the Russian drive, and a stalemate would ensue. With the Western Allies checked, possibly Stalin would go for an negotiated peace, perhaps a return to the status quo which had existed before the German attack in 1941. For the Germans, even a stalemated war was better than losing.

In any event, the repulse and defeat of the Allied invasion of Normandy was Hitler's last hope to avoid eventual defeat for Germany. He did not have the resources to fight a three-front war (if you include Italy). It would then be just a matter of time. Hitler realized this: On March 20, 1944, he told his principal commanders in the West, "The destruction of the enemy's landing is the sole decisive factor in the whole conduct of the war and hence in its final results."

In early June, all depended on the weather. The weather for Monday, June 5, was predicted by the Allied meteorologists to be stormy. Of course, Eisenhower had to make the decision a day before the actual invasion in order for the assembly and departure of the invasion to take place. The paratroops were scheduled to take off around midnight of June 4. On June 4, the weather prediction forced Eisenhower to cancel the invasion for the 5th. (Interestingly, Montgomery advised making the attack on June 5 despite the weather. It was a good thing that Eisenhower was in charge. An invasion on June 5 would have been a disaster.) A tentative decision was made to go the next day, June 6. The opportune days for the invasion were June 5, 6, and 7. If it did not take place during that period, it would be another two weeks before the proper conditions would be favorable again. In two weeks, anything could happen, particularly the loss of surprise if the Germans became aware of the situation. June 7 was somewhat questionable due to having to refuel the invasion armada.

So it was vitally important that the invasion take place on the fifth, sixth, or seventh. The fifth was already gone, and there was little hope for the sixth or seventh because of the weather. Late on the evening of June 4, Commander Stagg, the Allied Chief Meteorologist, reported to Eisenhower and his staff that a sudden turn in the weather forecast had occurred for Tuesday, June 6. The storm would occur on June 5 as predicted, but by the evening of the fifth, it would start to dissipate. On June 6, the weather, while still not good, would be much better than had been earlier predicted.

Eisenhower pondered his decision as the heavy rain dashed against the roof and windows. The course of the war might depend on his decision. Surely, thousands of lives were at stake if he made the wrong decision. There was only one man in the entire Allied world who could make the decision— Eisenhower. He decided to go on the sixth. In the most difficult decision of the entire war, Eisenhower had put everything on his own shoulders. He confirmed his decision early the next morning as the rain continued to fall heavily and the wind was shaking his camp. With this, the armada cast off and the paratroops were in the air in the first hours of June 6. Eisenhower visited the men of the 101st Airborne just before they took off. He had put his faith in his meteorologists. If they were wrong, a disaster would ensue.

After the final conference, Eisenhower wrote this note (just in case):

Our landings in the Cherbourg-Havre area have failed to gain a satisfactory foothold and I have withdrawn the troops. My decision to attack at this time and place was based on the best information available. The troops, the air, and the Navy did all that bravery and devotion to duty could do. If any blame or fault attaches to the attempt, it is mine alone.

The words of a selfless and great leader of men. I wonder if Hitler ever contemplated writing such a note.

One big advantage of invading on June 6 was that it caught the Germans entirely by surprise. The weather in the first week of June was so bad that the Germans felt an invasion would be impossible; their weather predictions called for continued bad weather in the days ahead. Allied meteorologists had the advantage of having bases in Greenland and Iceland to make their forecasts, which the Germans didn't have. Rommel was so sure of bad weather that he left his post and returned to Germany for his wife's birthday. Thus, the man charged with defeating the Allied invasion was not even there when it came. Surely, fate is a mysterious thing.

Thus, on the morning of June 6, 1944, the Germans were caught off guard and relaxed. It is very possible that Eisenhower took that into account in deciding to go, a secondary consideration that flowed from his decision to launch the invasion on June 6.

Three divisions of paratroopers (two American and one British) were dropped in the early hours of June 6. Eisenhower had been advised by his air commander, Leigh-Mallory, not to use the paratroop divisions, as he thought casualties would be horrific. Eisenhower thought the paratroops were crucial and decided to use them. (Leigh-Mallory was really not a highly competent man to be in charge of the air in such a huge and vital operation. He had not done a great job during the Battle of Britain. How he got this important position is a mystery.) While scattered out much more than had been anticipated (particularly the Americans), the paratroops wreaked havoc and seized critical points. They also diverted key German troops that were assigned to hold the invasion on the beaches themselves. In a spectacular and heroic action, men of the British Sixth Airborne Division captured the Orne River bridge on the left flank of the invading forces. They suffered severe casualties but accomplished nearly all of the tasks assigned to them. Overall, casualties were moderate, considering the danger of the operation. Eisenhower had made the correct decision, as the paratroopers played an important part in the success of the invasion.

Wray

Units such as that of Lieutenant Waverly Wray of the 505th Paratroop Regiment created big problems for the German defense. Lieutenant Wray's unit had helped seize Ste. Mere Eglise, a key junction road in Normandy near the beaches. Meanwhile, 6,000 German troops were forming nearby to attack Ste. Mere Eglise and then drive to the beaches.

Colonel Vandervoort, commanding officer of the 2nd Battalion of the 505th, ordered Lieutenant Wray and his company to attack the German flank and forestall the German advance. Lieutenant Wray decided to make a personal reconnaisance through the hedgerows. He heard guttural voices on the other side of the hedgerow. Wray rose up, aiming his M-1 at eight German officers gathered around a radio and told them, "Hands Up - Hande Hock." They made a break for it. Wray shot them all down. Meanwhile, two Germans behind him began firing at Wray. Bullets cut through his jacket and one cut off half of his right ear. Wray turned and dropped the German soldiers with one shot each.

Wray returned to his company. He put a mortar crew on the German flank and directed fire into the lanes and hedgerows most densely packed with the enemy. He then sent his company into an attack down one of the lanes. The Germans broke and ran. Wray and his men had stopped and turned back the attack on Ste. Mere Eglise. Such men as Lieutenant Wray were making a big difference in the Allied success. Unfortunately, in September, Lieutenant Wray, leading an attack in Holland, was shot and killed. He was a truly heroic soldier and man.

Men like Lt. Waverly Wray and his American comrades proved to be a big and unpleasant surprise for Adolph Hitler. He had issued an invitation to

America to join the war and now they had arrived at his doorstep. They came in force, abundantly supplied with ships, planes, tanks, guns, men—and courage. What Hitler thought in December 1941 was impossible, now was unfolding before him. His huge and arrogant miscalculation was about to explode in his face.

The Beaches

The weather on the morning of June 6, 1944, was about as Commander Stagg had predicted. It was better than the fifth, but still on the rough side. The waves in the English Channel were very choppy, which caused much seasickness among the troops on the landing craft. Most of them were glad to hit land, even if it was dangerous. The assault on the beaches was preceded by strong naval gunfire and air attacks by medium and heavy bombers. Unfortunately, most of the bombs from the air landed too far inland and did not help destroy the beach defenses.

Five different beaches were chosen for the invasion. On the western end, the Americans were assigned Utah and Omaha Beaches. For the east, the British and Canadians were assigned Sword, Juno, and Gold. The troops' assignment was to get ashore and go as far inland as possible on the first day to establish a workable and defensible beachhead.

On four of the beaches, Utah, Sword, Juno and Gold, the Allies assaulted the beaches and while met with resistance were able to move inland. By mistake, on Utah beach the Navy had landed the troops 2,000 yards south of the assigned objective. This turned out to be lucky, as the German defense was weaker where they landed. General Theodore Roosevelt, Jr., was on the beach leading his men.

On Omaha Beach, however, the Americans ran into a hail of fire. Unknown to allied intelligence, a new German division, the 352nd, had just moved into the area. The German defense was fierce and determined. Most of the American tanks had been swamped by the heavy sea. It was touch and go for several hours. Casualties mounted. At one point, General Bradley seriously considered discontinuing the attack on Omaha. At last, with the aid of naval gunfire and the heroic actions of men on the shore, they were able to move off the beaches and gain some ground inland. Omaha Beach was saved. General Norman Cota was one of the leaders of the men moving up from the beaches. The battle-hardened First Division had come through again for the Americans.

One company—Company A of the 116th Infantry Regiment, was composed of over 200 men, of which many came from the small town of

Bedford, Virginia. This group was in the initial attack and suffered terrible casualties; only several dozen survived, most of them wounded. It had been an awful day for Bedford, Virginia—one that would never be forgotten. . . . Meanwhile, British and Canadian troops to the east had made the furthest advances by reaching the vicinity of Caen, seven miles inland.

Hitler
June 6, 1944

On one of the most critical days of the war, the two Germans in key positions were Hitler and Rommel. With Rommel not even at his post, what about Hitler? The German plan for the defense of the invasion was a patchwork of ideas; no single determined plan existed. Von Rundstedt at Paris, charged with the whole Western Command, wanted to hold back from the beaches a strong reserve headed by Panzer divisions. In this way, once the direction of the invasion was determined, he would hurl his strong reserve into action and throw the invasion into the sea. However, Rommel, the man in immediate command, wanted to beat the invasion on the beaches themselves, and not allow any kind of foothold to be gained. He felt that the reserve von Rundstedt advised would be unable to make its way in time to the beaches due to Allied air power. Rommel had much experience in Africa with Allied air superiority, and he knew how effective it could be.

Hitler was undecided. For one thing, he did not know where the Allied attack would be. Thus, as in most cases like this, a compromise was reached. The beach defense was strengthened, and there was a reserve of Panzer divisions. In Normandy, one Panzer division, the 21st, was near the beaches. There were two Panzer divisions some miles from the beaches in reserve. Hitler himself was the only man who could move these Panzer divisions. Thus, while the Allies advanced with a single, coherent plan and a straight line command structure under Eisenhower, the Germans had no single plan and had three people in charge—Hitler, von Rundstedt, and Rommel. A decided advantage for the Allies. Time also was a key factor. The command structure of the Allies made decisive decisions—there was no delay. On the German side, time was also indeed a crucial factor. The events of the 24 hours of June 6 could decide the war. Each minute was precious.

Since Hitler was the absolute decision maker, and in the final analysis the commander of Germany, let us examine his actions on the critical day of June 6, 1944. Where was Hitler on the morning of June 6? He was asleep.

Hitler, somewhat like Churchill, worked late into the night and early morning; thus, he was a late riser. In the early hours of June 6, reports began coming into his headquarters of paratroop and other landings in Normandy. These reports were somewhat confusing; Jodl and his staff were not sure whether Normandy was the main landing or only a diversion for the real main landing at Calais, as the Germans had predicted.

Early in the day, von Rundstedt, convinced that Normandy was the real thing, asked for release of the reserve Panzer divisions to strike the Allied force before it could get settled—to hurl it back into the sea. Since Hitler controlled these divisions, von Rundstedt made his request to Hitler's headquarters; Jodl received the urgent request. Still unsure if this was the main landing or only a diversion, Jodl hesitated. It was Hitler's decision to make, and Hitler was still asleep. Jodl decided to wait until Hitler woke up. This was a great decision—for the Allies!

At noon, Hitler arose. One half of the precious day of June 6 was already gone. By that time, the invasion had been on for some hours and was making progress. By his attitude, Hitler didn't seem to be too perturbed; in fact, he seemed to relish the thought that finally the waiting was over and he could smash the Allies. In truth, he had a low appreciation of the Allied fighting power, and rightfully he had a high estimation of his own German Army. One against the other, Hitler felt he could win. (It is a fact, however, that many soldiers in the German Army in Normandy were not German. There were many Russians, Poles, Ukrainians, and other East Europeans. These men were not of the same caliber as ethnic Germans—some surrendered at the first opportunity.)

The main question at noon when Hitler was finally awake was what to do with von Rundstedt's request for the reserve Panzer divisions. It would take some time to get two of the three to the front under the circumstances. With Allied control of the air, their arrival time was uncertain. In any event, the quicker they started, the better. The need was urgent.

Hitler also had to decide whether to move elements of the Fifteenth Army at Calais westward to reinforce the forces in Normandy. Hitler pondered. Just as Eisenhower had to make a decision, Hitler now had to make a decision. The clock was ticking; time was running against Hitler. He, like Jodl, was unsure if Normandy was the main invasion point. Hitler overestimated the number of divisions the Allies had in England; in his mind, the number of divisions committed to Normandy was relatively small. This meant there was still a large number of divisions left in England—perhaps this large army was meant for the real invasion at Calais. Hitler hesitated.

Meanwhile, more urgent calls were coming in from von Rundstedt, demanding the release of the Panzer reserves—three divisions—to strike the Allies. Finally, at 4:00 p.m., Hitler released them to von Rundstedt. Too late! Hitler also did not send any of the Fifteenth Army to Normandy, leaving it in place at Calais.

On one of the most critical days of his and Germany's life Hitler was asleep and when he awoke he hesitated. If the Allies couldn't be defeated on the first or second day, they were not going to be defeated—the invasion would be a success. Hitler should have thrown everything he had at the invading forces as quickly as possible, including the Panzer reserve divisions and the units of the Fifteenth Army at Calais.

In delaying von Rundstedt's request for the three Panzer divisions and doing nothing with the Fifteenth Army, Hitler had lost whatever chance he had of defeating the invasion. Time and tide wait for no man. One could say that fear of Hitler by his officers had something to do with it. They were afraid to wake him up. Under similar circumstances, Churchill's men would have awakened him instantly. Rommel, driving by car, arrived back at his headquarters near the coast at 9:00 p.m.—too late! It is almost incredible that the man in charge of the immediate defense and defeat of the invasion forces was not even there. There can be no excuse for this huge error. The Germans knew an invasion was imminent, yet they seemed to be casual in their attitude. You can believe the Allies took it all very seriously.

The only Panzer division in the area, the Twenty-First, had been mobilized and waited all day for orders. They were itching to go, and they were equipped with the formidable Tiger Tank. Finally, they were told late in the afternoon to attack and throw the invaders into the sea. By this time, the Allies were on shore and in-depth defenses were in place. Still, the German attack was damaging. At one time, an element of the division reached the coast. In the meanwhile, in protracted fighting with the more numerous English forces, the division was being worn down. By the end of the day, the division was a spent and depleted force. Consider this: if this attack had been made by three Panzer divisions instead of one, and earlier in the day, what would have been the result? Fortunately for the Allies, that attack wasn't made.

On the decisive day of the war, June 6, 1944, both Hitler and Rommel failed. They both knew the importance of defeating the invasion, but their lack of action at a critical time is astounding. Maybe it is very possible that they had been outsmarted and outfought by the Allies. In any case, they suffered a resounding and decisive defeat on June 6, 1944. Roosevelt and Churchill deserve a great deal of credit for bringing this about. They had assembled the forces, appointed the best man possible and then let them fight the battle. Simple, but effective.

While Churchill, Roosevelt, and the Joint Chiefs had planned well, it was useless without proper implementation. In Eisenhower, Montgomery, and Bradley they had highly capable men to carry out their mission—and they did in a brilliant manner. The end of the first day found that the Allied forces had landed successfully and had gained a significant beachhead. No doubt Eisenhower and his staff were elated; to some extent, the hardest part was over. Now their task was to send reinforcements and materiel into the beachhead and build it up also to expand it, which they immediately proceeded to do.

On the other side, the Germans had missed their best chance of defeating the invasion. Now, they could only hope to contain it. They were sending reinforcements to the battleground, but Allied air attacks and French resistance forces slowed them up considerably. Hitler was still not sure this was the main attack. He left in place the entire Fifteenth Army of nineteen divisions that was stationed in the Calais area. Indeed, throughout the war, Hitler consistently overestimated the size of the British army. He still thought there were a significant number of divisions in England.

Therefore, on the one hand, we have the Allies with their forces concentrated in one push, while the Germans, having about the same number of men, are still dispersed. Hitler continued his mistakes—mistakes that came back to haunt him. Time and just about everything else was starting to work against the Germans. The Allies had the initiative on all fronts—the Germans were like the boy sticking his hands in the dike.

At this time, consider the actions of Roosevelt and Churchill before and during D-Day. Roosevelt, of course, was thousands of miles from the scene. He was vitally interested but, in his best judgment, had appointed General Eisenhower to conduct the invasion. He stood by and let Eisenhower do the job he was assigned. Churchill was close to the scene and met Eisenhower early in June, mostly to give him moral encouragement. He made no suggestions other than that he wished to be on one of the naval assault ships involved in the operation. Of course, this was a school boy idea and was rejected by Eisenhower. In fact, the King told Churchill that if Churchill went, he would go also. That ended that. Churchill pouted, but that was the extent of his direct involvement in the invasion.

The Allied decisions came quickly through one command. By the time the various German commands, including Hitler, could decided what to do, it was too late. Time was a precious commodity on June 6, and the Germans squandered not only time, but resources as well, in every way possible. They couldn't have done a better job for the Allies if they had tried. With command of the sea and air, the Allies could pick the point of their concentrated attack. The Germans did not know where the attack would hit, so they had to spread and thin their forces out. While the number of overall troops on both sides was about equal, the Allies had more men and power at the point of attack.

One big advantage the Germans had was the quality of their tanks, especially the Tiger with an 88 millimeter gun and heavily armored. The American Sherman Tank had thin armor plating and only a 75 millimeter gun. In one-on-one firefights, the Sherman had no chance. It would take five or six Shermans to equal one Tiger Tank—very frightening for the crews of the Sherman. The Americans were mass-producing the Sherman and were afraid that changing to a different model would delay production. Towards the end of the war, they had the much improved 90 millimeter Pershing Tank in limited numbers on the battlefield. However, in June, 1944, the better German tanks were a serious problem.

Naval gunfire in particular was a decided Allied advantage. It is not known how many Germans were actually killed by naval gunfire, but from accounts of the Germans themselves, it was terrifying, demoralizing, and effective. General Bradley had coaxed the United States Navy into beefing up its ships involved in the invasion to four battleships, four cruisers, and twenty-six destroyers. On June 6, at Omaha Beach when the situation was critical, the first positive message from the Army there was, "Thank God for the U.S. Navy!"

Meanwhile, Stalin was delighted with the events. Finally, the second front had actually happened. Surely, at times, he wondered if it would actually happen at all. The Russian Army was already advancing in the east, and the Normandy invasion would undoubtedly draw German resources from east to west. The pressure on Germany now would be from three directions—east, west, and south—as well as from the air above. The German Army, while still a great fighting force, was being dispersed to be beaten piecemeal. The combined resources of the United States, Great Britain, and the Soviet Union were much greater than Germany's. It was what Churchill foresaw at the time of Pearl Harbor and Hitler did not.

In arranging three great powers against him, Hitler was asking the impossible from the German people and his war machine. Hitler believed his will could conquer anything. But Churchill, Roosevelt, and Stalin had strong wills also—and they had the vast resources to back it up. Again, Hitler's complete underestimation of the Soviets and the United States had put him in the predicament he was now in. There was a large gap in power between the

Allies and Germany. Hitler's will could not produce more men, tanks, and airplanes—the things that win wars—than the Allies. A strong will is something, but it is not everything, as Hitler was to find out. On the 6th of June, 1944, the Allies had outthought, outfought, and done just about everything right, while Hitler and the Germans had done just about everything wrong.

1944 Post-Invasion

With the Allies ashore at Normandy, they continued to build up and expand their beachhead. As days went by and no other invasion occurred, the Germans began moving reinforcements into Normandy. Of course, by this time, it was too late. Rommel's plan to assemble a Panzer force and counter-attack could not be carried out. The Allies mounted attacks on the Germans continuously; each time Rommel tried to counter-attack, his forces were diverted to try to contain the constant attacks. Rommel and von Ronstedt were in despair. Their advice to Hitler was to make peace before the German front cracked wide open. Hitler told them to mind their own business. Von Rundstedt was replaced. In the meanwhile, on June 17, Rommel's car was struck by a British fighter plane and he was seriously wounded. After hospitalization, he was sent home.

He later was forced to commit suicide when he was implicated in the plot to assassinate Hitler. There was no direct evidence that Rommel was involved in the plot, but he was sympathetic to the effort. Rommel felt that the war had been lost and some accommodation should be made before the complete defeat and total destruction of Germany.

With the force rapidly building up, the Allies intensified their attacks on the German Army. The British in the Caen sector on the eastern end of the line mounted several strong armored attacks that were repulsed. The Germans concentrated nearly all of the Panzer divisions in that area to prevent a break-out. At about this time, a number of people on Eisenhower's staff, including the English Air Marshal Tedder, became dissatisfied with Montgomery. They thought he had made many boasts but had not come through on them—that he was too slow and over-methodical. They even suggested that Eisenhower fire Montgomery. Of course, this was impossible, as Montgomery was a hero to the British public.

In the meanwhile, at the American end, General Omar Bradley planned to break out of the Normandy peninsula with an all-out attack, "Cobra." This was basically the plan before the invasion began: that Montgomery would attract the main German forces, while the Americans would then break through on the weaker end of the German front.

On July 25, the attack began with strong support from heavy bombers. Unfortunately, some bombs fell short of their target inflicting many casualties on their own men. General McNair was killed. Most of the bombs did hit the German lines with devastating effect. The American infantry and armor pushed through the pulverized German defense. By the fourth day, they had achieved a clean break-through and were rolling south. Improvised German defense efforts could not stop the strong advance.

General George S. Patton assumed command of the newly formed Third Army to spearhead the American advance. General Eisenhower had several times saved Patton from being sent home. Patton often acted and spoke impulsively, which got him into great difficulty. Eisenhower had saved Patton's career for just the moment that was now developing. Patton was a master of tank warfare and hard-hitting pursuit—just what the situation called for. Patton's grandfather had served under Stonewall Jackson in the Confederate Cavalry. Just as Stonewall Jackson did, Patton believed in this hard-hitting attack and then pursuit to keep the enemy on the run.

Breaking out of Normandy through Avranches and Mortain, Patton was jubilant. According to earlier plans, a large part of his forces would roll west and secure Brittany. However, together with Eisenhower and Bradley, Patton changed the plan to meet new circumstances. The new plan was to send minimal forces west to Brittany, but send his main army south and then east to join an attack south from Caen by Montgomery, thus trapping the German Army. The junction would be Falaise.

Von Kluge, the new German commander, was alert to the danger. His military instinct was to pull back and create a new defensive line. Except for one thing: Hitler took over the battle. Unlike Churchill and Roosevelt, Hitler tried to control everything, even tactical battles. The Allies loved this. With the Allied Army streaming through the gap at Mortain near the sea, Hitler believed a strong westward attack at that point and reaching the sea would seal off the gap, thus trapping the Allied forces that had already gone through the gap. He ordered that newly formed units and also units from the Fifteenth Army at Calais turn and make the attack.

Eisenhower and Bradley were aware of German forces building for an attack on Mortain. Allied intelligence had broken the German cipher machine codes. This effort was code-named "Ultra." The Germans had thought their "Enigma" code was unbreakable. Indeed the Allies knew as much about what the Germans were going to do as the Germans did. (The only failure of this

Allied system was the Ardennes attack in December.) Eisenhower and Bradley decided to continue Patton's attack south and east below the gap, as previously planned. They stationed several divisions east of Mortain to meet the attack. This was a daring decision.

Von Kluge was dubious of Hitler's plan. Hitler was actually sending more men into the trap that was already developing to the south and east. If Hitler's attack failed, then all of these men could be lost. The whole German defensive front in France would be torn asunder; France would be lost. The Allied advance would go as far to the east as their supplies would take them—at least to the frontier of Germany itself.

Hitler's attack did fail. The Americans at Mortain, with the help of air power, beat off the repeated German attacks. The 30th Division under General Leland Hobbs particularly distinguished itself. Now, with Montgomery's forces finally on the move, heading south, and Patton's army turning east, the Germans were in a desperate situation. Von Kluge pleaded with Hitler to stop the attack at Mortain and pull all forces in that area back before they were surrounded. Hitler, at last, faced reality and ordered the retreat. The Germans fleeing southeast through the small gap at Falaise were repeatedly attacked by the Allied air force, causing large casualties.

The gap was not fully closed by the Allies at Falaise, which would have trapped most of the remaining German Army. Various reasons are given for this. Patton had reached his assigned position on time, but Montgomery did not; Montgomery was too slow. Another possible explanation was that General Bradley felt his forces were not strong enough to contain the head-long rush of the German retreat and would be overrun. In any event, a sizable number of Germans made it through the Falaise gap and escaped capture. Many of them did not. The German Army in Northern France had been virtually destroyed. There had been several hundred thousand casualties since June 6. Von Kluge committed suicide. Hitler at this time was greatly concerned that von Kluge was going to surrender; thus, when he heard of von Kluge's suicide, I'm sure he was greatly relieved. So much for von Kluge.

Again, Hitler's interference with the battle had played into the hands of the Allied commanders. On paper, Hitler's move against Mortain looked good, but in action it was a disaster. Again, Hitler's underestimation of the Allies was a factor. He was learning very slowly that the American Army could fight, and fight well. Hitler was improving his knowledge far too late, if at all. Another thing: Hitler's forces were not as strong as they had been in the past. He was trying to do too much with too little. Germany was one country trying to fight most of the world.

With the remainder of the German Army in Northern France in disarray, the Allies raced forward. Even Montgomery joined in the fast pursuit. The Germans didn't have time to set up any defensive lines because the Allied Army was moving so fast. Also, there were not enough German troops available to set up a defensive line, similar to their campaign against the French in 1940, except the other way.

The main problem with the Allied advance was that of supply, particularly gasoline for their armored formations. Many of their supplies were still coming across the beaches. Hitler ordered his troops in the port cities to hold them at all cost, which they did for a long period. It was just a question of time before the Allied advance would have to stop because of the supply problem. One of the main objectives now was the capture of Antwerp, which when usable as a port would be invaluable.

Eisenhower was not actually too enthusiastic about taking Paris. He knew that with supply as his main problem, this effort would be a drain. However, politically it was impossible not to take Paris; a revolt by the citizens there had already erupted. Eisenhower had promised General de Gaulle that French troops would be used to liberate Paris, so he sent the French Second Armored Division there. Hitler had order Paris to be used as a battleground and then burned. The German commander, Choltitz, refused to do this and surrendered his forces. Paris remained Paris, no thanks to Hitler. General Charles de Gaulle entered Paris to the acclaim of its citizens. The best of France had come back to France in triumph. The hated Swastika was torn down from the Eiffel Tower.

July 20, 1944

A number of German officers and some civilians had become disaffected with Hitler. They believed that Germany was losing the war— that Hitler would never surrender and Germany would be utterly destroyed. They preferred to end the war similarly to the way the First War ended. At the time of the Armistice on November 11, 1918, there were no enemy troops on German soil. German cities and industry were still in good order. Germany had surrendered then because it knew it was going to lose. The state, with the exception of the Kaiser, had been preserved.

The group that now wanted to end the war was not only upset with the war's progress, but they were aghast at Hitler's brutality. They felt Hitler was bringing shame to Germany. The only way to stop it, they concluded, was to assassinate Hitler. Their plan was a good one: Colonel von Stauffenberg, a heroic officer who had been wounded in North Africa, was now on Hitler's staff. On July 20 in his official duties, he attended a meeting of Hitler and his staff.

Colonel von Stauffenberg was carrying a briefcase with a time bomb in it. Maneuvering himself next to Hitler, he placed the briefcase within a few feet of Hitler and then left. Unfortunately, another officer who stood near Hitler shifted his stance, and his foot touched the briefcase. Since the briefcase was in his way, with his foot he pushed the briefcase further away from Hitler. The bomb went off as scheduled, but it was bad luck for the conspirators. Moving the bomb lessened its effect; the heavy top of the desk absorbed much of the blast. The building they were in was lightly constructed, especially the roof, which dissipated some of the blast. In any event, the plan failed to kill Hitler, who was slightly wounded in the arm and whose ears were affected. Naturally, he was shaken up. The conspirators assumed that Hitler had been killed and proceeded to finish their plan.

At this time, with Hitler in a state of shock, Goebbels in Berlin took over. His most important act was to reassure the outside world that Hitler was alive and unhurt. Thus, anyone who had been thinking of joining the conspirators would have second thoughts. Their fear of Hitler was great, and naturally so; if Hitler was alive, retribution would be quick and brutal. Goebbels also called Major Remer, the garrison commander in Berlin. This was an important call, as the conspirators were trying to get Major Remer and his troops to join them, thus taking over Berlin. Goebbels convinced Major Remer that Hitler was still alive; he even put Hitler on the phone to talk to Remer. The major prudently reaffirmed his allegiance to Hitler. This was the key moment in the whole situation.

Without Major Remer's cooperation, the conspiracy collapsed. It goes without saying that Hitler was infuriated by what he called the treachery of the conspirators. He ordered the immediate arrest of anyone even remotely connected with the plot. Many people arrested had no connection at all. All were executed, some by slow and tortuous methods. The conspirators had failed, but now they are considered heroes. This event showed that there were some Germans who were appalled at Hitler and his methods and risked their lives to stop him. If they had succeeded, many thousands of lives on both sides would have been spared. It is to their everlasting credit that they made the effort and paid for it with their own lives in the attempt.

The Invasion of Southern France

The original plan for the invasion of France called for simultaneous landings at Normandy in Northern France and also a landing in southern France near Toulon. However, the shortage of landing craft meant that the landing in Southern France, named "Dragoon," had to be postponed until August.

The troops would be American and French mostly withdrawn from the Italian Front, which was in Churchill's sphere of operations and under British command. After the capture of Rome on June 5, Churchill again began to have hopes of a breakthrough in Southern Europe. Thus, to have a large number of troops taken away to invade Southern France just when things were moving in Italy was appalling to Churchill. He had earlier agreed to the operation in Southern France, but now, with the advance picking up in Italy, he changed his mind. He believed it better to keep rolling northward in Italy and then into the Balkans, where there were strong partisan forces already operating. Of course, part of Churchill's thinking was that an Allied advance into the Balkans would forestall Stalin's take-over of the whole area. Once Stalin got in, he was in for good.

However, the Americans—Roosevelt, Marshall, and Eisenhower—insisted that Dragoon be carried out. They were skeptical of Churchill's Balkan adventure and viewed it as Churchill going off on a tangent again, another dispersal of forces, as Roosevelt would say. The Americans insisted they needed the ports of Southern France, particularly Marseilles, to supply the Western Front. It would also get more American and French troops into the main theater of operations. Naturally, the French forces would rather be fighting for their homeland than fighting in Italy.

The Americans were somewhat naive about political matters in Europe, particularly in southeast Europe. Churchill was certainly not. He was something of an expert, especially since his experience there in the First War. The Americans believed the front in France facing Germany was the battlefront where Germany would be beaten—the decisive front—and everything possible should be done to make the Allied attack in that area as strong as possible. Everything else was incidental. It finally came down to an argument between Eisenhower and Churchill. As Eisenhower has said, it was the one big argument he had with Churchill in the war. Churchill was known for keeping at it, once he started on something he believed in, trying to wear down the opposition with his oratory and persistence.

On this matter, it has to be said that both Churchill and the Americans were right. The Americans were right in that the Western Front was the decisive front and all the strength possible should be exerted there—and they needed Marseilles and the other ports in Southern France for supply purposes, as they were essential. Churchill was right in trying to get into Southeastern Europe before the Russians swept it up. It is questionable whether the Allied Army in Italy, even as strong as Churchill wanted, could have broken through the strong German defense line in Italy. Churchill's plan was a hope, while the Americans wanted a certainty in France.

As nearly all of the forces in Southern France were American and French, and not British, the Americans could do whatever they wanted to do. And they decided to proceed with Dragoon over Churchill's vigorous objections. One meeting between Eisenhower and Churchill lasted six hours over this subject. At this time, Churchill wanted the forces intended for Southern France to land instead in Brittany. Why, no one seems to know. Eisenhower would not budge and was backed up by Roosevelt and Marshall. Churchill was gradually losing his influence as the American forces got stronger and stronger.

At dawn on August 15, 1944, American and French troops landed on the French Riviera, supported by paratroops and naval gunfire from the American battleships. The landings were relatively unopposed, as the German presence was thin in this area. The Allies made rapid progress and captured Marseilles by the end of August. Churchill watched the landings from a British destroyer and telegraphed Eisenhower that he had admired the perfect precision and organization of the landing. In a letter to Marshall, Eisenhower commented on the message he had received from Churchill, saying, "He seemed to be most enthusiastic about Dragoon. When I think about all the mental anguish I went through to preserve the operation, I don't know whether to laugh or cry."

French and American troops, aided by the French Resistance, raced north and joined the right flank of Patton's army. This made a continuous Allied front facing east from Switzerland to the North Sea along the German frontier.

The Resistance Movement

In the countries of occupied Europe, the inhabitants had been stunned by the quick victory of the Germans. It took a while to recover their equilibrium, but slowly, resistance to the occupiers began. In particular, in occupied Russia, resistance became stronger and more effective with each passing day. Many Soviet soldiers had been bypassed in the initial Nazi onslaught. They took to the woods and joined with the local partisans. German retaliation was ruthless but could not stop the guerrilla movement. As their assault went further east into Russia, the partisan problem became even greater for the Germans. They had to divert many soldiers from the front line in order to keep their supply line open and suppress the resistance activities. It became a serious factor in the whole war. Of course, Stalin was doing everything he could to organize and supply the partisans. Nikita Kruschev was also involved in these efforts.

On May 27, in Czechoslovakia, the SS leader Reinhard Heydrich was ambushed and gravely wounded by Czech patriots. Several days later, he died. The following day at the Czech village of Lidice, all one hundred ninety-nine men in the village were rounded up and shot. The women and children of Lidice were sent to concentration camps, where they were all killed.

In the German Army itself, some officers were speaking out against the violence. A young officer, Michail Kitzelmann, who had won the Iron Cross for bravery, protested the atrocities being committed on the Eastern Front. Arrested and tried by court martial, Kitzelmann was shot by a firing squad at Orel on June 11.

In Greece, German forces were being increasingly harassed by Greek guerrillas. In retaliation, on May 24, three hundred twenty-five people, the entire population of the village of Pogonion, were shot. In France, as the day of invasion by England approached, increasing resistance activity was affecting the Germans. Power, telephone, and rail lines were being disrupted. The French were making it difficult for the Germans to respond to the threatened Allied invasion. More German troops were diverted from the coastal defense and reserve to cope with resistance activity.

In fact, all across occupied Europe, resistance forces were becoming stronger and bolder. Norway, France, Holland, Denmark, Poland, Italy, Greece, Yugoslavia, and Russia. Tens of thousands of German troops were tied down in trying to cope with the partisans. In the Balkans alone, twenty German divisions were battling the guerrilla forces. At various times during the war, between twelve and eighteen German divisions were tied down in Norway on occupation duties. The more territory the Germans occupied, the worse it got for them. They had managed to spread themselves too thin.

German retaliation for resistance action was swift and ruthless. In Paris, a twenty-two year old Communist, Pierre Georges, shot and killed a German officer. In reprisal, one hundred fifty people were rounded up and shot. In many areas of Northern France, escape routes for downed American and British air crews were in operation. Hundreds of allied airmen made it back to England. However, the cost was high to the partisans who helped them. At times, traitors infiltrated the groups and betrayed the brave men and women who were helping the airmen. Swift Nazi executions were the result. However, new routes would be set up, and the operation continued. This made Hitler furious; he had shot these men down once, and now he would have to do it all over again. One of the Frenchmen involved in dangerous operations was Francois Mitterand, who later became President of France. He himself had escaped from a prisoner of war camp and now was aiding escaped French prisoners of war and laborers.

After the invasion of Normandy, the French resistance movement was doing all it could to assist the Allies. In return, the Germans became even more barbarous, if that is possible. On June 10, 1944, in reprisal for a partisan attack on a military formation moving towards the Normandy beachhead, SS troops murdered six hundred forty-two villagers, including one hundred ninety school children. This was the village of Oradour sur Glane. Only two villagers managed to escape.

The Germans were having to fight not only on the Eastern Front, the Western Front, and Italy, but also in the occupied areas all over Europe. On June 6, the Second SS Panzer Division had been ordered to move from Toulouse in Southern France to reinforce Normandy. Repeatedly delayed by sabotage, the division didn't reach Normandy until June 18. These types of resistance actions were affecting German movements at every turn. They were helped greatly by British special teams that had parachuted into France to assist the resistance fighters. Many of these British were captured, tortured, and executed. Some of them were women who had volunteered. One of the airmen rescued was the American Chuck Yaeger, the man who later as a test pilot first broke the sound barrier.

In Holland, resistance fighters were increasing their activities. On April 11, 1944, in a precision raid by the RAF, a five story building in the Hague was bombed, destroying all of the Gestapo index card records of those active in the resistance movement. Unfortunately, 61 Dutchmen were killed in this raid. It had been impossible to warn them without endangering the success of the plan. Also in Holland, a senior SS officer, General Rauter, was killed by Dutch patriots. In reprisal, 263 Dutchmen were shot. A member of the German firing squad, Helmuth Seijffards, refused to take part and was arrested and later shot.

There were many episodes of heroic bravery under severe difficulties all over Europe involving the resistance movement. Many innocent people not involved in the resistance were killed in reprisal by the Germans. The Second World War was a total war and ended with a crushing German defeat and the destruction of much of Germany. Surely, they had brought it on themselves.

Defense Stiffening

As the Allied forces neared Germany, two things happened. One, their supplies were running out, and secondly, German resistance began to stiffen.

In addition, at this time, the V-1 and V-2 rockets began to be used against England in large numbers. These were a formidable terror weapon and inflicted many casualties. They had no actual effect on the battle itself; overall, it was a vengeance weapon. They had come too late. The huge effort that Hitler and the Germans had put into the rocket project was essentially wasted and had no effect on the outcome of the war.

Market Garden

The Allies in the West at this time in September, 1944, thought the war was almost over, that the Germans were in a state of virtual collapse. However, their supply problem prevented them from pushing forward on all fronts. Each general was clamoring for materiel, particularly oil, to keep the offensive going. General Montgomery advised Eisenhower to give him priority on supplies for his new plan to finish the Germans off. Instead of pushing east, Montgomery would go north into Holland, cross the Rhine at Arnhem, and push into Germany. This was a daring, and perhaps in retrospect, a foolhardy plan. However, Eisenhower agreed to it.

Eisenhower also thought the Germans were in a desperate condition. Since in the past he had had trouble getting Montgomery to move at all, he was glad to see him come up with a plan putting Montgomery in an offensive frame of mind. Moreover, German V-2 rockets were hitting London, launched from Holland.

Operation "Market Garden" was a plan whereby everything had to go just right for it to succeed. It involved crossing rivers at Nijmegen, Eindhoven, and at Arnhem on the Rhine. These crossings were to be carried out by the paratroop divisions, the American Eighty-Second and One Hundred First, at Nijmegen and Eindhoven and the British First Airborne at Arnhem. Arnhem was about sixty miles north of the Allied ground kick-off point. The route to Arnhem was through marshy woodlands, and a single road was the only means of moving Montgomery's armor and infantry north.

If any one of the operations failed, the whole operation failed. Probably the biggest problem was the single road north; if the Germans could concentrate enough forces to defend this single road north, the operation would fail. The paratroops were only lightly armed and could not hold out long against an armored attack. The whole plan was contingent on the thought that the Germans were collapsing.

The operation started off well, with one exception: Arnhem. The American paratroopers landed at Nijmegen and Endhoven and with heroic skill and courage seized both bridges. In addition, the British XXX Corps under General Brian Horrocks made good progress on the ground the first day. The Eighty-Second Division at Nijmegen under General James Gavin was to take the bridges across the Waal River at Nijmegen. This was a very important mission if the ground attack was to get through to Arnhem quickly. On September 19, the Eighty-Second had taken much of Nijmegen, but the approaches to the bridges were heavily defended.

Gavin and Horrocks decided that Horrocks would provide tank support for an attack on the bridges while Gavin crossed the river downstream in assault boats. Gavin would also hit the southern ends of the bridges. This attacking force would be under Colonel Ben Vandervoort. The crossing downstream by Major Julian Cook's Third Battalion would aim for the northern end of the bridges and was the most dangerous. The boats only 26 of them, were late, arriving at 1500 hours. They were of inferior quality, small, and mostly canvas. The Waal River at this point was 400 meters wide with a swift current. To make the attack with these few flimsy craft was almost suicidal. There were not enough paddles, so that many of the men would have to use their rifle butts as paddles.

Major Cook decided to make the attempt, realizing the importance of the mission. The boats began to cross and were met with a hail of fire. Many were hit, and there were many casualties; only eleven of the 26 boats made it to the other side. Cook led the attack with the remainder of his men, still under heavy fire. They took the top highway embankment and drove the Germans out. Meanwhile, reinforcements, the rest of his battalion, were crossing the river. Cook led the first wave in an assault on the bridges. His men came on fast. At the same time, Colonel Vandervoort's battalion was attacking the southern end and had started onto the bridges. Of course, the Germans had placed explosives and wired the bridges to blow them up, but Major Cook's men had cut all the wires. The Germans pushed the plungers, and nothing happened—the bridges were still there, intact.

Vandervoort, along with British tanks, crossed the bridges and joined Cook's forces on the northern side. The way was open for the ground assault to push on to Arnhem, eleven miles away. Lieutenant General Miles Dempsey, commander of the British Second Army, came up to shake Gavin's hand. "I am proud to meet the commander of the greatest division in the world today," he said.

The attack by the Eighty-Second on Nijmegen and taking the bridges intact is considered one of the greatest feats of the war. The paratroops were enraged that the British did not immediately push on to Arnhem and rescue the

First Airborne. The British made it half-way the next day but were stopped by strong resistance, including air power. It is hard to understand getting so close to Arnhem and not pushing through. While this was going on, the First Airborne had been having a very difficult time. The plan for this division was actually flawed from the beginning; the drop was not near Arnhem, but rather some miles to the west. While the drop went well, the Germans in that area reacted quickly. The division tried to move east to Arnhem but met resistance. Colonel Frost's battalion did get through and captured the north end of the bridge at the Rhine.

Several other adverse factors came into play against the Allied drive. General Model, now commander of the western front, had his headquarters in this area, and he took charge of and mobilized the defense immediately. Also, unknown to the Allies, two German Panzer divisions, survivors of Normandy, were refitting in the area. These forces were used by Model also immediately. The German reaction and its strength was a great surprise to the Allies. All now depended on whether the First Airborne at and near Arnhem could hold on until the ground troops reached them. The slowness of the XXX Corps in moving north has never been adequately explained. The American paratroops had, to some extent, paved the way north for the ground troops.

Again, we go back to the fact that there was only one road going north. With the marshy ground on either side, it was difficult to impossible for a long, mobile column to move forward except by the road. There was German resistance, not only at the front of the British column, but also by groups of Germans at scattered points east and west of the road. It was only necessary to knock out a few tanks to stop the whole column. Still, as mentioned, with their comrades at Arnhem in desperate straits and the fate of the whole attack depending on their swift advance, it seems that somehow they should have made faster progress. Perhaps if one had been there at the time, there would be a better understanding of the situation. With the Allied column mired only a few miles away, General Horrocks ordered the remnants of the First Airborne to break out southward, which they did. Approximately twenty-five hundred survivors made it back to the British lines. American paratroops aided in this endeavor. Market Garden had failed. The war would continue.

Montgomery did not seem to take any active part in the battle. He placed his confidence, it seems, in the commander on the spot. It would be interesting to speculate that if General George Patton had been directing the attack, it would probably have been successful. This is speculation only. Possibly the main explanation for the failure is that it was a daring mission based on the assumption that German resistance would be weak. It was much stronger than anticipated, so much so that it delayed and thwarted the operation. Bad luck also played a part.

During this period, by a Herculean effort, Hitler and his commanders had been able to build a coherent front on the western border of Germany behind the West Wall. This was a tremendous achievement under the circumstances. With Market Garden a failure and the supply situation still an important factor, Eisenhower directed Montgomery to open up Antwerp as a major port. Antwerp had been seized in early September in the Allied rush forward, but what had not been considered was that as Antwerp was an inland port, the seizure of the approaches was also necessary—unless they were taken, Antwerp was useless as a port.

The Germans understood this and had forces on the islands approaching Antwerp, particularly Walcheren Island. With these islands in German hands, Antwerp could not be used as an Allied port. Eisenhower had realized this earlier but had given priority to Market Garden. Now, with that behind him, he turned his attention back to opening Antwerp. The Canadian Army was assigned the task, a messy and back-water type operation, but very necessary. Attacks other than local were suspended until Antwerp could be opened. This gave the Germans a breathing spell and insured that the war would not end in 1944.

The Russian Front 1944

Russian pressure on the Germans continued in 1944. The Russians greatly outnumbered the German forces. While Hitler detested the idea of retreat, there was no other option, or his forces would be overrun. One advantage of retreat was that it shortened his defensive line. In his initial advance on Russia, the front line was relatively short. As he advanced further and further into Russia, however, the geography and thus the front became wider. That is one reason for the German defeat. As he retreated, it was the reverse. The front became less extended, still long but nowhere near as long as was at the time of Stalingrad.

Still, the Germans were now fighting on four fronts: the Russian, where they still had a large force; the Western, Italy, and the air war. The air war was pounding German cities to pieces, one by one. It is remarkable that the Germans were able to maintain a relatively high level of production under the weight of continued Allied bombing. Indeed, 1944 was their year of highest production for the entire war. Albert Speer, head of war production, was performing a miracle. Still, a large part of the Luftwaffe was needed to protect the skies above Germany, planes that were desperately needed on other fronts. Also, several hundred thousand military personnel were needed to man the anti-aircraft batteries and other defenses. Transportation and oil were critical targets; and more and more, the Allied air forces made them a priority. Oil, in particular, was vital to the German war effort; without a sufficient amount of oil, the war was over.

The Russian offensive had now crossed into Poland—the war was getting closer to home for the Germans. With the approach of the Russians, the citizens of Warsaw staged an armed revolt; of course, they were lightly armed. They fought heroically and held out for the approaching Russians to save them. However, when the Russian Army got near Warsaw it stopped. The Poles were desperate. Even Roosevelt and Churchill pleaded for Stalin to advance and save the Poles before it was too late. No reply from Stalin; no action by Stalin. The Poles in Warsaw were crushed by the Germans.

Why didn't the Russians intervene? The prevailing opinion was that Stalin considered the people in revolt, and they were not his kind of people. Rather, they were Polish patriots whose leanings would probably be with the West. This was one way of getting rid of them; let the Germans do it. When the Russian Army moved in, it would be easier to establish the Polish Communists in a government under the control of Stalin. Diabolical.

After taking Warsaw, the Russians continue to advance westward, nearing the border of Germany itself. All the mistakes Hitler had made were now at his doorstep. The Russians had come a long way from their disastrous defeats in 1941 and early 1942. Under Stalin, the Red Army had waged a terrific and now successful struggle against the Nazis under Adolph Hitler, who had aided them with his huge mistakes at Moscow and Stalingrad.

Surprise Attack - The Ardennes

In September, 1944, when things seemed to be falling apart for the Germans on the Western Front, Hitler was making plans for the future. It is rather uncanny that he was planning a great attack at the same time the Germans were in terrible condition. Hitler was undoubtedly correct in his decision to attack on the Western Front. The time would be December. In particularly, his decision to attack from the Ardennes was a brilliant tactical decision. At this point in the war, Germany was definitely losing and retreating on all fronts; at this rate, it was just a matter of time until it was defeated. Actually, at this time, no matter what he did, Hitler was going to lose the war.

However, in his plan, Hitler had adopted the potential possibility of dealing to the Allies on the Western Front a serious setback. Hitler's planning was outstanding: he was going to hit the Allies in their weakest spot. The only problem with his plan was that he did not have the overwhelming strength to make it successful. Several years earlier, it may have been possible, but not now. Also he was counting on the slow reaction of the Allied leadership, such as the French in 1940. However, in December, 1944, he was not fighting the French or their leadership. He was up against a very competent group of Allied leaders—Eisenhower, Montgomery, Bradley, Patton, and their very capable subordinates. Also, he was fighting a very tough and battle hardened American Army. Actually, the forces Hitler could accumulate for the attack were not as strong as he had had in the past. Still, it was a considerable force.

Hitler believed that once the Allies reached the German border, they would have to stop and regroup due to lack of supplies. During this period, he planned to build up a new offensive army—in fact, two armies, the Fifth and the Sixth Panzer Armies. He would attack from the Ardennes, the same place he had already had success in 1940. His plan was as follows: In December, the weather would be bad, thus reducing or negating the large advantage of the Allied air force. Considering the Allies thought that Germany was on its last leg, a large offensive at this time would catch them utterly by surprise. Such surprise can create chaos, as in 1940 with the French. Hitler knew that the Allies had only four or five divisions covering an 85 mile front. He would rapidly push through, moving west and then northeast. His objective: Antwerp.

If he could achieve that objective, he would cut off the British Army and part of the American Army north of the breakthrough. The two wings of the Allied armies separated, he would destroy the northern forces just as in the 1940 campaign. He would win victory in the West; this was his last chance, and he was determined to give it all he had. Literally, his life depended on it. With the surprise element and the swiftness of his attack, he was counting on paralyzing the Allied command. By the time the Allied command reacted, it would be too late.

Hitler's generals wanted to have more limited objectives in the attack, as they felt their forces were not strong enough to take Antwerp. Hitler, as usual, overruled them—it was all or nothing. Hitler was taking a huge risk, in that he was using his last reserves. If the attack failed, he would have none left to stop both the Western and the Eastern Fronts.

Earlier, Eisenhower and Bradley had considered the Ardennes and decided to send only limited forces there. One reason was that the terrain was so bad for a German attack. Perhaps they should have considered that in 1940 the Germans attacked France from the Ardennes. Possibly, they did consider it, but felt the circumstances were different now. With the forces at their disposal, they felt they would be more effective on the offense to the north and south of the Ardennes, leaving the Ardennes a rather isolated area. They felt there was little chance of a German assault in this area, but if miraculously the Germans did such a thing, the allies could contain them by bringing in forces from the north and the south. They still considered a large assault from this area very unlikely. They thought the Germans incapable of mounting a serious attack anywhere.

The Allied intelligence did not even consider a major attack from the Ardennes—the Germans were too weak. It would be impossible for the Germans to accumulate enough forces to mount a large attack. Needless to say, Allied intelligence was stunned and incredulous when the German advance began.

On December 16, 1944, the Germans attacked and achieved complete surprise. The Allied air force was not able to help due to miserable weather conditions. Hitler's gamble had gotten off under favorable conditions for the Germans. Only one thing went wrong. The forces of the five American divisions thinly scattered across the front fought back stubbornly. Due to the hilly, wooded nature of the country and the presence of few roads, small groups of defenders could create a strong defense. Instead of running over these relatively few defenders, the Germans found themselves caught up in firefights all along the front. They had thought they would easily run over the thin American line— Hitler had again underestimated the Americans. The first several days were critical to the Germans; they wanted to reach the Meuse River as fast as possible and turn north towards Antwerp. The faster they advanced, the less time the Allies would have to react.

The small number of American troops in the Ardennes was upsetting the entire German timetable. For example, the 110th Infantry Regiment under Colonel Hurley Fuller was attacked by the entire Forty-Seventh Panzer Korps. The 110th put up a brilliant fight before being overrun by vastly more numerous German forces. (Colonel Fuller was captured. Later, he would lead American prisoners of war in their forced marches in the east part of Germany under terrible circumstances. He witnessed the brutality of the advancing Red Army taking vengeance on German civilians.)

Meanwhile, in the late afternoon of December 16, Eisenhower in Versailles received news of the German assault; Bradley happened to be there with him. Bradley thought it was just a local attack and was not too concerned. As the day went on, more German units were noted in the attack, a sizable number of units. Eisenhower concluded it was not a local attack, but rather a large one, and that it had to be stopped.

He immediately ordered Bradley to send the Seventh Armored Division from the north to help out and to call Patton and have the Tenth Armored Division to head north to the southern Ardennes. Patton objected, and was told, "Ike is running this damn war; do what you are told," which Patton did. At this time, the Allies had nearly all of their forces in the front lines. There were no actual reserves, not unlike the French in 1940. There were two airborne divisions, the 82nd and the 101st, that were refitting from the Holland campaign. On December 17, the two divisions were ordered to the Ardennes, particularly the 101st under General McAuliffe to Bastogne, a key road hub in the southern Ardennes. Contrary to Hitler's belief, the Allied commander (Eisenhower) had reacted quickly and vigorously to stop the German advance. It was just in time.

The Seventh Armored arrived at St. Vith in the North Ardennes just ahead of German forces coming in. St. Vith was an important junction, and the Germans had to have it. A delay here would be critical to their plan. St. Vith and Bastogne were key points the Germans had to have quickly to sustain their offensive momentum.

General Haislip and General Clark of the Seventh set up their defense along with remnants of the divisions that had been defending the Ardennes, one of them a strong combat armored unit of the Ninth Division. They formed a horseshoe defense to protect it from all sides except the western side. The Germans attacked in piecemeal fashion but could not break through. Some German units bypassed St. Vith to the north and south. The defense of St. Vith was causing the Germans a great deal of trouble.

However, two regiments of the American 106th Division had been cut off on the Schnee Eifel to the east of St. Vith. The commander of the 106th, General Alan Jones, headquartered in St. Vith, had thought the Seventh Armored was going to attack and rescue the two regiments of seven thousand men and did not pull them back.. However, the Seventh had its hands full defending St. Vith. Thus, the men of these two regiments were captured by the Germans. It was the biggest American setback in the Battle of the Bulge. It was not really General Jones's fault—just the brutal fortunes of war. Meanwhile, on December 23, the pressure on the Seventh Armored was too much to endure; they were almost surrounded. They were ordered to retreat through the small gap that remained, which they were able to do. They had done a great job.

During this period, Eisenhower had a meeting with Bradley and Patton on the 19th concerning an American attack from the south by the Third Army toward Bastogne, which would hit the German flank. General Patton promised to attack on December 23 with at least three divisions. This would be a remarkable achievement and showed the distinguished ability of General Patton.

When Eisenhower returned to his headquarters that night, his staff had come up with an idea. Since the front was virtually broken in two, Bradley's First and Ninth Armies were north of the breakthrough with the Third Army south of the bulge. It would be difficult for Bradley to communicate with, much less command, these separate armies. The staff's idea was to turn all forces north of the bulge over to the command of General Montgomery, and those left south of the bulge would remain under Bradley's command. The staff thought this would simplify and clarify the command situation.

Also, the British XXX Corps of five divisions was not in the front line in the north. If the Germans actually crossed the Meuse and headed for Antwerp, this unit was in the ideal place to stop them. As the XXX Corps was under Montgomery's command, this would fit in nicely with the new command set-up. General Bedell Smith, Eisenhower's assistant, was incensed when the staff brought him the plan. However, he calmed down and thought it was his duty to present it to Eisenhower. Eisenhower studied the map. He knew if he followed his staff's recommendation, it would cause controversy, particularly with the Americans; the American generals did not like Montgomery. But he decided to do what he thought was right and agreed with the staff's recommendation.

Montgomery immediately assumed command of all the forces in the north, which actually was the bulk of the Allied Army. Bradley retained control of those units south of the bulge, mainly the Third Army. Bradley didn't like it, but could not deny the logic of the move. (Later, when Montgomery claimed credit for his role in stopping the attack, it made Bradley furious, and rightly so.)

Thus, Hitler again was wrong about the quick reaction to events by the Allied high command. Instead of panicking, the Allies and Eisenhower were reacting in a cool, professional manner to the surprise attack. It was not going to be 1940 all over again for Hitler. It was Montgomery who ordered the Seventh Armored at St. Vith to retreat and, according to them, saved their lives. Some people may make adverse remarks about Montgomery, but not the men of the Seventh Armored. They were thoroughly grateful to him.

The German Sixth Army in the north, under General Sepp Dietrich, was making little progress because of the tough defense, particularly at St. Vith and Monschau. Dietrich could not turn the corner on the American defense and thus head to Meuse and Antwerp. In short, his drive had stalled. American reinforcements from the north were moving south to blunt and then stop the German drive by Dietrich.

However, to his south, Manteuffel's Fifth Army was making some progress. Hitler decided to reinforce Manteuffel's army. Overall, American resistance continued strong along the whole front. As mentioned, the nature of the Ardennes with heavily wooded terrain, few roads and bridges made it good defensive territory, and the Americans were fiercely fighting the attacking Germans. Some American troops that were captured were mowed down by the Germans at Malmedy. The news of this spread along the American front and made them fight even harder.

Units such as Lieutenant Lyle Bouck's platoon of eighteen men were typical. Lieutenant Bouck's small unit was stationed at Lanzerath, a small village in the center of the German attack. His platoon was attacked on the morning of December 16. Wave after wave of German infantrymen were mowed down by Bouck and his men—four hundred Germans were cut down and lay in heaps along the ground. However, Bouck's unit was running out of ammunition. Finally, in another large attack, Bouck's unit was overrun, and Bouck himself was wounded and captured. This small unit had played a significant part in blunting and delaying the enemy advance. The same thing was occurring at many other places along the line.

A rather unusual group of heroes in the Ardennes battle were American engineer units. Normally not designed as front line fighting units, the engineers played a significant part in delaying and stopping the German advance. Colonel Joachim Peiper, commander of the elite First SS Panzer Regiment, led the German attack. His spearhead unit was scheduled to advance quickly, penetrate the American defense and reach the Meuse River within a few days of the initial attack. In the meanwhile, his advance would disrupt and cast into confusion the Americans with the quickness and shock of his attack. Peiper was the ideal man to lead this attack—young, aggressive, hard driving, ruthless, and a fervent Nazi. If anyone could reach the Meuse, it would be Peiper.

Starting early on the morning of December 17, Peiper's aggressive drive met with success, overrunning several American units and making fast progress; already, his reinforced regiment was causing consternation to the Americans by the speed of its advance. He had achieved a breakthrough. Peiper's unit was accused of perpetrating the Malmedy massacre, that is, the execution of several hundred American prisoners. After the war, Peiper and some of his men were put on trial and imprisoned for these crimes.

On December 18, Peiper's drive to the Meuse continued—until he ran into the Fifty-First American Engineer Battalion at Trois Ponts. This was a very important point, as it had three bridges over the Ambleve and the Salm Rivers. Peiper desperately need to capture these bridges to get to the Meuse.

The Fifty-First set up its meager defense as best it could and waited for Peiper. And when Peiper approached, they opened fire. Peiper did not know how much strength he was faced with. After destroying several German tanks, the engineers blew up the bridges. As Peiper said later, "If we had captured the bridges at Trois Ponts intact and had had enough fuel, it would have been a simple matter to drive through to the Meuse River that day." One action by a courageous group of engineers had thrown the entire German timetable off balance.

Thwarted at Trois Ponts, Peiper diverted his forces toward Werbonnet only four miles away. Between him and his objective was Lienne Crick, which, despite its small size, was unfordable. Just before Peiper's kampgrujspe arrived, a squad from the U.S. 291st Engineer Combat Battalion blew another bridge in his face. Stymied in his push to the west, Peiper's attack faltered. Heavy units of American divisions in the area now began to close in on the stalled Peiper. Eventually, he had to cut his way back eastward to the German lines with only a fragment of his men.

One German officer said they could have been successful if it hadn't been for "those damned engineers." A fitting tribute to a courageous group of young Americans. Units such as these all along the Ardennes front were blunting and defeating the German attack.

Further to the south, the 101st Airborne Division had been sent to Bastogne on the evening of December 18 just in the nick of time. The Germans were only a few miles away, moving west towards Bastogne, and if they had moved more quickly, they could and should have beaten the Americans to Bastogne. An American combat command of the Tenth Armored Division arrived at Bastogne shortly after the 101st. The two units saved the day on the southern part of the front. The Germans made piecemeal attacks on Bastogne but were repulsed. In the interest of time, they decided for the moment to bypass Bastogne and head west to the Meuse. American units at Noville, just north of Bastogne, put up a great fight, thus delaying the Germans. Colonel James La Prade and Major William Desorby led the gallant defense. Colonel La Prade was killed, and Major Desorby was wounded. In addition to delaying the German attack, the Americans inflicted serious casualties on the attacking enemy.

The Eighty-Second Airborne was used to fill in the open gap in the bulge, along with other units from the American First and Ninth Armies. As always, the Eighty-Second did a splendid job under General Gavin.

The German drive, stalled in the north, also began to slow down in the center. One reason was fierce resistance; another was the shortage of roads. They were also having fuel shortages. Finally, the German drive came to a halt. At Celles the Second Panzer Division had been destroyed by American armor. Hitler refused to accept defeat; he ordered Bastogne, now surrounded, to be captured at all costs. Meanwhile, General Patton's attack from the south began on December 23, as promised, with the objective of relieving Bastogne. Through difficult terrain and bad weather, the attack made slow but steady progress and, urged on by Patton, relieved Bastogne on December 26. The Battle of Ardennes was over, although hard fighting was still going on.

With this last fling of the dice, Hitler lost all hope of winning the war. He had used his last available reserves, and now most of them were casualties or prisoners. He pulled the remnants back from the bulge to his starting line. The last main offensive German action of war was over. It was rather remarkable that the German soldiers could still fight effectively, even though they knew they had almost no chance of winning. Their very last chance was now gone. Hitler was playing his last cards and losing everywhere—time was running out on him and on Germany. Perhaps the German troops fought well because they had now reached their own soil and, to some extent, were fighting for their own homes. The Germans were a very disciplined army and believed in following orders, perhaps too much so. They continued to fight for four more months. Many were casualties in a hopeless cause. One man had brought them to this: Adolph Hitler.

There were two main reasons for the German defeat in the Ardennes. (1) The German forces assigned were not large enough and powerful enough to achieve their mission. The German generals had warned Hitler of this beforehand, but he wouldn't listen. (2) The Americans fought a terrific battle, in particular small unit actions such as Lieutenant Bouck's. The Allied commanders acted quickly and effectively to stop and turn back the German attack. Individual American soldiers had fought bravely and refused to yield. They won the battle.

Churchill and Roosevelt had no direct involvement in the Battle of the Bulge. At this point, to a large extent, the war was out of their hands. They had appointed competent commanders, and now it was up to them to fight and finish the war. Hitler was still up to his usual old game of trying to run everything—with fewer and fewer good results.

The Air War

In 1940, the British knew that they had no chance of defeating the German Army in Europe by themselves, and at that time they were by themselves. But they were determined not to just stand on the defensive, but in some way to take the offensive. The only way they could do that was in the air. They devoted a great part of their limited resources to the air, and in particular to heavy bombers—the Halifax and the Lancaster four-engined planes.

Lord Trenchard, the air chief of the R.A.F. in the First War, was still influential through the twenties and thirties. His view was that the war could actually be won through the air, that is, by heavy bombing of German industry, transport, and indeed, German cities. He considered that the bombing would so disrupt the economy and the daily existence of a country that it would have to surrender. In effect: create havoc. Many people espoused this idea, so much so that the British devoted large resources to the R.A.F., which consisted of over a million men. Many Americans also believed in the air war, particularly General Billy Mitchell. Although discredited at the time in the 1920s, his ideas were largely carried out by the Americans later. A large part of American resources were also devoted to the air, and in particular, to the heavy bombers, the B-17 Flying Fortress and the B-24 Liberator.

The B-17 was a particularly formidable airplane. With machine guns in all parts of the plane, it presented a great defensive aircraft. In formation with other B-17s, it could put up a tremendous amount of fire against attacking aircraft. Confronting the B-17s the Germans used the fast flying Messerscmitt-109 equipped with two 20 millimeter cannons and two machine guns. The Fockewulf 190 armed with four 20 millimeter cannons and two machine guns were also used in these attacks. Attacking in large numbers, with their concentrated firepower and speed, they had the advantage over the slow flying B-17s. The addition in 1944 of the American P-51 Mustang as fighter escort to the B-17s helped the Americans in the furious air battles.

The Germans and the Russians did not develop a four-engined long-range plane; their planes were more of the tactical variety; that is, they were designed to gain superiority in the air over the battlefield and assist their armies. The Germans and the Russians were at each other's throat in close combat and did not actually need long-range bombers.

In 1941, the British began to attack Germany by air, intensifying their attacks as the year went by. On May 20, 1942, one thousand heavy bombers attacked Cologne; three days later, a similar attack was made on Essen, the home of the Krupps munitions works. The Americans began their attacks in 1943 by the Eighth Air Force, based in England. The British bombed by night in order to hold down the losses. The Americans bombed during the daylight. They knew the risk was greater but felt they could achieve more accurate bombing in daylight. Also, the defensive firepower of the B-17 could fight off German attacks. It wasn't planned this way, but it became a war of attrition between the heavy bombers and the Luftwaffe, with each side taking heavy losses.

One particular attack by the R.A.F. achieved devastating results. Starting on July 24, 1943, Hamburg was hit by a mass attack, which continued for six days. The U.S. Air Force also participated in daylight attacks. The city was virtually destroyed, over forty-five thousand people were killed, and two-thirds of the population had to be evacuated. The shock waves of these attacks on Hamburg spread all over Germany. Goebbels was almost in a panic. Everyone was furious at Goering, who became less visible each passing day. The attacks by the British and the Americans was costly indeed to the attackers as well. In one raid on Schweinfurt, the Americans lost sixty planes with ten men aboard each. During the war, both the Americans and the British lost approximately seventy thousand men each, a very high percentage of the men actually engaged.

The air war was very hazardous duty for the men in the air. The Americans developed a system whereby after twenty-five missions the men were sent home to train other airmen. In the R.A.F., it was thirty missions. Considering the fact that on some missions ten percent of the planes were shot down, it is easy arithmetic to see that chance of making twenty-five missions was small. I am sure that the men making these missions understood that, but they carried out their tasks with fortitude and courage. They were determined to do their part to defeat Hitler, no matter what, even at the risk of their own lives. It took a man like Winston Churchill to appreciate and understand the feelings of the men involved. I quote him as follows:

I would like to express my respect and appreciation for the officers and men who fought and died in this fearful battle of the air, the like of which has never before been known, or with any precision imagined. The moral tests to which the crew of a bomber were subjected reached the limits of human valor and sacrifice. Here chance was carried to its most extreme and violent degree above all else. There was a rule that no one should go on more than thirty raids without a break. But many who entered on their last dozen wild adventures felt the odds against them were increasing. How can one be lucky thirty times running in a world of averages and machinery? Detective Constable McSweeney, one of the Scotland Yard officers who looked after me in the early days of the war, was determined to fight in a bomber. I saw him several times during his training and his fighting. One day, gay and jaunty as ever but with a thoughtful look he said, 'My next will be my twenty-ninth.' It was his last. Not only our hearts and admiration, but our minds in strong comprehension of these ordeals must go out to these heroic men whose duty to their country and their cause sustained them in their superhuman trials.

I have mentioned facts like the Americans had 60 of their large Fortress aircraft destroyed out of 291, and on another occasion out of 795 aircraft dispatched by British bomber command against Nuremberg 94 did not return. The American Fortress carried a crew of ten men and the British night bomber seven. Here we have each time six or seven hundred of these skilled, highly trained warriors lost in an hour. This was indeed ordeal by fire. In the British and American bombing of Germany and Italy during the war, the casualties were over a hundred and forty thousand, and in the period with which this chapter deals there were more British and American aircrew casualties than there were killed and wounded in the great operation of crossing the Channel. These heroes never flinched or failed. It is to their devotion that in no small measure we owe our victory. Let us give them our salute.

There is no way to say anything better about this than Churchill's.

To illustrate how close Mr. Churchill's remarks came to the actual battle, and in particular his remark, "here chance was carried to its most extreme and violent degree above all else," the author relates what happened to my brother, Lieutenant William C. Stewart, Jr., to whom this book is dedicated. Lieutenant Stewart, or Billy as he was known to us, was a bombardier on a B-17. He was killed in the air over Berlin on September 12, 1944, nine days short of his twenty-first birthday. I would have to say he was the finest young man I have ever known and was by far the most outstanding member of our large family.

Earlier in 1944, after making a number of hazardous missions, he received the Air Medal. His crew was then switched to more safe missions, evidently reconnaisance type. However, in a letter to us on August 11, 1944, Billy said he did not feel useful on these missions as a bombardier was not really needed. He was going to ask to transfer back to a bombardment unit.

We were informed in late September, 1944, that he was missing in action. Shortly thereafter, we learned that of the crew of ten, four had gotten safely out of the plane before it went down. We naturally hoped and prayed that Billy was one of the four. However, some weeks later, we were informed that he had been killed in action.

Almost a year later, we received a letter from the navigator on the flight, Lieutenant Donald Marsh, who had been a prisoner of war during this time. Lieutenant Marsh relates the details of my brother's last flight, which shows how accurately Mr. Churchill's remarks fit the actual circumstances. Here is the letter. It speaks for itself.

Hamilton, Ohio
July 10, 1945

Dear Mrs. Stewart,

I was flying with your son on September 12. Mother showed me your letter some time ago and I would have have written sooner, but this is a very hard letter for me to write. I feel certain that I shall re-awaken memories you have of your son. However, maybe I can be of some help by telling all I know about him.

He had flown three or four missions as bombardier on my crew. Since I am a navigator, he and I flew together in the nose of the plane. We got along very well together and I enjoyed flying with him.

We were on a long and hard mission on September 12. At about 11:30 our formation was broken up a little by flak and about the same time German fighters attacked us. The attacks were from behind us, so Lieutenant Stewart and I in the nose could do nothing but wait. We were hit badly and soon the left wing and the bomb bays were afire. Two twenty millimeter canon shells burst in the nose, and I believe one of them slightly wounded Lieutenant Stewart. However, we both buckled on our parachutes and went to the door of our compartment. The engineer and copilot were at the escape hatch when we got there. The engineer's feet were badly shot up. After those two had gotten out the pilot came dragging his parachute which had bursted open. We helped him gather up the chute in his arms. Then as I was ready to dive out the hatch, the plane started to spin and dive. This threw me away from the hatch and then back over it and out. Lieutenant Stewart was thrown back up into the nose of the plane. If we had had a few seconds longer, I feel certain he too could have gotten out. Just after I got out the plane exploded.

Four of us were brought together after the Germans had captured us. We all hoped that the others would turn up alive. I had not given up hope until I got home and learned what had happened.

If I may be of any other help to you, please let me know, Mrs. Stewart.

Yours Sincerely,
Donald C. Marsh

This letter from Lt. Donald Marsh was the last our family heard about Billy's last flight until 56 years later in 2001. At this point I was going through some of Billy's last letters and noticed they were addressed to the 367th Squadron of the 306th Bomb Group. My son, Vance Stewart, Jr., found on the Internet that there was 306th Bomb Group Association, the secretary being Russell Strong of Charlotte, N.C. I called Russell and mentioned that Billy was a member of the 367th Squadron. To my amazement Russell replied that he was also a member of the 367th and was on the mission of September 12th, 1944, as navigator on Lt. Adam's plane. He said Billy's plane was in formation on his left just next to his own. After 56 years I now learned a tremendous amount of information on the mission of September 12, thanks to Russell. He provided me with many records and accounts of that day which he recalled very well as he said it was his roughest mission. I appreciate Russell's help in providing me with some picture and understanding of the events that happened that day.

As mentioned, Billy was a member of the 367th Squadron of the 306th Bomb Group. On that day, September 12th, the 306th had 36 planes in the air along with scores of planes from other Groups. The 306th lost a total of nine planes that day, 2 shot down by anti-aircraft fire and 7 by fighter air craft. These terrible losses all occurred within a few minutes as the Group was first hit by anti-aircraft fire and then about 25 Focke-Wulf 190's attacked from above. These fighters then made another attack from below with deadly effect, principally caused by their 20 mm cannon fire. The 367th Squadron was particularly hard hit losing five out of nine of its B-17's. Russell Strong's plane was one of the four survivors. This was one of the hardest missions of the 306th Bomb Group.

The following day a report was compiled on the individual losses based on accounts by the pilots of the planes that made it back. It is remarkable that these pilots could observe what was happening to their falling comrades while they themselves were under intense enemy fire. Sometimes the pilots of several planes would report on the same plane that went down. In the report below the name of the pilot of the lost plane is mentioned first followed by the air craft number. This stark report gives us some comprehension of what our young airmen faced. The report gives us a greater understanding of the air war and of the whole war itself. The history of these times calls that these events be recorded and all our airmen be remembered.

HEADQUARTERS 306TH BOMBARDMENT GROUP   D-A-1
Office of the Intelligence Officer
United States Forces

APO 557
13 September, 1944

SUBJECT: Intelligence Narrative - Aircraft Losses
Mission: RUHLAND, 12 September, 1944

TO: Commanding Officer, 306th Bombardment Group (H)

The 306th lost nine aircraft, seven to fighters (one A/C, #093-V, pilot Donkin, crash landed in England) and two to A.A. gun fire. These losses occurred just north east of Berlin at approximately 1130 hours. A.A. fire accounted for two A/C just before the fighter attacks. Below is the consensus of information from returning crews on each A/C:

Major FARWELL, A/C 690-W
Lt. Brown says this A/C hit by A.A. gun fire N. Berlin, 5240W - 1340E at 1126. 9 chutes, one of which appeared not to open. No fire, smoke, or explosion. Lts. Eros and Lingwall agree A/C hit by A.A. gun fire.

Lt. DONKIN, A/C 093-V (367th)
Hit by fighters. Maintained lead for a while then told Gassman to take over. Crash landed 5 miles S.E. of Manston. 4 bailed out over England. Two dead. Four with some injuries. Three not hurt.

Lt. BARR, A/C 969-X (367th)
Lt. Gassman's crew says that A/C exploded as a result of direct hit on #3 engine. Lt. Breed's crew says that A/C had all four engines on fire. 3 chutes. A/C peeled off, not seen any more. Lt. Risk says this A/C on fire. Hit by fighters. Exploded. 1 chute.

Lt. BAILEY, A/C 065-Z (367th)
Lt. Adam says this A/C down to fighters. 1130 hours. 6-7 chutes. Might have been 042 instead.

Lt. WHITE, A/C 042-P (367th)

Lt. Adam says possibly this A/C down to fighters at 1130. 6 to 7 chutes.

Lt. WEGENER, A/C 278-K (367th)

Lt. Adam says this A/C hit by fighters, 1130 hours N. Berlin. Went off to left. Four chutes. Possibly more. Lt. Gassman says #3 engire on fire. Slid off to side. Not observed any longer. Lt. Risk says this A/C tail assembly shot off. Dropped out of formation, 1128.

Lt. SASSER, A/C 368-0

Lt. Underwood says the A/C down 1135 hours, NE Berlin. #3 engine hit by A.A. gun fire. A/C spiralled down to clouds. No fire. 5 chutes observed. Lt. Lacy says this A/C hit by A.A. gun fire before fighters arrived. #2 and #4 engines out. Under control. No chutes. 1127 hours.

Lt. GATES, A/C 5...-W

Lt. Schoenbachle. says this A/C hit by fighters 1... hours. Flames from radio room back. No chutes observed. #3 engine on fire.

Lt. FREEMAN, A/C 180-K

Lt. Hutchinson says this A/C hit by two fighters. A/C dropped back on fire. No chutes observed to come from A/C, but two noticed in area. Could not follow afterwards. Just NE of Berlin, approximately 1130 hours. Lt. Alyea says this A/C hit by fighters 1128. Broke in half. No chutes observed.

JOHN A. BAIRNSFATHER,
Major, AC,
Group S-2.

◆ ◆ ◆

The 306th Bomb Group normally consisted of seventy-two B-17's. Records of the 306th from 1942-45 show that a total of 177 of its planes were lost. No words can express the enormity of the ordeal or the sacrifice of the brave young men who flew these planes. They are all heroes.

Fortunately as the air war went into it's later period, German air opposition, particularly in aircraft, began to wear down due to their heavy losses in men, material and fuel. Allied fighter escort planes, by extending their range, were doing a very effective job of shielding the bombers to the target and back. The Eighth Air Force and the R.A.F. had won the air war over Germany.

Suffice it to say the air arm, both tactically and strategically, was decisive in the Allied victory in the West. These men did not die in vain. Along with the destruction of the German economy and industry, the Luftwaffe was constrained to put a large part of its air force in the air over Germany. These planes had to be pulled from both the Eastern and Western Fronts, assuring air superiority for the Allies on both fronts. The Germans were straining their resources in all directions and losing in all directions: on the ground, in the air, and on the sea. They chose to fight the world and were now paying for Hitler's ignorance for what he had stirred up against them, too late, too late.

6

The Pacific War

Roosevelt and Churchill

After the Battle of Midway in June, 1942, the United States, with limited resources, seized the initiative. The war against Japan in the Pacific was primarily waged by the Americans. The Japanese were bogged down in China; each success they achieved there led them further and further into the interior—a bottomless pit. The Chinese fought sporadically at times, but relied on geography to help them. China was a little like Russia—the further you got into it, the worse off you were. Still, China absorbed thousands of Japanese soldiers and aided to that extent.

Rather stupid strategy on the part of the Japanese. They should have concentrated all of their forces on stopping the Americans. The hundreds of thousands of Japanese troops in China were completely wasted and had no effect on the war. At the end of the war, with their homeland almost destroyed and occupied by a foreign power, I wonder if the Japanese considered their Chinese adventure was worth it.

Churchill and Roosevelt had different attitudes about China. Churchill, immersed in the war in Europe, was not interested in China—in fact, he thought it was more of a liability than an asset. He felt that China was in the backwater of the war and could have no effect on its outcome—that the resources and efforts devoted to China were wasted and could be better used elsewhere. In his six volume account of World War II, China is scarcely mentioned. It is said that once, Churchill remarked about the Chinese, "I don't bother them and they don't bother me." It may have been good for the Americans to have had this philosophy before going into Vietnam.

Roosevelt, on the other hand, was very committed to and sympathetic to China. China was one of the main reasons America was brought into the war. The American public was also sympathetic to the Chinese people, who had been so severely mistreated by the Japanese invaders. Roosevelt viewed China as an important country vital to victory in the Far East. He tried his best to get supplies to them to sustain China's war effort, even though it was exceedingly difficult to do so. Roosevelt felt the war in China was tying down hundreds of thousands of Japanese troops that otherwise could be fighting the United States.

Chiang Kai-shek

The nominal leader of China was Generalissimo Chiang Kai-shek, the President of the Republic of China and its commander-in-chief. The word nominal is used because China was actually split into two groups—Chiang's forces and the Communists under Mao Tse-tung. At times, the Communists cooperated with Chiang, and at other times they operated on their own. The United States recognized Chiang as the leader of China and conducted its affairs with China through him. The Americans did have some liaison men working with the Communists in order to spur their war effort against Japan.

Chiang's major thought during the war was to hold his government together, to build up his forces with the aid of America, and then settle accounts (that is, crush) the Communists after the war with Japan was over. In the meanwhile, he would cope with Japan the best way he could, fighting sporadically and withdrawing into the interior. Of course, Roosevelt was hoping China would take a more active part in the war and was urging them to do so. As mentioned, he was supplying them with war materiel as best he could over a tenuous supply route.

At Marshall's request, Roosevelt appointed General Joseph Stilwell to lead the American representation in China. This proved to be something of an unfortunate choice. Stilwell was a rather abrasive, combative type personality in a post which required delicacy and diplomacy. He was trying to carry out his assignment of getting China to be more aggressive in fighting the Japanese, while Chiang was dragging his feet. Chiang felt the Japanese were much stronger and better organized than the Chinese and that more battles would only lead to more Chinese defeats. Chiang was still thinking about holding his forces intact to deal with the Communists after the war. Stilwell had an impossible job under the circumstances. He was openly contemptuous of Chiang, which naturally resulted in a bad relationship between the two. Finally, Chiang could stand it no more and requested Roosevelt to remove Stilwell. Roosevelt had no choice but to do so.

In the meanwhile, there was another American in China helping the Chinese in their war against Japan. He was General Claire Chennault, a very colorful and dynamic figure. Before Pearl Harbor, Chennault had organized a volunteer group of American pilots to come to China and fly for the Chinese—the America Volunteer Group, otherwise known as the Flying Tigers. Although relatively small in number, this group was very effective and inflicted serious damage to the Japanese air force in China. Chennault and his men became well known to the public and were regarded as heroes.

Upon America's entry into the war, Chennault's group was combined with additional air units to form the Fourteenth USAF, with Chennault as commander. This was still not a large force, but it was very effective. Chennault became a favorite of Roosevelt because he was actually accomplishing something in a complicated situation. Chennault continually asked for reinforcements and supplies, as he felt he could deal a major blow to Japan in this area of Asia. Chennault was disdainful of fighting the Japanese on the ground in China and wanted to direct all American efforts to the air campaign. This brought him into open conflict with Stilwell. Chiang liked Chennault and his ideas, and he definitely didn't like Stilwell—which resulted in Stilwell's removal.

The Americans had the idea of using China as a base for B-29 air attacks on Japan and made a major effort to do so. Some attacks were actually made. However, the great difficulty in getting supplies, fuel, planes, etc., into China made it impractical to mount large attacks on Japan using China as a base. With the capture of the Marianas Islands in the Pacific, it was much more practical to use them as bases for air attacks on Japan.

In the latter part of the war, Roosevelt realized the limitations of Chinese involvement and resigned himself to doing the best he could to keep them going in a difficult situation. After the war ended, Chiang tried to impose his authority over the whole of China, including the Communists. The morale and organization of Chiang's army was poor, while the Communists were very tough and dedicated to their cause. In the battles that followed, Chiang's army crumbled and the Communists were victorious and took over all of China.

America's efforts in China had come to naught in the end. It was mostly Chiang's fault, as his government was filled with corruption and was not popular with the Chinese people. America didn't lose China; Chiang did. Roosevelt's efforts on behalf of China during the war did propel China into the forefront of the nations of the world. It was Roosevelt's effort that placed China on the five-member Security Council of the United Nations, along with the United

States, England, France, and the Soviet Union. Actually, Roosevelt was proved to be right about the potential of China.

Guadalcanal

Meanwhile, in the Southwest Pacific, the U.S. Marines landed on Guadalcanal in the Solomon islands on August 7, 1942, killing the few nearby Japanese that had recently landed and captured the airfield. Japan wanted Guadalcanal as an air base to cut off supplies and reinforcements to Australia. They also wanted to sustain their offensive movements. The battle for Guadalcanal was fierce and bloody, lasting six months. This battle was a test for both sides: whoever won would be considered the strongest side, indicating the outcome of the war. One might say it was the Stalingrad of the Pacific.

There were a series of naval battles off the coast of the island. The Japanese were successful in most of these battles, particularly those involving night actions. Admiral Nimitz appointed a new officer to command the U.S. naval forces in that area. William "Bull" Halsey, an aggressive, fighting admiral, was just what Nimitz wanted. The naval battles continued; now, they were fought mostly in regard to the re-supply of the Japanese army on Guadalcanal. The Japanese were losing the war on the ground. Their suicide attacks were just that—suicide. Their ranks were being depleted rapidly.

Slowly, with the aid of air power from Henderson Field on Guadalcanal, the tide began to turn in favor of the Americans. The Japanese were now sustaining severe losses on the ground, but also in the naval war. A war of attrition was working against the Japanese. Each side was throwing in reinforcements, but American sea and air power began to sink most of the supplies and men Japan sent. It was becoming impossible for them to supply and reinforce their thinning contingent on the island, so they pulled out. They had lost the test; possibly the handwriting was on the wall for them. Guadalcanal, along with Midway, were the turning points in the Pacific War. From here on, it was all downhill for the Japanese.

The Japanese high command in Tokyo was well aware of the consequences of these defeats. Tension was high. So much so that several high officers got into a fight and brandished their swords at one another. In a conference with Tojo, General Tanaka lost all control and shouted at Tojo, "What are you doing about the war? We'll lose it this way you damn fool!" Tojo was stunned.

There were other Japanese who were stunned as well, particularly those who had fought at Guadalcanal. They had been very surprised at the fighting spirit and courage of the Americans, that the Americans were willing to fight to the death for their country, just as the Japanese. The Japanese had not counted on this. They had met their match and even more at Guadalcanal.

In the meanwhile, in New Guinea, General MacArthur was also frustrating the Japanese drive to take Port Moresby. Taking the offensive, MacArthur used his limited forces of Americans and Australians to bypass Japanese strongholds and leave them to starve and wither on the vine—the leapfrog strategy. Allied air power again played a large part in his success. In one action, American planes sank twelve out of sixteen ships trying to bring reinforcements; four thousand Japanese troops were drowned. It was called the Battle of the Bismarck Sea.

With defeats at Guadalcanal and in New Guinea, the Japanese had reached the end of their offensive strengths and had lost the initiative. To lose the initiative in this kind of maritime war was, in effect, to lose the war.

The Death of Yamamoto

Admiral Yamamoto, the "victor" at Pearl Harbor, decided to visit Rabaul and raise the morale of his forces. He decided on April 14 to visit his various commands in that area and rejuvenate them in the fight against the Americans. His visit from Rabaul to the Solomon islands was broadcast over the radio to the Solomon bases—of course, in code. This broadcast was indeed unfortunate for Admiral Yamamoto, to say the least. The Americans had broken the Japanese code and intercepted and decoded the message. Commander Layton, Pacific fleet intelligence officer, took the intercept to Admiral Nimitz immediately. Nimitz believed the elimination of Yamamoto would be a severe blow to the Japanese, especially psychologically. Nimitz was unsure what to do. He forwarded the information to the highest command in Washington: President Roosevelt. The answer spelled the end of Admiral Yamamoto.

American air units at Henderson Field, Guadalcanal, were alerted to attack Yamamoto's plane as it approached Buin at the southern end of Bougainville. Sixteen P-38 Lightnings were assigned to do the job. Yamamoto's plane and another carrying his staff were punctual, arriving at 11:35 a.m. over Buin. The Americans were waiting for them, and both planes were shot down. Yamamoto was killed outright. His body was found, his fingers still clutching his ceremonial samurai sword, so the legend goes. Pearl Harbor was still being avenged. Yamamoto's death dealt a severe blow to the whole Japanese nation. The man who had started the war was now gone. Victory for the Japanese was slipping away; the death of Yamamoto was just a portent of things to come.

Japan on the Defensive

The Japanese were now in the predicament of garrisoning and defending the numerous islands across the whole central and southwestern Pacific Ocean—virtually an impossible task without command of sea and air. Their extensive victories early in the war were now coming back to haunt them. Since the United States was now on the offensive with superior naval and air forces, it could pick and choose where it would strike next. Thus, it could concentrate greatly superior forces at the point of attack and was bound to be successful. "Get there firstest with the mostest," as General Nathan Bedford Forrest had said in the Civil War.

The Americans, with the initiative, were able to bypass large Japanese bases such as Rebaul and Truk. Thousands and thousands of Japanese were left behind to starve, completely ineffective to the war. By repeating these same successful tactics, it was only a question of time before the main islands of Japan would be reached.

There was one strategic question for Roosevelt: which route to take across the Pacific to Japan. He had his very competent General MacArthur attacking from the southwest Pacific to the north in the direction of the Philippines. The central Pacific was more in the naval sphere, with aircraft carriers and Marines under another very competent officer, Admiral Nimitz.

Which route to take? Many of Roosevelt's advisors, including MacArthur and Nimitz, believed that the Americans should concentrate their forces in one big push rather than two dispersed actions. The Central Pacific route actually seemed the most direct and shortest route across the Pacific and to Japan itself. MacArthur pointed out that to bypass the Philippines would be morally unacceptable. The Philippine people and the Americans were friends; America had already promised the Philippines their independence in 1946. The Filipino people were suffering under the Japanese; moreover, there were hundreds of Allied prisoners there, some dying daily of starvation.

Roosevelt was in a dilemma. He had two highly competent officers who were very successful in their drives against the Japanese. He decided to leave well enough alone. Since both drives were showing such major successes, why not continue with success? This was another big decision Roosevelt made, and it was right. While Hitler and Japan were making big mistakes, Roosevelt was making good decisions. One large advantage of two separate drives in separate regions is that it kept the Japanese wondering where the Americans were going to strike next. It was like a one-two punch.

Indeed, in its simplest terms, this whole war was somewhat like a boxing match. Japan, the courageous lightweight fighter, was standing toe-to-toe with America, the courageous heavyweight fighter. In this kind of fight there could be only one certain winner. It was not a question of whether Japan, the lightweight fighter, would fall, but how long it would take. How much pounding from the heavyweight could it absorb before falling?

Across the Pacific

With the capture of the Marianas Islands by the forces of Admiral Nimitz, Japan proper came within reach of American heavy bombers—the B-29s. This was one of the decisive factors in the war. The attack on the Marianas was preceded by an attack on the Gilbert Islands, particularly Tarawa. Tarawa was needed, as it had the only air base in the archipelago. The attack was made by the Second Marine Division under General Julian Smith. Tarawa was defended by forty-five hundred tough troops under Admiral Deiji, whose orders were to fight to the last man. Tarawa was a very strong defensive position with deeply entrenched bunkers.

A preliminary bombardment was made by three battleships and other vessels, to little effect. The Marines landed on the north side of the island and met a terrific resistance. It took almost three days of fierce fighting to overcome the Japanese, who were virtually wiped out to the man. Over one thousand Marines were killed and twenty-one hundred wounded; this was a staggering number of casualties. It cast a chill over the American command, considering that there were many islands between Tarawa and Japan. However, Nimitz was determined to correct the mistakes of Tarawa and continue his campaign across the Central Pacific.

He attacked the Marshall Islands and with better preparation was able to seize them with many fewer casualties than at Tarawa; again, the Japanese fought to the last man. The few prisoners captured were usually wounded or so stunned by the bombardment that they were incapable of fighting.

Task force 58, a large fleet under Admiral Mitscher, attacked and neutralized the large Japanese base at Truk on February 17 and 18. Over two hundred seventy Japanese planes were lost on the ground and in the air, along with a number of naval vessels sunk. The Japanese were fighting hard, but were being overwhelmed by American power. The advance on the Marianas was relentless. The Japanese knew they had to stop the Americans from occupying the Marianas; it was critical to the defense of the home islands of Japan. The Marianas, consisting of Saipan, Tinian, and Guam, were Nimitz's main objective. They would be bases for the next naval move on Japan, but more importantly, they would be air bases for the B-29. The B-29 was a long-range bomber which would reach Japan itself.

The invasion was planned for June, 1944, under the command of Admiral Spruance, the victor at Midway. The largest force yet assembled in the Pacific was slated for the operation. The initial attack was to be on Saipan on June 13. A large group of battleships bombarded the island for several days, achieving some results. The Second and Fourth Marine divisions went ashore on June 16 and came under intense fire; however, by the next day, forty thousand troops had landed.

Meanwhile, the Japanese Navy had planned an all-out assault on the Americans, particularly by air. These naval attacks would be augmented by planes from ground bases in the area, particularly Guam—indeed, a formidable assault. The Japanese fleet was under the command of Admiral Ozawa. Over 450 planes were available in the naval attack alone. U.S. submarines spotted the advance of the Japanese fleet and alerted Admiral Spruance. The huge American fleet was prepared and waiting for the Japanese attack. Spruance's main objective was to cover the Saipan landing force and not be lured away from that task. Many have since criticized Spruance for not steaming west and attacking the Japanese fleet. Nevertheless, Spruance felt his first duty was to protect and keep secure the American beachhead on Saipan. Admiral King later told Spruance he had done the right thing and praised him for his decision to protect the beachhead.

The first wave of 64 Japanese planes made the initial attack, of which 42 were shot down. Almost no damage was incurred by the American fleet. The next wave was 128 planes, of which 97 were shot down. The third and fourth waves consisted of 129 planes, of which 80 were shot from the skies. No damage was inflicted on the Americans. Of the 373 aircraft that Ozawa had launched, 240 were downed, in addition to the 50 that were destroyed by American air attacks on Guam. Many others were lost to various causes. The American fighter defense and heavy anti-aircraft fire had all but destroyed the attacking planes. This defensive victory by the Americans was called "the Great Marianas Turkey Shoot."

Meanwhile, the American submarines were attacking Ozawa's fleet. His flagship, the new carrier Taiho, was struck and eventually sank. The carrier Shokako, one of Pearl Harbor's assailants, was also hit by torpedoes and sank. In an attack by Mitscher's planes, another carrier, the Hiyo, was sunk and several other vessels were seriously damaged. On the 20th, Ozawa withdrew his fleet to the west. It was still a large force; however, there were only 35 aircraft left in the entire fleet. The cream of Japanese aviation had been wiped out. After this battle, the Japanese Navy was always short on pilots and aircrews. The best were gone, and the incoming men were rushed into service and were under-trained. They became sitting ducks for the more numerous and experienced American fliers.

On Saipan, Japanese suicide attacks were no more successful than they had been on Guadalcanal. The last Japanese committed suicide, including Admiral Nagumo, who had commanded the Pearl Harbor attack. Revenge in all its fury was overtaking and consuming the Japanese. After the fall of Saipan, the Americans attacked Tinian and Guam, which were overcome despite fierce resistance. Typically, the last Japanese unit on Guam did not surrender until September 4, 1945, when the war was over.

The Battle for the Marianas resulted in a tremendous victory. Japan was now in range of American bombers. The government of Hidiki Tojo resigned. The Japanese recognized the magnitude of the Marianas defeat. Now, Yamamoto, Nagumo, and Tojo were gone. The instigators of the war were paying the price for their tremendous misjudgments. The whole Japanese nation itself would soon have to pay for the militarists' bombastic mistakes that took them into a war they could not win.

Churchill and the Pacific

Churchill's role in the Pacific war was very limited. His objective was, first of all, to stop the Japanese drive, based in Burma, against India. This he did. After India was saved, that whole theatre was really academic in the war against Japan, other than psychologically and for prestige. If the islands of Japan itself were defeated and occupied, the rest of their captured empire was gone. If you kill the head, the rest of the body is dead also. This is what happened when Japan surrendered; the British walked into Singapore without a shot being fired.

Frankly, the British and Japanese battle in Burma was a waste— thousands of casualties on both sides in an area that had no effect on the outcome of the war—the whole thing was a total waste. Both Britain and Japan were guilty of the same mistakes: fighting for the sake of fighting. Earlier in 1943, Churchill had said he hated jungles—which go to the winner anyway! With this attitude, it is a wonder that Churchill allowed the tortuous advance through the Burmese jungles.   It is also true that Australian forces in the latter part of the war were attacking bypassed Japanese garrisons in the southwest Pacific. This, too, was unnecessary and a waste of men's lives and materiel. General

Blamey, the head of the Australian army, is said to have been responsible for this; General MacArthur did not favor these attacks. However, MacArthur did form an assault on Borneo by the Australians, which was completely unnecessary. These British and Australian resources should have been used elsewhere in more vital areas.

The British did send a strong fleet to the Central Pacific naval campaign, consisting of four carriers, two battleships, five cruisers, and fifteen destroyers. They made a significant and valuable contribution. In particular, the British carriers had armored flight decks which made them less vulnerable to Japanese air attacks.

Other than stopping the Japanese drive against India, I don't think Churchill was particularly interested in the war against Japan, especially after Singapore. Of course, he wanted to win, being Churchill. He realized, however, that this was an American sphere of operations; moreover, with the British all-out effort in Europe, he did not have enough resources for this part of the world. Great Britain was no longer a world power. Actually, in World War II, the only world power was the United States.

Leyte Gulf

MacArthur attacked the island of Leyte on October 20, 1944. The Japanese were determined to make a decisive stand in the Philippines; if they couldn't defeat the Americans there, where could they stop them? Admiral Nimitz and General MacArthur combined their commands for the assault on the Philippines—MacArthur in charge of ground troops and Bull Halsey in charge of naval forces. Leyte is in the central Philippines, and the Allies believed at first that the Japanese would concentrate their defense on the main island of Luzon. However, the Japanese leadership decided to fight it out for Leyte on the ground and on the sea. This being the case, the battle of Leyte would decide the fate of the whole Philippine Islands.

Indeed, the Imperial Japanese Navy had decided to make Leyte the decisive battle of the war. They knew that if the war continued in its present trend, they would lose. The loss of the Philippines to the Americans meant that their oil supply from the south would be cut off. Without oil, the navy was useless; hence, the war was lost. So they decided on an all-out gambling attack to destroy the American beachhead at Leyte and regain the initiative at lease defensively. The risks were great, but the risk of doing nothing was greater.

At this stage of the war, Japanese naval air strength was very weak, which made victory for them impossible. Nevertheless, they would try with the fleet they had left. Somewhat like British Admiral Phillips near Singapore. Their plan involved a three-pronged attack. They took into the plan an understanding of Bull Halsey's personality: to attack, and especially to attack enemy carriers. The Japanese had a fleet of six carriers under the command of Admiral Ozawa. The only problem was they had very few aircrews to man them. Attrition had taken its toll; Ozawa's was almost a ghost fleet. Of course, Halsey didn't know this. The Japanese decided to use this weak force of carriers as a lure for Admiral Halsey. Coming down from the north and then turning back, they would pull Halsey's fleet north, away from the Leyte beachhead.

The main Japanese battleship fleet under Admiral Kurita, with almost no air support, would approach Leyte from the west, pass through the San Bernardino Strait, and then south to destroy the beachhead. Another smaller force of Japanese warships, under Admiral Nishimura, would approach Leyte from the west and then south of Leyte through the Suriago Straits and also attack the beachhead. If everything went right according to plan, it just might work. If the American fleet wasn't pulled north by Ozawa's carriers, Kurita's fleet would be at Halsey's mercy and would be destroyed.

Halsey learned of Kurita's approach from the west from submarines which attacked and sank the heavy cruisers Atago and Maya. Halsey's aircraft attacked and scored some damage and sank the battleship Mushashi. Momentarily, Kurita turned his fleet around and back to the west. Halsey's pilots reported exaggerated damage to Kurita's fleet and that it was retreating. At that time, Halsey learned of Admiral Ozawa's fleet of carriers to the north. Here was his chance to finish off the remainder of the Japanese carrier fleet. Halsey ordered his entire fleet north to pursue and destroy Ozawa's makeshift fleet—thus uncovering the Leyte beachhead. Halsey had fallen for the lure, as the Japanese had hoped.

Meanwhile, Kurita had turned back east on his original mission and headed for Leyte Gulf. The only thing that stood between him and destroying the beachhead was a small group of destroyers and escort carriers. The small escort carriers were used for support of ground operations and were not suited for heavy naval action.

Let us return to the south to Admiral Nishimura's fleet of battleships and cruisers, the third prong of the attack, entering the Surigao Strait south of Leyte. Admiral Kincaid with a number of American battleships (some of which had been salvaged from Pearl Harbor) were waiting for him. In a night battle, the Japanese fleet was virtually destroyed by Kincaid's forces. This left Kurita's fleet as the only hope for Japan. Kurita was proceeding south down to Leyte gulf, approaching the beachhead, when he was attacked by three American destroyers, the Hoel, the Johnston, and the Roberts. In an heroic but suicidal mission, these small ships were attacking the entire Japanese fleet, mainly to buy time for their comrades. They were all sunk. At the same time, planes from the escort carriers were launched and inflicted significant damage on Kurita's fleet.

Far to the north, Halsey had caught up with Ozawa's decoy fleet and was on the verge of destroying it. Meanwhile, Kincaid, Nimitz, and the whole American Navy were wondering where Halsey's fleet was with the American beachhead uncovered. Finally, Nimitz, who usually stayed out of tactical matters, wired Halsey to move south and rescue the beachhead. By this time, Halsey was hundreds of miles to the north and would take some time to get there. At the time, Halsey was furious with the interference by Nimitz just as he was going to wipe out Ozawa's carrier fleet. Halsey did not realize the seriousness of uncovering the American beachhead at Leyte. Spruance wouldn't have made that mistake.

Meanwhile, Nimitz and Kincaid were not the only ones wondering where Halsey's fleet was. There was another admiral at this critical point in the battle who was wondering the same thing. That was Admiral Kurita. The attack of the destroyers and the escort carrier planes had delayed Kurita's advance toward Leyte gulf; they had also caused some damage and disarray to the Japanese fleet. There was some disarray in the mind of Admiral Kurita at this time also. He could feel Halsey coming, but he didn't know how far away he was. If Halsey's fleet was nearby, Kurita's fleet would be trapped and destroyed. "Never take counsel of your fears," said Stonewall Jackson. Beset by indecision, Kurita at last made up his mind. He turned his fleet away from the beachhead, headed north, and escaped.

Many mistakes were made on all sides, but at the end of the day, it was a tremendous American victory. Four Japanese carriers, three battleships, ten cruisers, and eleven destroyers had been sunk. American losses were light. Despite Halsey's travails, the Japanese Navy's overwhelming defeat was such that it never recovered. For the rest of the war, the Japanese Navy was all but through. This was its last big battle. One could say the war, for all practical purposes, was over for Japan.

Kamikaze

During the Philippine campaign, the Japanese made their first Kamikaze (Divine Wind) attack on October 21. The Kamikaze was an attack in which the Japanese pilot deliberately flew his plane into a surface ship with bombs attached. In other words, a suicidal mission—the pilots took off with only enough gasoline for a one-way trip. This tactic was very effective and was actually the only way the Japanese could inflict serious damage on the American fleet.

There was a definite advantage to the Kamikaze tactic. The Japanese did not have enough trained pilots; the Kamikaze pilots needed little training—elementary training was enough to get the job done. To realize that when you took off, your objective was to crash yourself and your plane into a ship must have been frightening, even to the tough and dedicated Japanese pilots. They went ahead anyway.

These attacks inflicted many casualties upon the Americans, and caused serious problems. As they got closer to Japan, the Kamikaze attacks greatly intensified, particularly at Okinawa. These desperate efforts, while troublesome and, to some extent, horrifying to the Americans, could not affect the outcome of the war. Japanese lives were wasted, dying for their emperor, who, as time would tell, was really a pathetic and very ordinary person whose life was not worth that of a single one of those brave young men.

The Japanese learned a great deal from World War II, particularly what not to do. For fifty years since then, they have not had a military, and they seem to be getting along very well without it. No one would even consider "dying for the Emperor." Perhaps, to some extent, these young men did not die in vain after all.

Post-Leyte

After prolonged and severe fighting, General MacArthur defeated the Japanese on Leyte and then proceeded to invade Luzon. The Japanese fiercely defended Manila, which was practically destroyed in the fight. MacArthur loved Manila, and this hurt him deeply. The remaining Japanese, under General Yamashita, still a considerable force, withdrew into the hills, where they were isolated and ineffective. Losing the Philippines was almost a death blow to the Japanese. American and air bases there could effectively cut off the flow of supplies and oil going from the south to Japan, thus crippling what was left of their war machine. Again, any fighting south of the Philippines was totally unnecessary.

The American submarines played a major part in the defeat of Japan. In 1944 alone, they sank 603 ships. During the war, a total of one 1,314 Japanese ships were sunk by American submarines, or 57 percent of all of Japan's shipping losses. It is conceivable that over a period of time, American submarines could have won the war by themselves, cutting off virtually all supplies going into Japan. An island nation, Japan was almost entirely dependent on imports; without them, it would literally starve and freeze to death.

Thus, at this stage of the war, the Japanese had lost almost all of their navy; the Americans in the Philippines had cut their supply line; and the B-29s in the Marianas Islands were poised to begin bombarding Japan itself. Pearl Harbor was a bittersweet victory for the Japanese. The power unleashed by the attack on Pearl Harbor was crushing Japan. Time was inevitably working for the Allies and against Japan; Roosevelt had received the first blow, but he was dealing out the last ones. With much of their resources devoted to the European Theatre of operations, Roosevelt and the Americans were advancing steadily on Japan itself. Japan was about to be overwhelmed by American power.

Roosevelt's greatest talent in World War II was in mobilizing the full power of the United States and exerting it all over the world. In addition, he seems to have had an uncanny knack of picking outstanding men to lead his forces: Marshall, Eisenhower, MacArthur, King, Nimitz, and their subordinates, Bradley, Patton, Halsey, and Spruance. The power was there; Roosevelt mobilized it, set the course, and then turned it over to his very competent military leaders. It was a tremendous accomplishment. The man who some years earlier had been thought of as a lightweight proved that he was anything but. In this war, he seemed to do everything right—and on top of that, he was an inspirational leader. America was well served by Franklin D. Roosevelt; no one could have done a better job. Ask the Japanese.

MacArthur—The Pacific War

General Douglas MacArthur and Admiral Nimitz were President Roosevelt's top men to lead the war in the Pacific. Let us examine one of the truly most unique men in the war—Douglas MacArthur. MacArthur was one of the best officers the United States has ever produced. It can also be said that he was the most controversial one, a very complex individual. Vanity, it seems, was his main offense—not incompetence.

Douglas MacArthur grew up in the Army. His father was General Arthur MacArthur, an Army officer who won the Congressional Medal of Honor for leading a charge up Missionary Ridge at Chattanooga during the Civil War. He later went on to serve in the Philippines and became governor general of the islands in 1900. He had a very distinguished career. Douglas grew up in this atmosphere; the Army was his life. He also grew up with a deep attachment to the Philippines.

MacArthur was at the top of his class three our of his four years at West Point, graduating with the highest marks ever received there. His record at West Point was similar to that of Robert E. Lee. In the First World War, Douglas distinguished himself as an officer in the famous Rainbow Division. Among the many awards he received for courage and excellence were seven Silver Stars (a record), two Distinguished Service Crosses, and the Croix de Guerre. He won two Purple Hearts for wounds suffered in action and became the youngest Brigadier General in the Army. General Pershing admired MacArthur, although later their relationship became strained. MacArthur came out of the war with the best prospect for the future in the entire Army. He became superintendent of West Point, and in 1930 President Herbert Hoover appointed him Chief of Staff of the Army, the youngest man ever to hold this top job. Dwight D. Eisenhower became one of his aides.

When Roosevelt became President, MacArthur violently disagreed with his plans to cut back the Army as a means of dealing with the Depression. Roosevelt and MacArthur clashed personally. They were two titans, but Roosevelt had the final authority. Eventually, MacArthur could stand it no more and went back to the Philippines as military advisor to President Manuel Quezon.

In March 1941, with war clouds gathering, MacArthur was restored to the active list as a Major General (later Lieutenant General) and was appointed U.S. Army Commander in the Philippines. A very intelligent decision by Roosevelt. War began on December 7, 1941. MacArthur was the right man in the right place, not only for himself, but also for the United States. Despite his personal difficulties with MacArthur, Roosevelt appointed him because he felt MacArthur was the best man for the job—a tribute to Roosevelt.

The war did not start off too well for MacArthur. Even though Pearl Harbor had been bombed eight hours earlier and the news had reached the Philippines, MacArthur's air force was caught on the ground. One hundred aircraft were destroyed. In a flash, the air defense of the Philippines was gone, and hence, to a large extent the Philippines was gone.

The blame for this terrible occurrence could be shared by many; it was due mostly to the confusion of the moment. Everyone was rushing around; plans were being made; and at this point, Japanese bombers appeared overhead. The three top men in charge were General MacArthur, General Lewis Brereton, his air commander, and General Sutherland, MacArthur's Chief of Staff. There seems to have been some breakdown in communication between Sutherland and Brereton—many blame Sutherland. In any event, precious time was lost. Miraculously, MacArthur was not blamed for the disaster, even though he was commander-in-chief. Roosevelt was smart in overlooking this matter; he wanted to save MacArthur for the future, realizing MacArthur's distinguished ability.

Several days after the bombing, Japanese troops began landing at Lingayen Gulf on northwestern Luzon. General MacArthur wisely withdrew his troops into the Bataan Peninsula. Manila was occupied by the Japanese on January 2, 1942. The Americans still held Corregidor, the island fortress in Manila Bay from which MacArthur commanded his forces who were fighting heroically on Bataan.

On February 22, 1942, Roosevelt, through General Marshall, ordered MacArthur to leave the Philippines, turning over his command to General Jonathan Wainwright. MacArthur objected but was overruled. He left Corregidor on March in a PT boat with his family and a few aides. He was awarded the country's highest decoration, the Congressional Medal of Honor. It is the only time in history that both a father and a son have won this high honor. At that time, with defeat everywhere, America needed a hero. With Bataan holding out so gallantly, MacArthur was awarded this high honor. He went on to become a legend.

MacArthur arrived in Australia expecting to find a gathering force which he could lead back to attack the Philippines. Instead, he found virtually nothing at all. He was very disappointed; he would have to start from scratch. However, he did make a speech to the Filipino people—"I shall return." He was entirely sincere in this remark; he intended to return, come hell or high water. At the time, the Japanese were winning everywhere and things looked very bleak for the Allies. They needed someone to inspire them at this dark time, and MacArthur was just the right man to do it.

He began by turning back the Japanese attack at Port Moresby in New Guinea. This was the high water mark of the Japanese offensive in the southwest Pacific. After this defeat, they were on the defensive. MacArthur began to build up his forces with army, air force, and naval units. He was constantly badgering the War Department for more resources. He knew that the European Theatre was being given the first priority; this didn't stop him, and he eventually got what he needed.

As time went on and as his forces increased, MacArthur began his "leap frog" strategy in New Guinea and elsewhere—that is, landing past Japanese strongholds in less well defended locations. This succeeded in cutting off those strongholds and left them to wither on the vine. It also resulted in far fewer casualties for MacArthur troops. He was very proud of the relatively low casualties in this campaign, and rightly so.

MacArthur's destination was the Philippines. He loved the Philippines and the Filipino people. The thought of their suffering under the Japanese, as well as the defeat of America in the Philippines in 1942, was something he couldn't stand. It had to be made right. MacArthur detested losing, and he was not going to lose—it wasn't in his heritage.

At his conference with President Roosevelt in Hawaii on July 26, 1944, MacArthur persuaded Roosevelt to attack the Philippines instead of Formosa, favored by Nimitz and the Navy. The attack would be made on Leyte in the central Philippines. Earlier, Admiral Halsey had noticed in air attacks across the entire Philippines that the Japanese seemed particularly weak in the Leyte area and recommended it for the initial attack. This was approved by higher authorities as well as MacArthur. Leyte was to be attacked on October 20, 1944. Roosevelt and Churchill happened to be meeting at the time and quickly agreed to speeding up operations in the Philippines—a quick adjustment by the Allies.

In attacking Leyte, MacArthur was given full support by the Navy. This would be an all-out effort by both services, the Army and the Navy. Huge resources were now at MacArthur's command. He successfully invaded Leyte, and with the Navy's tremendous victory over the Japanese fleet at the Battle of Leyte Gulf, he went on to Luzon. Again, he was successful, and the large Japanese force under General Yamashita (the victor at Singapore) went into the hills.

Manila was finally captured on March 3, 1945, after a fierce struggle with Japanese die-hard marine units. Manila was practically destroyed needlessly in the fighting; thousands of Filipino civilians were killed, many shot or bayoneted by the Japanese. Remember, in 1941 when MacArthur retreated to Bataan, he left Manila an open city, which saved it from destruction. Not so the Japanese: the atrocities they committed were horrible. When MacArthur saw the destruction in Manila, he broke down and wept. Later, he would write in regard to the taking of Manila, "To others it may have seemed my moment of victory and monumental personal acclaim, but to me it seemed only the culmination of a panorama of physical and spiritual disaster."

With all his victories, there can be one valid question regarding MacArthur's tactics: that is, his non-use of the Australian army. He did use Australian units in New Guinea, but after that campaign he did not. There were five divisions of fine Australian troops that he could have used in the Philippines and other northwest attacks. Instead, after New Guinea, it was an all American operation. Why didn't MacArthur use Allied troops, as Eisenhower was doing so effectively in Europe?

There were possibly two reasons why MacArthur didn't use Australian troops. (1) MacArthur wanted direct control over his forces. With an all American effort, there was no one to consult or defer to other than Marshall and Roosevelt. With Australian troops came Australian generals and politicians. MacArthur wanted himself to be entirely in command. In particular, he didn't like General Blamey, the head of the Australian Army. (2) MacArthur felt he didn't need Australian forces. His own American forces were being greatly increased as time went on. In short, MacArthur thought he and the United States could do the job effectively on their own. Of course, he was successful, as the record bears out. Still, it can be said if the splendid Australian troops had been employed in the Philippines, American casualties would have been fewer, and victory achieved possibly more quickly.

In any event, General MacArthur achieved brilliant success during World War II. Churchill called him the best military man of the war. With the occupation of the Philippines and Okinawa, the Americans began their buildup for the invasion of Japan itself, and the culmination of the entire Pacific war.

The man that President Truman and General Marshall chose to head the land invasion was General Douglas MacArthur. No one else was even considered. MacArthur was one of the giants in American efforts in World War II. He is in the same league as Roosevelt, Marshall, Eisenhower, and Nimitz. He accomplished everything he set out to do, sometimes with very limited resources. He represented the entire Allied world in accepting the Japanese surrender on board the USS Missouri in Tokyo Bay. It was certainly appropriate that he do so.

MacArthur was a very controversial man, mostly because of his personality. He was imperious, overly dramatic, and flamboyant, and he seemed to thrive on publicity. At times, he was arrogant, even with his superiors. He was one of a kind.

Iwo Jima
The Last Steps to Japan

November 28, 1944, was an important day in the war; it was the first day of B-29 attacks from the Marianas on the Japanese homeland—attacks that were to end eight months later in the almost total destruction of Tokyo and other major Japanese cities. It was the beginning of the end for Japan. Sadly and tragically for Japan, the only light at the end of the tunnel was the terrific glare from the atomic bombs dropped upon Hiroshima and Nagasaki.

Personally, the author wishes there had been some other way than this to end the war and is only grateful that he did not have to make this decision.

The Marianas were 1,300 miles from Japan, a round trip of over 2,500 miles, just about the ultimate range of the B-29. Too close for comfort. Situated on a direct line half-way between the Marianas and Japan was the small volcanic island of Iwo Jima. It would be a perfect emergency landing ground for B-29s about to run out of fuel or damaged in the air strikes. For this reason, and also to use it as a fighter base to accompany the bombers on their raids, it was determined that Iwo Jima must be taken.

Iwo Jima was an island about eight miles square with no vegetation and beaches were covered with soft volcanic ash. At the southern end of the island was Mount Suribachi (500 feet), a rocky extinct volcano, soon to become a place never to be forgotten in American and Marine Corps history. The Americans knew that Iwo would be heavily defended, but they did not know the extreme lengths the Japanese had gone to fortify and defend the island. Over twenty-three thousand men under Lieutenant General Kuribayashi were dug in the underground bunkers and maze of trenches.

After several days of intense shelling by battleships and air attacks, the Americans of three Marine divisions began landing on February 19, 1945. It was as savage a battle as Tarawa, perhaps worse. The Japanese had zeroed in on every yard with inter-lacing lines of fire. Even American tanks were being destroyed by the dozens. Iwo turned out to be the toughest battle in Marine Corps history.

On February 23, Mount Suribachi was taken despite intense fire that caused heavy casualties. Associated Press photographer Joe Rosenthal made an unforgettable photograph as the Marines planted the American flag at the summit. A monument to the moment now stands in Washington, D.C. to commemorate this inspiring event. The battle for Iwo Jima continued for several horrible weeks, ending in the complete defeat and destruction of the Japanese. Of their 23,000 defenders, only two hundred survived as prisoners.

The Americans also sustained very heavy casualties, a total of almost 20,000 men, of which over 5,000 were killed. It was an American victory, but at a tremendous cost in human lives. If the Japanese were to fight like this on a much larger scale when their main islands were eventually attacked, the combined casualties for both sides would be in the millions, a prediction the Americans took into account before using the atomic bombs.

The capture of Iwo did prove very useful to the American Air Force, as hundreds of B-29s made emergency landings there, saving thousands of lives.

Its capture proved to be worth the awful casualties, but surely the Marines and their families would never forget the terrible battle of Iwo Jima and its price.

Okinawa
Final Stepping Stone to Japan

The final objective for the Allies in the war against Japan was Japan itself. No one wanted to have to invade the Japanese main islands, but if it had to be done, it had to be done. The whole goal of the American military from Midway on was the advance against the home islands of Japan. Many hard battles had been fought in the advance across the Pacific, but now the final goal was in sight.

There was one obstacle—and also opportunity—left: Okinawa. This island was a member of the Ryuku chain of islands about three hundred sixty miles south of the main islands. It was considered by the Japanese to be an integral part of Japan and indispensable to its defense. To reach the main islands, it was necessary for the Americans to conquer Okinawa. Once occupied, it could serve as the springboard base for the attack on the home islands. Thus, both the eyes of the Japanese high officials and those of their counterparts on the American side were fixed on Okinawa. For America, if they won Okinawa, it might not be necessary to undertake the very costly invasion of the main islands. Their occupation of Okinawa would signal to the Japanese that they were beaten and things could only get worse.

Moreover, Okinawa, occupied by the Americans, would effectively cut off virtually all supplies coming in to Japan. Oil, coal, iron, food, all the essentials would be stopped. Not only could the American base at Okinawa stop nearly all war materiel coming from the south, but also its naval and air attacks would stop traffic coming in from China, Manchuria, and Korea.

Japan, an island country with very limited natural resources, was dependent on imports for its life. The American bases in the Philippines were already slowing down the flow of materiel, and now with the Okinawa base, it would virtually shut down all materiel coming into Japan. Of course, American submarines were working the entire route and wreaking havoc on Japanese shipping. Thus, the battle for Okinawa was a matter of life or death for Japan. They had over 100,000 troops stationed there, ready to face the American assault. Moreover, Japan intended to use masses of Kamikaze in an all-out effort to destroy the American fleet.

Realistically, the Japanese should have earlier brought home, as best they could, all their troops from other areas—China, Burma and the South

Pacific. They should have had over 200,000 troops on Okinawa, rather than 100,000, to have any chance of winning this decisive battle. With this larger force, they could have made a strong effort to drive the Americans into the sea. The war was not going to be won or lost in China or Burma—it could be lost at Okinawa on their doorstep. The Japanese leaders were unwilling to give up their far outposts in order to try to save their own home islands. They could not face up to the stark realities of their situation. Pretty stupid. This was a big help to the Americans.

On April 1, 1945, after ten days of intense naval and air attacks, they landed on the west coast of Okinawa. It was the largest amphibious landing of the war after Normandy. Three Marine and four Army divisions were involved. Surprisingly, the invaders were met by only a minimum of resistance. The Japanese were going to make their stand on the north and south ends of the island, particularly on the south. Marine units pushed north and, after some hard fighting, were able to overcome Japanese resistance in that area. However, the Army units moving south began to encounter strong entrenched resistance and faced slow-going. The Japanese were fighting as fanatically as ever. Marine units joined the Army divisions in the southern fight. The campaign slowed down to a war of attrition—the type of battle the Japanese could not win.

In the meanwhile, at sea, hundreds of Japanese Kamikaze pilots hurtled their planes at American ships in suicidal dives, inflicting serious damage to scores of ships in the huge American fleet. But, the fleet was so large that it could take these hits and keep going. Almost five thousand American seamen were killed in these attacks. However, the result of this Japanese effort was that the Kamikaze unit of pilots was shattered.

At this point, the mighty Japanese battleship Yamato, the world's largest battleship, put out to sea to attack the American fleet, escorted by a small fleet consisting of one cruiser and eight destroyers. It, too, was on a suicidal mission; there was only enough fuel for a one-way trip. Alerted to the approaching Yamato, Admiral Spruance dispatched hundreds of planes to attack. Three hundred planes attacked the Yamato from all directions. After innumerable hits from bombs and torpedoes, the mighty Yamato rolled over and disappeared. Of her crew of 2,767 men, 2,488 were lost. Most of her escort was also sunk. They had accomplished absolutely nothing except to end the Japanese Navy as any kind of force in the war.

The ground campaign forged on day after day with heavy casualties on both sides, mostly Japanese. Towards the end of the battle, the American commander, General Simon Buckner, was killed by an artillery shellburst. Four days later, the Japanese commander, Lieutenant General Mitsuru Ushijima committed suicide. Many other Japanese, seeing the end approaching, also killed themselves.

After eighty-two days of bitter fighting, the battle was finally over. More than 100,000 Japanese had been killed. Surprisingly, over 7,000 were taken prisoner. The American casualties on land and sea numbered 12,000 killed and over 30,000 wounded. But Okinawa was now in American hands. In effect, the war was over: Japan could not win. It was a matter of when and how she would lose.

Roosevelt's strategy of attacking from the south with MacArthur and across the central Pacific with Nimitz had succeeded brilliantly. The one-two punch had overwhelmed the spread out Japanese defense at every point and kept them confused as to where the Americans would strike next. It had also distracted the Japanese from their most vital task—the defense of the area around Japan itself. The Japanese were fighting everywhere and then the Americans were right in front of them. It must have been a shock.

It is possible to speculate that Japan could now be defeated without having to invade the main home islands or to use atomic bombs. With continued heavy air attacks from B-29s and naval carriers, the whole of Japan could be flattened. American battleships could bombard with 16 inch shells the port cities such as Yokohama. Cut off from oil, coal and food, the entire Japanese population would be in a state of starvation and exposure. It would seem under these circumstances that at some point, the Japanese would have to surrender. Who knows what would have happened or how long it would take? In the end, the Americans did not have to invade the home islands, and the war was brought to a quick conclusion, thereby saving the lives of millions of people.

Five Americans

It should be noted that five future American presidents served in the Pacific War—all in the Navy. They were John F. Kennedy, Richard M. Nixon, Gerald R. Ford, Lyndon B. Johnson, and George H. Bush. Two of these men particularly distinguished themselves: John Kennedy and George Bush. John Kennedy's story is well chronicled. He was the young commander of a small torpedo boat, PT-109, which was rammed and sunk by a Japanese destroyer. By his cool and courageous actions, young Kennedy helped in saving his crew. Later, he would become a Congressman, a Senator, and in 1960 was elected the first Catholic President of the United States. (Contrary to the opinion of some, the Pope did not take off from Rome and rush to take over the United States.)

Less well known is George Bush's adventures as the youngest commissioned naval airman in the Navy—he was given his wings just short of his nineteenth birthday. On September 2, 1944, Bush's plane, piloted by Bush with a crew of three, was making a bombing attack on the island of Chichi Jima in the Bonin Islands. The plane was hit and caught fire, filling the cockpit with smoke. Bush told the two crewmen behind him to bail out and headed the crippled and burning plane out to sea. He definitely did not want to be captured by the Japanese, who were known for their brutal treatment of prisoners.

As flames from the wings approached the cockpit, Bush bailed out, hitting his head on the tail as he dove from the plane. He was cut but not seriously wounded. By very good fortune, his life raft had somehow fallen along with Bush into the Pacific. Making his way to the life raft, Bush began paddling furiously as best he could away from the island. He had heard that on this island the Japanese had reached the point of cannibalism. A Japanese patrol boat was sent out to pick up Bush, but his fellow pilots circled overhead and attacked, turning the boat back.

Bush was, in the meanwhile, trying to locate his two crewmen, but could find no sign of them, which caused him great distress. The planes overhead had called for help to rescue Bush. Several hours later, much to his relief, the American submarine Finback broke the surface nearby and pulled him in. Ensign Bill Edwards of the Finback filmed Bush being pulled from the water and his first, understandably shaky, steps on the submarine's deck. He was a tall, very young American naval pilot who, along with thousands of others, was risking his life in the service of his country.

Bush was entitled to be rotated home, but insisted on being sent back to his carrier, the USS San Jacinto. Altogether, he flew 58 combat missions and received the Distinguished Flying Cross. America is indebted to George Bush and the many other young Americans who, likewise, performed their duty with valor, serving their country very well at a critical time in its history. George Bush went on to become a Congressman from Texas and a Vice President of the United States, and in 1988 was elected President of the United States. Both Kennedy and Bush faced dangerous and disastrous circumstances with coolness and courage—perhaps those qualities brought them to the highest office in the land.

7

War in Europe—The Beginning of the End

Roosevelt and Hitler

The Atomic Bomb

It is ironic that if Hitler had been a normal person, Germany would probably have been the first country to develop the atomic bomb. By his racial prejudice against the Jews and other minorities, Hitler lost the race for the atomic bomb. He lost the services of Einstein, Szilard, Fermi, Frisch, Peerils, Wigner, and Teller, among others. He not only lost their services for his cause, but he also drove them to the Allied side. Each of these men played a critical part in the development of the atomic bomb. To cite one of these, consider that Leo Szilard was the first to propose the idea of a nuclear chain reaction, which was crucial to the development of the atomic bomb.

In 1939, these men were very concerned that Germany would gain the lead in developing the bomb. German scientists such as Otto Hahn and Fritz Strassman had already been working on the research for a number of years. In addition, occupied Czechoslovakia had large uranium deposits. In August, 1939, Szilard, Wigner, and Teller went to see Albert Einstein and persuaded him to write a letter to President Roosevelt to warn him of the danger. This precipitated the American program to build the bomb.

The effort started very slowly. America at that time was not in the war, and the need did not seem urgent. In Russia, Igar Kurachitov also alerted his government that an atomic bomb must be made. This was achieved some years later with the help of intense espionage of the United States program.

As war approached, the United States' interest in the atomic bomb intensified. Roosevelt was particularly concerned about what might happen if Hitler got it first. During 1941, American scientists visited Britain and were impressed by the work of Frisch and Peerils. These American scientists included

Arthur Compton, Ernest Lawrence, and Vannevear Bush. They recommended to Roosevelt that the Americans and the British work together in a crash program to build the atomic bomb.

Roosevelt approved and appointed General Leslie Groves to head the mammoth project. Groves appointed Robert Oppenheimer to head the scientific project, the actual building of the bomb. Robert Oppenheimer assembled a brilliant team of scientists, including the refugees from Europe and British scientists, who worked at a remote camp in New Mexico called Los Alamos. Many of the scientists working diligently on this project hoped that the final result would be that an atomic bomb could not be built. They were afraid of the consequences if it did work. A sort of a positive-negative outlook. Not only many brilliant scientists, but also billions of dollars were devoted to this project. It is amazing that with all this, the project was kept a secret until the bomb was actually used in 1945.

Meanwhile, in Germany, contrary to the fears of the American atomic team, work was progressing very slowly on the development of the bomb. For one thing, Hitler did not seem to have a lot of interest in it. Perhaps his brain could not absorb all the scientific details of the project. Perhaps he was too busy running every aspect of the actual war. It is possible that he thought the development of the atomic bomb would take such a long time that the war would be over by the time it could be achieved. Remember, in 1941 and 1942 the Germans were winning. One of Germany's leading physicists, Werner Heisenberg, was pessimistic that a bomb could be built at all. However, he and his team did begin work on it. His project received a serious setback when a heavy water plant at Vemork, Norway, was sabotaged by Norwegian patriots. Also, the Germans overestimated the resources that would be needed to build the bomb. With Hitler showing little interest in the project, it began to falter. Finally, the resources committed to it were diverted to other things such as the V1 and V2 rockets.

Where Roosevelt had seen the potential of the atomic bomb, Hitler had not. On this everything hinged. Whoever invented the atomic bomb first and could produce it in sufficient numbers would win the war. If Germany had it first, about ten bombs would have crushed and demoralized the entire Allied army on the Western Front in 1944. One or two atomic bombs dropped on London in 1944 would have created havoc. The war may have and probably would have had a different outcome.

Thankfully, Hitler did not develop the bomb. Roosevelt did. Two bombs were used on Japan in August, 1945, terrifying not only the Japanese but also the whole world. Japan, beset from all sides, surrendered a few days later.

Japan had already lost the war, but the atomic bombs undoubtedly hastened their surrender.

Hitler again had made a crucial mistake. On the other hand, Roosevelt had put all the scientific power and resources of the United States behind the project. Roosevelt's first concern was to beat the Germans in developing the bomb. He had no idea where they were at any time in their program. He had to assume that with their typical efficiency, Germany was working hard on this crucial project In any event, Roosevelt did a tremendous job in handling this very important project. He recognized the situation, turned it over to the best brains available, and gave them all the resources they needed. Roosevelt was doing a lot of things, and doing all of them right.

The (Decision) to Use the Atomic Bomb

The author is only grateful that he was not asked to play any part in making the decision to use the atomic bomb. Everything connected with this decision was bad; there were no "pros" and "cons," only horrible results. It was a dilemma without precedent in world history. The word *decision* is in parentheses because in effect, there was no precise time that a decision was made whether or not the bomb would be used. In building the bomb, a momentum had been created that led to the inevitable use of it—why build it if not to use it? The immediate question did not appear to be whether to use the bomb, but rather where to use it. The only top American leader who questioned using the bomb was Eisenhower.

Certainly, the question had been raised, particularly by the scientists working on the bomb, of how it would be used. It was proposed to first advise the Japanese that we had the bomb, and then use it on a remote area as a demonstration of its effectiveness. This idea was rejected because of the uncertainty that the bomb would actually work as planned. If it failed, it would make America look foolish and damage its credibility. Also, it was possible that even if it worked in a remote area, the Japanese would not be suitably impressed—they could suppress the news of the bomb so as not to alarm the public.

It was decided by all involved at the highest levels that the only way to fully demonstrate the power of the bomb was to use it on Japanese cities without any warning. If it failed, no one would know the difference. The rationale for using the atomic bomb was simple: It would bring a quick end to the war.

Faced with the invasion of the main islands of Japan, the leaders of the United States had to look back on the earlier battles involving the Japanese:

Tarawa and, most recently, Iwo Jima, where the Japanese had fought to the last man and inflicted severe casualties on the American troops. With over two million Japanese soldiers defending the home islands, American casualties would be staggering. Some suggested between 500,000 and a million.

The battle for Japan would become a battle of annihilation—with the Japanese civilians caught in the middle. Japanese casualties, military and civilian, would be enormous—in the millions—and the country would be virtually destroyed. It is true that the American casualties were foremost in the minds of the American leaders, but certainly they understood the whole picture.

So it came down to dropping several atomic bombs, thus killing several hundred thousand people, which would end the war quickly; or, invading the home islands which would result in millions of casualties over a drawn-out period of time. Both choices were terrible; it was down to which one was the least terrible.

(If President Truman had decided not to use the atomic bombs and proceeded on an invasion of Japan that resulted in 500,000 casualties, what would have happened in the United States? That is, if after the invasion news leaked out that we could have bombed two Japanese cities and ended the war with no invasion and no American casualties.

My speculation is that there would probably have been the greatest outcry of indignation and controversy in American history that these 500,000 casualties could have been prevented.)

In looking at these facts, the American leaders proceeded on the premise that using the bombs would end the war quickly and save lives in the long run. Thus, the bombs were used on Hiroshima and Nagasaki, and the traumatic effect on the Japanese did bring an end to the war in a very short time. There is no doubt that not having to invade the home islands of Japan and fight a terrible yard-by-yard land battle did prevent an immense number of American and Japanese casualties. This is not an attempt to minimize the awful suffering of the people of Hiroshima and Nagasaki, only to put it in some horrible context. Horrible circumstances in an altogether horrible war that was not necessary in the first place.

The Yalta Conference

On February 4, 1945, Roosevelt and Churchill met Stalin at Yalta in the Crimea. The war with Germany was entering its last phase, and all three men were looking to the future. At this time, the relationship among all three was good. All had worked together to first stop Hitler and now to crush him. Good feelings abounded. All three knew that without the others, they would not have arrived at this stage. They hoped, at least Roosevelt and Churchill did, that the bonds forged in war would continue into the future. It must be said that Churchill was already beginning to have doubts. Stalin, of course, has his own agenda—as time would tell.

The three main topics at the conference were Poland, the war with Japan, and the founding of the United Nations organization. To all effects, the Polish question had already been decided. The Red Army occupied Poland and was pushing westward. Nothing could change this fact; to get the Soviets out of Poland would require military action by Churchill and Roosevelt, and this was out of the question. The western border of Poland was open for discussion. To make up for land in the east lost to Russia, Poland's western boundary was moved west to take in the eastern region of Germany. This, too, was mostly already decided by the Soviets and the Red Army.

Next, the question of the government of Poland was discussed. Stalin had installed his own Communist Polish government in Warsaw—the so-called Lublin Poles. Churchill and Roosevelt tried to get Stalin to enlarge this government with leaders from the exiled Polish government in London. They felt an obligation to this group which had furnished thousands of soldiers to the Allied armies in the west and Italy. They had fought bravely and well. Stalin virtually cut off all discussion about the makeup of the Polish government. However, he did agree that popular elections could be held after the war to establish a democratic government. This was the best that Churchill and Roosevelt could do—and it was a great deal if, indeed, Stalin had carried out his promise, which he did not.

As for the later charge that Churchill and Roosevelt had sold out Poland, this was untrue. No one in Britain and the United States wanted World War III over Poland. The only way to get Russia out of Poland was with military force, and Churchill and Roosevelt had no intention to do that—it was unthinkable. As Roosevelt told Admiral William Leahy, "Bill, I did everything I could."

In regard to Japan, Stalin informed Roosevelt that a few months after the end of the German war, Russia would enter the war against Japan. This was good news for Roosevelt; Japan was fighting fiercely, and the more pressure exerted on them, the better. Of course, Stalin expected to gain from his participation, and he did. Russia's entering the war did have a psychological effect on the Japanese and influenced their ending the war in August, 1945. It was one more very bad thing that was happening against Japan at this time. The roof had fallen in on Japan.

The United Nations framework was effectively established at Yalta. The fact that the United States was a founding member meant that the United Nations would be a positive factor in the future of world peace. It could not solve all the problems, but it was still a very worthwhile organization. It would be headquartered in New York City.

An additional topic at Yalta was the Russians' request that the Allied Air Force attack large cities in eastern Germany that were railroad and transportation hubs supplying the German forces on the Eastern Front. This was already on R.A.F. Commander "Bomber" Harris's agenda. One of these cities was Dresden, which was heavily attacked on February 13 by the R.A.F. and the American Air Force. The results were similar to what had happened in Hamburg in July, 1943—that is, the city was virtually destroyed and thousands of people were killed. As a result of the controversy over the attack, Churchill ordered a cessation of this type of raid a few weeks later.

As the Yalta Conference broke up, Churchill, Roosevelt, and Stalin could feel good overall about their accomplishments, not only at the conference but also over the last three and one-half years. They had worked well together and had come a long way from the dark days of 1941 and 1942. Their main objective had been the defeat of Hitler, and they had done it. Unfortunately, after the conclusion of the war, Stalin reverted to his old ways—that is his and Lenin's dream that Communism should rule the world. Thus, the beginning of the Cold War. One thing about the Cold War is that it is much better than a hot war, which really no one wanted, particularly now that atomic weapons were on the scene.

Communism eventually failed in Eastern Europe and in the Soviet Union. Its inherent defects were: the lack of incentive to work and a failed agricultural system. Without enough food nothing else matters. The Communist system could not compete with the free enterprise system.

The containment policy of the United States plus Communism's own basic defects caused it to implode internally. The people of the Soviet Union and Eastern Europe turned away from the oppressive Stalinist style of government. In the end, Hitler and Stalin, both tyrants, had failed—primarily because of their own viciousness and lack of humanity.

Industrial Production
USA Arsenal of Production

In organizing the USA for war, Roosevelt did a phenomenal job, particularly in organizing its industry. The Great Depression, had struck American industry a crippling blow. Demand for products was at a low ebb.

However, the large corporations were barely able to stay in business, companies such as Ford, General Motors, Boeing, Douglass, U.S. Steel, and Firestone. In 1941, when the United States began to gear up for war, these and other companies were ready. They were working at under capacity, but their framework was intact; their production potential was enormous. The automotive and aircraft facilities were particularly set up to produce on a massive scale.

After Pearl Harbor, these companies turned away from civilian production and put all their resources into the war effort. Roosevelt and his advisers let them know what they wanted, and these companies, in an all-out effort, turned it out. Mass production lines turned out huge quantities of war materiel. Since many Americans were unemployed, there was a large labor pool to draw from, including millions of women. American war products began to show up all over the world, even in remote China, flying in over the Himalayan Mountains, the Hump, as the flyers called it. On these very dangerous missions, many planes took off and were never heard from again.

During the war, the U.S. produced 296,000 planes, 87,000 tanks, 2,400,000 trucks, 17,400,000 rifles, and 315,000 pieces of field artillery. In 1944 alone, the U.S. produced 96,000 planes—more than the combined production of Germany, Great Britain, and Russia. Supplies to Great Britain and Russia were critical to keeping these countries in the war. Even Nikita Kruschev said the Russian advance westward would have been impossible without American trucks.

Great Britain and the Soviet Union also did a remarkable job in war production, particularly Russia, with so much of its industrial heartland overrun by the German attack. Miraculously, Stalin moved his production further east to the Ural Mountains, out of reach of the Germans. The Germans had no idea that the Soviets were capable of doing this—that is why they continually felt that Russia would run out of materials and were on their last leg.

All three of the Allies not only fought very well in the field, but also organized their industries in an outstanding way. The United States' vast production tipped the scales in favor of the Allies. Japan was never able to get its war materiel produced on a mass scale. Evidently, they thought that their sensational early victories would make it a short war. In fact, compared to the United States, Japanese war production was pitiful—one main reason they lost.

Meanwhile, in Germany, war production in the first years of the war was not impressive. The Germans had not geared up their industry for mass production of weapons; indeed, some civilian goods were still being produced. Unfortunately, in February, 1942, Albert Speer was appointed by Hitler to head German war production. Speer was Hitler's personal architect; he also staged very effective mass gatherings, such as the Nuremberg Rally. Albert Speer turned out to be an industrial genius. With increased Allied bombing, Germany incredibly doubled, then tripled its war production, admittedly from a low starting base. One can only wonder what Speer would have achieved if there had been no Allied bombing to contend with.

Next to Hitler, Speer was the most dangerous man for the allies to consider in Germany. Certainly, the war would have ended sooner without Speer in control of German production. Hundreds of thousands of casualties, including German, occurred because Speer prolonged the war. It is possible that some would say this statement is unfair to Speer, but it is a fact. It should be remembered that Speer was an avowed Nazi and supported Hitler until the final days of the war, when it was evident that Germany had lost. To show Speer's ability, for instance, in 1944, Germany turned out almost 40,000 planes—an incredible amount, considering the Allied bombing as well as shortages of materials and labor. Speer had made himself, in effect, the second most powerful man in Germany—almost indispensable.

German production was being consumed as soon as it came off the production line. Eisenhower ordered the Allied Air Forces to attack and cripple the Deutsche-Reichbahn, the German rail system. By January of 1945, rail traffic was down to 25 percent of normal capacity. Fighting on four fronts—the Western Front, Italy, the Eastern Front, and the air war—was more than even Speer could cope with. Moreover, they were running out of trained men to use the equipment. The shortage of oil was a major problem for the Germans. No matter how many planes and tanks were produced, without oil and the rail system, they were useless. The Allied bombing, plus the fact that the Russians overran the Romanian oil fields, drastically reduced Germany's oil supply. In addition to the crippling and virtual destruction of the rail and oil system, Germany was being crushed from every direction. Hitler's dreams were being turned into Germany's ashes.

It is possible that Albert Speer may not have been an actual war criminal, but he certainly helped Hitler to continue the war longer than necessary. His efficiency in a terrible cause was bad for everyone concerned, including Germany. Speer was fortunate that he was not executed after the war trials at Nuremberg. He received a long prison sentence of 20 years, which he served in full. After coming out of prison, Speer wrote a book titled *Inside the Third Reich*, in which he tried to exonerate himself of Hitler's monstrous crimes. Speer may not have committed these crimes, but he was undoubtedly an accomplice.

In the end, the overwhelming might of the Allies was too much for one country. Germany should never have started a war it had virtually no chance to win, particularly with Hitler in command, trying to fight the world. As Ludendorff said at the end of the First War, "After all, we cannot expect to fight the whole world and win." It was happening again to Germany under Hitler, who had learned nothing from this previous experience. The results would be the same, only this time, most of Germany was destroyed.

Hitler and the Death Camps
The Final Solution

Adolph Hitler to the Reichstag, January 30, 1939:

> "If the international Jewish financiers. . . should again succeed in plunging   the nations into a world war, the results will be. . . the annihilation of the Jewish race throughout Europe."

As the Allies rushed into Germany and Poland, they were astonished to find a number of concentration camps—rather, extermination camps. They were also shocked by the magnitude and horrendous cruelty of these operations.

It is with difficulty that the author brings up the subject of "The Final Solution." It is hard to believe that mankind would act in such a barbarous fashion. Over the course of history, murder has been committed time and again, but never on such a large and thoroughly organized scale. A total of six million Jews were exterminated in the period of World War II. The Jewish population of three million in Poland was almost completely wiped out—men, women, and children.

How did Hitler become so obsessed with his hatred of the Jews? No one really knows; who knows what went on in his twisted and evil brain? Perhaps his parents were anti-Semitic; perhaps during his impoverished youth some incident occurred that turned him against the Jews. We know that at the end of the First War, Hitler was enraged at the German surrender; he refused to accept defeat. He believed some treachery was the cause of Germany's loss. He looked for scapegoats to blame and fixed on the Jews. After a while, he came to believe and become inflamed by his own propaganda. His hatred seemed to build and feed on itself.

At some point, the idea of eliminating the entire Jewish population of Europe evidently occurred to him. The Germans were a master race; everyone else was inferior, and in particular the Jews, according to Hitler. What is so tragic about this is that not only Hitler, but also thousands of Germans participated willingly in this organized mass murder of millions of innocent people. How could they do it? The only explanation the author can think of is that the people who perpetrated this atrocity were so obsessed with hatred themselves that they were crazy—no rational human being could commit these barbarous acts. Another explanation is just that there are bad and evil people in this world.

The idea of killing all the Jews was termed *The Final Solution*. Hitler turned it over to the SS, particularly Goering, Himmler, and Reinhard Heydrich.

During the early part of the war, Heinrich Himmler assembled a special command called the Einsatz groups. At the start of the war, their job was to follow the army into Poland and isolate the Jews into ghettos. At the beginning of the Russian campaign, their assignment was changed to start the first phase of the "final solution"—that is, the extermination of the Jews. Following the war and at the war criminal trials, the following exchange took place between Russian Judge Nikitchenko and Einsatz Leader Ohlendorf:

The Judge: For what reason were the children massacred?
Ohlendorf: The order was that the Jewish population should be totally exterminated.
The Judge: Including the children?
Ohlendorf: Yes.
The Judge: Were all the Jewish children murdered?
Ohlendorf: Yes.

In response to further questioning, Ohlendorf described how a typical killing took place.

'The Einsatz unit would enter a village or town and order the prominent Jewish citizens to call together all Jews for the purpose of "resettlement." They were requested to hand over their valuables and shortly before execution to surrender their outer clothing. They were transported to the place of execution, usually an anti-tank ditch, in trucks—always only as many as could be executed immediately. In this way, it was attempted to keep the span of time from the moment in which the victims knew what was about to happen to them until the time of their actual executions as short as possible.

'Then they were shot, kneeling or standing, by firing squads in a military manner and the corpses thrown into the ditch. I never permitted the shooting by individual, but ordered that several of the men should shoot at the same time in order to avoid direct personal responsibility.'

After witnessing several of those executions, Himmler himself became physically ill. Later, in the spring of 1942, an order came from Himmler to change the method of execution to "gas vans." (It is distressingly remarkable how German companies aggressively competed to build these and other larger "factories of death.") Ohlendorf said his Einsatz Group accounted for over 90,000 victims. Another Einsatz Group in the north accounted for 229,052 victims. Its commander, Franz Stahlecker, apologized to Himmler that the number would have been greater except for the heavy frosts which made executions more difficult.

It is reported that over 600,000 Russian Jews were massacred by the Einsatz Groups in Russia. Bad as it was, this was only the prelude to the mass executions that were to be carried out in Himmler's concentration camps on a huge scale.

In January, 1942, Heydrich convened a meeting of various representatives of the SS and outlined the plan. Himmler was also involved in discussions with his subordinates in this regard. Thirty concentration camps were constructed. The largest was Auschwitz; others included Dachau, Buechenwald, Triblinka, Relsec, Sibibor, and Chelmno. Many of these were in Poland. Gas chambers were the principal means of execution. The prisoners were led to believe that they were going to be given a shower; they had no idea what was to befall them. When they did, it was too late. At Auschwitz, in a macabre scene, an orchestra of young female inmates played Viennese waltzes in order to lull the unsuspecting victims. The Germans, with their customary efficiency, managed to perform the ghastly work in a highly organized manner and on a vast scale.

The outside world knew that something bad was happening but had no idea of the monstrous scale and technique involved. Even if Churchill and Roosevelt knew of it, there was scarcely anything they could do about it except win the war as quickly as possible, which they did. As the war moved into Germany and Poland, the Allied armies began capturing the death camps. They were shocked beyond belief at what they found. The majority of the German people probably did not know of the vast scale involved in this operation. However, one wonders what they thought when their Jewish neighbors suddenly were all disappearing, never to be heard from again. The shame of this incredible crime does belong to Germany, as it was Germans who carried it out.

The only positive thing to come out of this, if you can call it that, is that nearly all of the murderers paid for their crimes: Hitler, Goering, Himmler, Heydrich, and many more. It is scant consolation to the murdered victims of their horrible atrocities. For centuries to come, when the name Hitler is mentioned, it will forever be related to the holocaust of six million innocent people.

Roosevelt
Warm Springs, Georgia

As the war was nearing its end, President Roosevelt was very tired. He had a cottage at Warm Springs, Georgia, where he went in early April, 1945, to get some rest. Many people had noted on his return from Yalta that he looked especially frail and wan; it seemed the spark had gone out of him. Around noon on April 12, he was sitting for a portrait and took a break to pursue his stamp collection. Suddenly, he grabbed his head and said, "I've a terrible headache." These were his last words. He was pronounced dead a short time later of a stroke. Franklin D. Roosevelt was a casualty of the war, the same as if he had been killed on a battlefield.

Word spread quickly of his death, and Americans just couldn't believe it. The man who seemingly had been with each one of them for over twelve years as President was gone. The American public must have thought that Roosevelt had been President for so long that he would continue there forever.

Although he had many enemies, he had a much larger number of friends and supporters. He had been elected president a record four times. As his funeral train made its way northward hundreds of miles to Washington, almost the entire route was lined with Americans, the average people whom he had helped, paying homage to a great friend and leader. He was buried at his home in Hyde Park, New York.

Before the war began in December 7, 1941, President Roosevelt had brought the country intact through the worst depression in history. In war, he united and mobilized it in a tremendous effort to defeat Germany and Japan. It is incredible that one man could accomplish so much. He was a great peacetime leader and a great wartime leader. At the end of the war, the United States was the greatest power in the world. Roosevelt deserves to be remembered on the same level as two other great American presidents: George Washington and Abraham Lincoln.

Harry S. Truman

On April 12, 1945, almost at the conclusion of the war with Germany, Franklin D. Roosevelt died of a stroke. All Americans were shocked, even those who were opposed politically to Roosevelt. Everyone in America knew that Roosevelt was a great leader and was doing an excellent job of directing the war. Hitler and Goebbels were jubilant; they thought this might change the American effort that was helping to crush Germany. They were grasping at any straw at this time. After the first shock wore off, the American people thought, "What next?" And then they remembered that the Vice President automatically took over as President.

It is a fact that some Americans didn't even know who the Vice President was. The first reaction of the ones that did know may have been to clutch their heads. Harry S. Truman was now President of the United States. In a comparison of Roosevelt and Truman, there was a huge difference in the minds of the people. Actually, the public knew very little about Harry Truman besides, maybe, his picture. At first thought, he seemed to be nowhere in the same league with Franklin D. Roosevelt. Actually, Roosevelt had been president for so long and was such a commanding figure, that no one paid much attention to who was vice president during all of his terms in office.

Now, unbelievably, one of them was President Harry S. Truman. There was a sinking feeling among the American people, even those who didn't like Roosevelt. What was known of Truman was not exactly favorable. He gave the impression of a nondescript senator who seemed just sort of ordinary. That he should take the great Roosevelt's place seemed unthinkable—but there it was. Truman was now in the Oval Office. Roosevelt was gone.

Harry S. Truman was born in Lamar, Missouri, in 1884 to poor parents in a semi-rural area. His family soon moved to Independence, Missouri, just east of Kansas City. (Abilene, Kansas, the home of Dwight D. Eisenhower, was not far away.) Harry had poor eyesight as a child and had to wear glasses. This prevented him from playing ordinary games and sports with the other children. As a result, Harry spent much time by himself. He began going to the library and developed a particular interest in history books. He became a well read young person. His father had a difficult time making ends meet, and Harry spent a great deal of time working on the farm. Later, when asked if he thought his father was a failure, Truman said, "Any man whose son becomes President of the United States is never a failure."

World War I was something of a welcome relief for Harry. He became a captain in the Artillery, went to France, and participated actively in some of the big American offensives there. According to all, he did an excellent job and won the respect of his men. Upon returning home, he and a partner opened a men's haberdashery store in Kansas City. The store failed, and Truman worked diligently over the years, finally paying off all debts connected with the store. Harry married his childhood sweetheart, Bess Wallace, on June 28, 1919. It is interesting that Truman's mother-in-law made it plain that she never thought Truman was good enough for her daughter, even after he became President of the United States. That's how it went for Truman—he was always underestimated.

Kansas City was run at that time by the political machine of Tom Pendergast. About this time, Pendergast was searching for someone to be the county judge, and Truman was recommended, mainly because of his war record. With Pendergast's help, Truman was elected and applied himself vigorously to the task of improving conditions in his area. Truman said that at no time in his career did Pendergast ask him for any favors at all. As County Judge, Truman won a reputation for honesty and efficiency.

In 1936, there was an opening for the United States Senator, and Truman ran for that high office. He was elected with Pendergast's strong support. As he began his duties in Washington, Truman found that he did not receive much attention or respect from his fellow senators. They regarded him as "Pendergast's man." However, with his diligent work and friendly personality, over the years Truman became a valued and respected member of the Senate. He was re-elected in 1940.

Truman had almost no contact with President Roosevelt while he was a Senator. When the war began, Truman became head of a Senate committee to investigate waste and corruption in the billions of dollars spent on the defense build-up. He performed an outstanding job on this and received much favorable publicity. His rating with his fellow politicians increased favorably. Still, he had virtually no contact with Roosevelt.

With the election of 1944 coming up, many Democrats, particularly those in the South, were dissatisfied with the incumbent Vice President, Henry Wallace. They viewed him as too liberal and something of a nut. Many Democrats feared that Roosevelt might not live through his fourth term—they definitely did not want Wallace as President. Roosevelt was told that Wallace would be unacceptable as his vice presidential running mate. His political aides, one of them being Robert Hannigan from Missouri, recommended Truman.

Hannigan asked Roosevelt whom he would like as his vice president. Roosevelt took a piece of paper and wrote, "I would be glad to have either (Supreme Court Judge) William O. Douglas or Harry Truman." Hannigan knew that Roosevelt's recommendation for vice president was critical and presented the note to the secretary as, "I would be glad to have either Harry Truman or William O. Douglas as Vice President." The fact that Truman's name now came first made all the difference in the world.

Truman was nominated (much to his astonishment) and was elected Vice President along with Roosevelt as President in November, 1944. It became increasingly obvious to those around Roosevelt that his health was declining rapidly. Yet, Truman had only two short meetings with Roosevelt before his death on April 12, 1945. In short, Truman had no preparation at all for this very important job. For one thing, he knew nothing at all about the development of the atomic bomb.

Fortunately, Truman took over as the war with Germany was almost over. All the planning and decisions in this regard were already done. Truman pledged himself to carry on the policies of Franklin D. Roosevelt and to prosecute the war against Germany and Japan as vigorously as possible, which he did. Truman, a modest and plain speaking man, fooled a lot of people. He turned out to be a great president. Though from a humble background, he was very intelligent and also tough. He helped conclude the war against Germany, and Japan was finished by August of 1945. After Roosevelt's death, the country under Truman did not miss a beat in its determination and effort to win the war. Truman seemed to be an ordinary man, but he was not. The country was fortunate to have him at this time.

After the war, Truman initiated the Marshall Plan for Economic Aid to Western Europe, which helped it to survive—and perhaps kept it from going Communist. He also started NATO, the North Atlantic Treaty Organization of Western Europe, Canada, and the United States. This proved a bulwark against the expansion of Communism for over forty years. He also integrated the armed forces, which was the first big step in the civil rights movement for black Americans. Truman was elected President in his own right in 1948. This election was one of the biggest upsets in American history. Truman won because he waged an outstanding campaign as an underdog. No one gave him a chance except a very few friends and Truman. It seems everyone sold Truman short all along the way, except Truman and history. Truman was an honest, down-to-earth, plain-spoken man who was later revered by his countrymen, particularly for these qualities. Some later Presidents were measured by Truman's standards and did not measure up—which made Truman look even better.

In the early part of the year 2000, 58 eminent American historians gathered to rank in order the best of the 41 presidents. The rankings were (1)

Abraham Lincoln; (2) Franklin D. Roosevelt; (3) George Washington; (4) Theodore Roosevelt; (5) Harry Truman. (Eisenhower was ninth on the list.) Truman, the "little" man from Missouri, had fooled everyone—he had done a magnificent job.

This era produced three of the greatest men in American history: Franklin D. Roosevelt, Harry S. Truman, and Dwight D. Eisenhower. America was indeed fortunate to have these three men during one of the most critical times in its history. Indeed, the whole world is indebted to these men. Without them, the course of history might have been entirely different and entirely ominous in the extreme. They played a vital role in destroying Hitler and also in thwarting Stalin's ambition to absorb all of Europe.

Germany Crushed

In February of 1945, the Allies in the West were getting ready for the final push against Germany. Of course, the winter weather was a considerable obstacle. The Russians were approaching the German border, threatening Berlin. In Italy, after capturing Rome, the Allies were continuing their slow advance to the north. Hitler was being pushed into a corner from all sides—Germany's worst nightmare.

Somehow, in all his wisdom, Hitler had arranged for Germany to fight almost the entire world. His insular thinking, his egomania had led to all this. Hitler had proven to be a powerful, smart man who went beyond his limits. He didn't have the world view of a Churchill who was always thinking on a grander scale. Hitler was great at smashing what was in front of him, but incapable of seeing the bigger picture, except as he wanted to see it. His limited education and experience was not enough in what proved to be a world war.

In February, despite the weather, the Allies began to advance in the West. Resistance was still strong, but Hitler's insistence on not yielding any ground played into Eisenhower's hands. As the Allies approached the Rhine, hundreds of thousands of German troops had been surrounded and captured. As the Allies closed against the Rhine, the last barrier to Germany, they received a terrific break. Elements of the Ninth Armored Division arrived at Remagen and were amazed the bridge across the Rhine was still standing. General Hoge told his troops to rush the bridge and cross it. Of course, the troops felt that at any minute the bridge would blow up in their faces; nevertheless, they bravely rushed across the bridge and made it to the east side. The few Germans there made a somewhat futile resistance and then surrendered—more American units poured across the bridge and enlarged the bridgehead.

Bradley was elated and called Eisenhower about what to do next; this unexpected gift wasn't in the plan. Eisenhower was also elated and told Bradley to push across five divisions to enlarge the bridgehead. It was almost too good to be true. The Allies had looked on the Rhine as a formidable defensive barrier and now with one stroke it had been breached.

Hitler was infuriated. He had all the officers connected with the defense executed. What was equally disturbing to Hitler was that he had no reserves to throw at the bridgehead—Hitler had run out of men and units. There were about five German tanks in the area, and Hitler told them to rush to the scene—thus, he who once was one of the most powerful men in the world was now almost a corporal again. Meanwhile, Patton was attacking to the south and in a rush crossed the Rhine at Oppenheim on March 23.

Montgomery, in the north, always one for the planned, sure-thing battle, assembled a large force including paratroopers for his attack across the Rhine. He treated it like another invasion of Normandy. With a tremendous artillery barrage and air attacks, his troops crossed the Rhine at Wesel on March 24. Patton was delighted that he had beaten Montgomery across the Rhine with no preparation at all. The German front, with no reserves and stretched to the breaking point, showed signs of collapse.

Winston Churchill was there with Eisenhower to witness Montgomery's crossing of the Rhine, the last barrier to Germany. He was overjoyed at the Allied success. He told Eisenhower, "My dear General, the German is whipped. We've got him. He is all through." The next day, Churchill crossed the Rhine and stood on German soil. It had taken five years of tremendous struggle, but he had persevered and won.

Meanwhile, Bradley had built up his forces at Remagen and attacked northeast; Montgomery also attacked from his bridgehead. The Ruhr and 300,000 German troops were surrounded—General Model committed suicide. With the German western front now collapsing at nearly all points, the name of the game was pursuit as one large German city after another fell to the Allies. Still, at some points, the Allied troops ran into fanatical German resistance, mostly from the SS—Major General Maurice Rose, commander of the Third Armored Division, and one of the most outstanding American officers, was killed near Paderborn in the last few weeks of the war by one of these fanatical groups.

Hitler, now in his bunker in Berlin, was frantically trying to stem the tide but had nothing to do it with. He still poured over his maps and made plans, but it was obvious to all it was hopeless. On February 3, the Russians reached the Oder River, only 35 miles from Berlin. They also continued their attacks all along the entire front. As the Allied forces pushed across Germany, they were shocked when they found the numerous concentration camps. The condition of the people still living and the stacks of dead bodies was horrifying to the troops. They couldn't believe that anyone could commit these terrible atrocities. Many of the SS guards were summarily shot. It was something that no one could ever forget.

After the collapse of the Ruhr pocket, the Allies advanced eastward. When their spearheads reached the Elbe River, they were 100 miles from Berlin, and there didn't seem to be too much in front of them. At that time, the Russians, who were less than thirty miles from Berlin, began their attack to take the city.

Eisenhower was faced with a decision whether to drive to Berlin or not. Churchill and the British were urging him to attack; Churchill was worried that the Red Army and Stalin would take all the credit for defeating Germany if they took Berlin. The Red Army had already occupied much of Eastern Europe, and Churchill wanted to put a damper on their progress and influence. Already, there was a growing problem with Russia over Poland. With the death of Roosevelt, Churchill's influence had become less in Allied actions. He did not have the personal relationship with Truman and Marshall that he had enjoyed with Roosevelt.

Eisenhower pondered his decision. His forward elements of several divisions had reached the Elbe, but the entire Army group had not. Eisenhower was not exactly sure what kind of resistance he would face—to bring up sufficient forces would take time. The Russians were at the point of assaulting Berlin; they had already begun initial attacks. General Bradley pointed out that an attack and battle for Berlin could cost as many as one hundred thousand casualties. (Indeed, the Russians did have casualties of several hundred thousand men in this attack on Berlin.)

Another factor was that Allied intelligence predicted that Hitler and his fanatical followers would set up an enclave in the mountains of southern Germany and the Alps and fight to the last man. Of course, later this was found out to be only a vague idea of some of the Nazis. At the time, though, the Allies took it seriously and directed some military efforts in that direction to prevent it.

All of these things Eisenhower had to consider with regard to moving to Berlin. Probably the main factor that influenced him, besides the potential casualties involved, was that the occupation zones had already been laid out. Berlin was in the Russian zone. If the American Army attacked and took Berlin, it would, after leaving a small force there, have to turn and retreat back to the

American occupation zone. Summing all of this up, Eisenhower decided not to go for Berlin. Under the circumstances, it was the right decision.

Later, some would question this decision, but that was hindsight. It must be remembered that at the time, Russia was a valued ally. The Red Army and Stalin had put up a terrific battle against the Germans. So far, for the most part, American and Britain had gotten along well with the Soviets. It was thought at the time that good relations would continue. No one could foresee that Stalin would break nearly all of his promises made to Roosevelt and Churchill.

After its capture by the Russians, Berlin itself was occupied by troops from all four countries (including France) and divided into zones. Berlin was 110 miles east of the boundary of the Allied occupation zone for Germany— thus, it was an island in a Communist sea. After the war, it remained a focal point of tension between the Allies and the Soviets. Several times, it looked as if war over Berlin was imminent.

◆ ◆ ◆

In later years, the sharp contrast of prosperous West Berlin as compared to the drabness of Communist East Berlin was very obvious to everyone. This situation, plus the events surrounding it, would eventually lead to the reuniting of all Germany and contributed to the break-up of the entire Soviet Union. Perhaps the division of Berlin in 1945 was a blessing in disguise.

8

The Reckoning

The Final Days of Hitler and Nazi Germany

The death of Roosevelt on April 12 had no effect on the rapid advance of the Allies across Germany. Montgomery headed for Bremen and the Baltic Sea. Bradley pushed ahead in the center and established bridgeheads across the Elbe. Patton's Third Army and the Seventh Army under General Devers rushed south and east. On April 24, elements of the First American Army met the Russian army at Torgau on the Elbe. The war for all intents and purposes was over, but hard fighting continued.

Meanwhile, the Red Army was advancing into Austria and occupied Vienna on April 13 after a bitter struggle. Some American troops under Patton thrust into northern Austria at Linz. Perhaps because of this, and also prodding by Churchill and Truman, Stalin decided to keep his agreement on Austria, and it was divided into four zones—Russian, English, American, and French. A few years later, Austria regained its independence and became a neutral country, like Switzerland. Austria had had enough.

On April 16, Russia launched its offensive to take Berlin with a huge bombardment. The Russian forces greatly outnumbered the beleaguered Germans, and it was just a question of time and bitter fighting before they took Berlin.

On the southern part of the front, Red Army forces had entered Czechoslovakia and were fighting their way towards Prague against strong resistance. In the latter part of April, Patton's troops approached the northern Czechoslovak border, then moved inward, reaching Pilsen, not far from Prague. Churchill urged Eisenhower to lunge forward and take Prague. This would bolster the Allied cause in that country. Eisenhower hesitated; his understanding or assumption at the time was that Prague and most of Czechoslovakia would be taken by the Russians. It is very likely he consulted with General Marshall on this. In any event, Eisenhower didn't take Prague, which he could have done. Perhaps he was trying to maintain good relations and to prevent an accidental clash with the Soviets. Churchill was very upset by this and rightfully so. It is possible to say that the Americans were somewhat naive in political matters.

Thus, the country that in March, 1938, at Munich had almost caused a world war now was lost in the shuffle—very sad for the Czechs, as they eventually became a Communist country dominated by Russia. Edward Benes, the President of Czechoslovakia at the time of the Munich crisis, had set up a provisional government in London during the war that was recognized by the English, Americans and Russians. He returned to Prague at the end of the war, but his government was undermined and then replaced by the Communists. Of course, Stalin was behind all this.

In Berlin, heavy fighting was continuing. In one of his craziest decisions of the war, Hitler sent his best surviving Panzer divisions to fight the Russians in Hungary. Hitler had many more troops fighting in Hungary, Austria, and Czechoslovakia than he had at Berlin. Perhaps at this stage, out of anger and frustration he had become irrational. Frankly, I think I should say more irrational, as Hitler really at the core was not a rational man to begin with.

At this time, Hitler lived in an underground bunker beneath the Chancellery Building at Berlin. There with him were Goebbels and his shrunken Army General Staff. Hitler continued to hold daily military meetings with his generals, sometimes moving non-existent units to scattered places. The dike was breaking. Hitler's empire that once covered nearly all of Europe was now reduced to a basement in shell-shocked Berlin.

Hitler had put all his faith in a counter-attack against the Russians around Berlin by General Steiner. The only problem was that General Steiner's meager forces existed mostly on paper and in Hitler's mind. When Hitler found out there would be no attack by General Steiner, he went into a rage. His last slender hope was gone. All of Hitler's twisted plans, hopes and scheming had come down to this—catastrophic defeat and disaster.

Each day as the battle for Berlin continued block by block, Hitler could hear the guns and explosions getting closer. The Russians were sustaining heavy casualties, but they gained ground each day. It was just a matter of a short time before the Chancellery itself would be overrun. The Allies were advancing rapidly on all fronts as the German army was showing signs of collapse, particularly on the Western Front. German soldiers much preferred to be taken prisoner by the Americans and British rather than by the vengeful Soviet Army. Refugees clogged the roads, moving west in fear of the Soviets.

At this time, Hitler received a cable from Hermann Goering, the number two man in the government. Goering wanted to know if, since Hitler was surrounded in Berlin, he (Goering) should take over the government. This really infuriated Hitler. What was strange about Goering's telegram was that there was actually no government to take over—only scattered, disintegrating fragments.

Hitler determined not to be captured alive, particularly after seeing what the Italian partisans had done to Mussolini. After his capture, Mussolini and his mistress were shot numerous times and their bodies hung grotesquely upside down from lamp posts in Milan. As his last days approached, in a bizarre ceremony on April 29, Hitler married his long-time mistress, Eva Braun. They had a short marriage. The next day, April 30, at about 3 o'clock in the afternoon, they retired to a room where they committed suicide. Eva Braun took cyanide. Hitler shot himself through the head. (Hitler was not made of the same stuff as Churchill, who would have gone down fighting.)

Hitler's and his wife's bodies were carried outside the Chancellery, put into a ditch, and burned, a fitting end to an evil man. Goebbels, his wife and five children also committed suicide. Himmler and Goering did so as well. Goering's death occurred just before he was about to be executed. It was a complete mystery how Goering, under close scrutiny, had obtained the cyanide to kill himself. Speculation was that an American guard had given it to him— never proved.

Thus, the end of Adolph Hitter; a violent man, he died a violent death. With his death, the war was over, although scattered fighting continued for a few days. The new head of government, appointed by Hitler before his death, was Admiral Donitz. Donitz sent General Alfred Jodl to Eisenhower's headquarters to surrender. The Germans surrendered unconditionally on May 7, 1945. The European war was over. The one thousand year Reich had lasted just twelve; it fell 988 years short.

During those years, particularly beginning in 1939 with the start of the war, Hitler and Germany had caused untold millions of deaths and tremendous damage all over Europe. Thankfully, by the strong efforts of millions of people, his terrible regime had been smashed. As leaders of the people fighting Hitler, the Allied leaders, Churchill, Roosevelt, and Stalin, had met the challenge and defeated Adolph Hitler.

Churchill, Roosevelt, and Stalin had done a great job in overcoming Hitler. Their strategical plans had been very effective and had brought about the destruction of their enemy. However, you can have great strategical plans, but without execution they are meaningless. Churchill, Roosevelt, and Stalin had to have highly competent men to carry out their plans. First of all, they had to choose the right people—and they did an excellent job in this. In particular, there are four men that stand out: Eisenhower, MacArthur, Nimitz, and Zhukov. All of these men had one thing in common: they were successful.

Consider that Eisenhower, an obscure lieutenant colonel in 1941, was in 1944 leading the Allied invasion of Northern France. This is incredible. During this period, Eisenhower had successfully invaded French North Africa, Sicily, and Italy. After making the brilliant invasion of Normandy, he was successful in the Battle for France and then in the Battle for Germany, which led to the defeat of Germany.

Eisenhower received this cable from General Marshall a few days after the end of the war. As you remember, Marshall was an austere, remote, and tight-lipped officer. The cable stated:

> You have completed your mission with the greatest victory in the history of warfare. You have commanded with outstanding success the most powerful military force that has ever been assembled. You have met and successfully disposed of every conceivable difficulty incident to varied national interests and international political problems of unprecedented complications.

Eisenhower, Marshall said, had triumphed over inconceivable logistical problems and military obstacles.

> Through all of this, since the day of your arrival in England three years ago, you have been selfless in your actions, always sound and tolerant in your judgments and altogether admirable in the courage and wisdom of your decisions.
>
> You have made history, great history for the good of mankind and you have stood for all we hope for and admire in an officer of the United States Army. These are my tributes and my personal thanks.

From a man not given to outward shows of emotion and who took a rather stern and business-like approach to everything, this is very high praise. Marshall knew better than anyone the trials and difficult situations that Eisenhower had faced, and in this cable he showed his true admiration and respect for Eisenhower, the man he had chosen to lead the American Army in Europe. He had not misplaced his faith, and Eisenhower had not let him down in any way.

Eisenhower has had many critics, most saying that other men under him had really accomplished the victories—but as he said after the war, "I don't know who deserves the credit for the victory in the West, but I certainly know who would have got the blame if we had lost."

MacArthur and Nimitz led the American drive across the Pacific, and if you asked the Japanese after the war, I think they would say objectively that MacArthur and Nimitz had done a pretty good job of it. Both MacArthur and Nimitz in 1942 had to start from scratch, which they did—they stopped the Japanese advance and then took the offensive themselves. Remember, most of America's men and resources were being committed to the European Theatre; MacArthur and Nimitz had to make do with what they had.

MacArthur defeated the Japanese in New Guinea and began his successful drive to the Philippines—bypassing large Japanese strongholds. Nimitz, in a brilliant action at Midway, defeated Yamamoto's fleet and then began his drive across the Central Pacific. MacArthur's and Nimitz's forces arrived at their destination in Tokyo Bay on September 2, 1945, with the complete surrender of Japan. It is difficult to impossible to see where they made any mistakes at all.

Marshall Zhukov and Stalin were the men, along with the brave soldiers of the Red Army, that saved the Soviet Union. The Germans, with 150 divisions, had made a tremendous attack which was almost successful. Zhukov always showed up at the right time and in the right place—of course, directed there by Stalin. Zhukov had defeated the Germans at Leningrad, Moscow, Stalingrad, and then in the drive to Germany and the Battle of Berlin. He was the Germans' worst nightmare.

Under Churchill, Roosevelt, and Stalin, these four men had been indispensable in winning the war. Hitler had many very competent generals, but he chose to ignore their advice and run the war himself—and look at the results, tactically and strategically. Hitler was convinced that the Germans were invincible. Maybe they weren't supermen after all.

Final Tally
Strategical Mistakes in World War II

The final tally of Strategical mistakes in the war shows that Hitler won on that score by a huge majority. The final tally was:

Churchill	**0**
Roosevelt	**0**

Stalin	<u>1</u>
Total	1
Hitler	6

Stalin's strategical mistake was the allowing of large armies of the Red Army to be surrounded and destroyed in 1941. The ferocity and efficiency of the German attack had a great deal to do with this.

Hitler's six strategical mistakes obviously had a direct effect on the outcome of the war. With all the enormous forces he had arranged against him Hitler could not afford to make any mistakes—particularly when his opponents were making virtually none. With all these huge mistakes, Hitler and Germany had no chance of winning the war.

Decisive Mistake 1. The failure to knock England out of the war in 1940. Perhaps the English and the R.A.F. had something to do with this. After defeating France, Hitler didn't seem to know what to do about England. England was still alive and fighting back when America entered the war—this meant a two-front war for Germany. Germany could not win a two-front war. Hitler should have known this; certainly, his generals did.

Decisive Mistake 2. The failure to knock Russia out of the war in 1941. The initial mistake occurred when Hitler attacked Greece and Yugoslavia in April, 1941. His timetable for the attack on Russia was set back by five to six weeks that were precious later in 1941 in Russia. Again, Hitler's impulses and the rage to strike back got the better of him—if there was any better.

However, the most decisive mistake was, against the advice of his generals, he turned away from the attack on Moscow in August. Instead, Hitler chose to send a large part of von Bock's central army south to help encircle a large Red Army in the Ukraine. Von Rundstedt's army was heading north and joined von Bock's to complete the encirclement. This was a great tactical success; hundreds of thousands of the Red Army were captured. However, it was a disastrous strategical mistake. Russia could replace men, but it could not replace Moscow.

In August on the Central Front, the time had been right for an immediate advance on Moscow. At that time, Stalin had relatively few troops left to oppose von Bock. A strong attack by the Germans at that time before winter set in would have captured Moscow.

Moscow was the central city and the hub of the Soviet Union. This would have been a strategical decisive defeat for the Russians and would have fragmented their defense. The government would have to be moved. It is very possible that Hitler could have negotiated peace with what was left of the Russians—a peace very much in Germany's favor. Possibly something like the one he had concluded with the French in 1940. The Russians would then be a non-factor in the rest of the war. With this development, one could say that Hitler had won the entire war. Britain was alone and had no chance of defeating Germany. The whole outcome of the war would have been different.

Decisive Mistake 3. The declaration of war against the United States on December 11, 1941. As mentioned, when the Japanese attacked Pearl Harbor, this brought about a declaration of war by the United States against Japan. The United States didn't declare war on Germany; the war at that point was between Japan and the United States. Hitler could have and should have done absolutely nothing. Why bring another huge power in against him? Also, the United States had made the decisive difference in World War I. There was all to lose and nothing to gain by bringing America into the European war.

Hitler declared war on America on December 11, 1941, giving the flimsy reason that the United States was already engaging in the war by supplying England and attacking German submarines. This was a reason but not a good reason to bring the might of a huge country in against him. He was already fighting Britain and Russia. On December 10, 1941, he was facing about two percent of America's power. On December 11, by declaring war, he was now facing seventy percent of American power—not a good move. (Of course, the other thirty percent of American power was directed against Japan.)

There may be several reasons why Hitler declared war on the United States.

1. He totally underestimated the power of America. Wars are not won by contempt and ignorance of your opponent.
2. He thought Japan would fully occupy the United States in the Pacific. After all, hadn't they just won a stunning victory at Pearl Harbor?
3. He hated Roosevelt.
4. In his egomania, he thought he could win, no matter what.
5. The total of the first four.

It is safe to say that in the first weeks of December, 1941, seemingly at the height of its power, Germany had lost the war. First, Hitler's army had been stopped and turned back at the gates of Moscow, insuring that Russia would remain in the war. Second, Hitler had brought into the European war a great power, America. Hitler was now fighting Great Britain, Russia, and the United States all at the same time. A very good way to lose a war. In fact, mathematically, as Churchill perceived, at that time Hitler had lost the war.

Decisive Mistake 4. The failure of the attack on Russia in 1942. The large army that Hitler attacked Russia in 1942 was very strong indeed—its objective was Stalingrad on the Volga. This would effectively occupy a large part of the Soviet Union and also cut off the Caucasus and its oil. Without oil, the Red Army would be immobilized along the entire front and thus defeated.

The campaign started off well. The German army was gaining much ground every day against sporadic and ineffective resistance. The Russians had expected the Germans to attack Moscow and were unprepared in Southern Russia. As the attack rolled along relatively easily, Hitler made another fateful decision, perhaps one should say a fatal decision. He became overconfident; he thought the Soviets were collapsing when actually they were retreating. He decided to split the army into two parts, a disastrous mistake. Army Group B under von Paulus would continue eastward and take Stalingrad. Army Group A under von Kleist would split off and directly attack the Caucasus.

By his dispersion of his army, Hitler lost on both fronts. If he had continued the attack as originally planned with one large army objective Stalingrad, he would have been successful in taking Stalingrad. He almost did it with only half of his army. In taking Stalingrad and Astrakhan, he would hold the Volga all the way to the Caspian Sea. He would have cut off and then taken the Caucasus, which by itself could not have held out. He very possibly would have won the war against Russia at this point.

As it was, Hitler took a tremendous defeat at Stalingrad, the turning point in the war in Russia. His generals barely saved Army Group A in the Caucasus. The war with Russia could not be won and hence was lost.

Decisive Mistake 5. Failure to defeat the Allied invasion of Normandy on June 6, 1944. In 1944, the war in the west hinged for both sides on the invasion of Northern France. If Hitler could inflict a smashing defeat on the invasion forces and throw them back into the sea, he would have won a tremendous decisive victory. The psychological effects alone would be huge, not only with the English and the Americans, but also with the Russians. Defeated in the invasion of Northern France, the efforts of the English and the Americans would probably be set back several years. Who knows what could happen in a war in several years? Anything could happen.

The decisive day of the invasion was D-Day itself, June 6. If the Allies could get ashore and establish a significant beachhead, the invasion would be a success. If strong German reinforcements did not come up immediately and counterattack the first or at least the second day, the Germans had failed to defeat the invasion. The allies would be in France to stay—the second front would be a reality. Again, in a two-front war Germany would inevitably lose.

Hitler, undecided about how to defend Northern France, had compromised his defense plan between von Rundstedt's and Rommel's plans. Von Rundstedt's plan was to have a strong Panzer reserve some distance from the shore line, and when the exact point of invasion was determined, the reserves would attack and throw the Allies into the Channel. Rommel's plan was to have all forces close to the beach and throw the Allies back into the sea at the shoreline.

Hitler compromised between the two plans, which dispersed his defending force and resulted in the failure of the entire effort. Looking back, if he had done one or the other, he would have done better. Since he did neither, his defense was a failure. In addition to everything else, the German command situation was flawed from the beginning. Too may chiefs, too many layers, and too much Hitler.

When von Rundstedt called Hitler's headquarters early on June 6 to release the reserves, Hitler was asleep. One-half of the decisive day was already gone before he woke up. After he finally woke up shortly after noon, Hitler couldn't decide what to do. When he finally decided to release the Panzer reserves at 4 o'clock in the afternoon, it was too late. The invasion would probably have been successful without Hitler's slowness, but it would have certainly helped the Germans greatly to have three Panzer divisions rolling toward the beaches early on June 6—at least they would have had some chance. With the Allied invasion victory, success in the West was virtually assured for the Allies. Hitler had failed again.

Decisive Mistake 6. In total, Hitler somehow managed to bring the power of Britain, America, and Russia against him. Somewhat similar to the First War, only worse, as in this one Russians did not fall out as in 1917. Each mistake Hitler made seemed to lead to another big one. When he invited America into the war, he had not finished off Britain and Russia; he himself had forged a coalition against Germany. In addition to everything else, Hitler was a coward. He insisted that men in far-off posts, such as Stalingrad and Tunisia, fight to the death. One reason for this was to keep the war as far away from himself as possible; his no retreat policy was also in the same vein. He was trying to keep distance between himself personally and his enemies. He only killed himself when the Russians were less than two hundred yards away. He was hoping for a miracle.

In looking at all of his mistakes, the biggest mistake Hitler made was number two, the failure to knock Russia out of the war in 1941. His armies were poised in August to attack Moscow. There was relatively little at that time to oppose them. They could have done it; they could have captured Moscow in 1941. With the Russians out of the war, the entire situation would have changed. Hitler lost the war right then and there by his decision to turn south away from Moscow.

Hitler started off by picking off countries one by one. Somehow, that strategy got lost along the way. Possibly it was because Britain, America, and Russia wouldn't cooperate. They fought back—together. They were just as tough as the Germans, and there were more of them. Hitler could not afford to make mistakes, which he did in abundance. Earlier in the war, Hitler actually had chances to win the war. If he had successfully invaded England in 1940, he very probably would have won the war. If he had defeated Russia in 1941 or 1942, he probably would have won the war. He didn't win these battles and in bringing America in against him, lost the war.

Churchill, Roosevelt, and Stalin proved to be much smarter than Hitler. They didn't make the mistakes that would beat them. Maybe Hitler was just a corporal after all. A sometimes brilliant corporal, but still a corporal.

There were a number of turning points in the war. Midway and Guadalcanal in the Pacific, the Battle of Britain, and the defeats of Hitler at Moscow and Stalingrad. The author believes the number one turning point of the war was December 7, 1941, at Pearl Harbor, a day that Roosevelt said would live in infamy. Pearl Harbor brought America into the war—it was a disaster, but getting America into the war turned out to be a monumental and fatal disaster for Japan and Germany. While Japan made the attack, Hitler, in a move that defies all logic, jumped in and declared war on the United States. Little did he know what lay ahead.

Adolph Hitler

"There are two possibilities for me: To win through with all my plans, or to fail. If I win, I shall be one of the greatest men in history. If I fail, I shall be condemned, despised and dammed."

—Hitler to Speer, November, 1936

Adolph Hitler had a strange life, to say the least. A starving, uneducated art student in Vienna, at times he was reduced to begging from his few acquaintances. When the First War started, Hitler was elated and enthused, along with most of the German people.

Hitler served meritoriously on the Western Front and rose to the rank of corporal. Near the end of the war, he was gassed, temporarily blinded, and sent to the hospital. As he recovered in the hospital, he learned that Germany had surrendered. He was stunned; he couldn't believe it. No one could beat Germany; surely there must be treachery somewhere. In his twisted mind, looking for someone to blame, Hitler focused on the Jews and Communists. This was not only wrong, but very unfair to the Jews—thousands of Jews had served in the German army and had fought bravely. No matter to Hitler, his fury turned to hatred and a burning passion for revenge.

As he was still in the army, he was assigned to investigating the many small militant groups in Munich. The army was anxious to forestall and squelch the revolutionary activity that was sweeping Germany at the time. Hitler did join one small radical group, the National Socialist Party; in a short time, he was its leader. In 1923, the numbers of his party had grown substantially, including air ace Hermann Goering. Hitler then led a Putsch to topple the Bavarian government. Police and army units opened fire, and some of his supporters were killed. Hitler was tried and sent to prison. In prison, where he had comfortable quarters and was treated like a guest, Hitler wrote Mein Kampf. He laid out his philosophy, which was mostly hatred and violence. The book's turgid prose was not widely read until years later when it was too late.

Between 1924 and 1932, Hitler continued to enlarge his number of supporters; he had decided to take over the national government by legitimate means. The Depression, starting in 1929, also hit Europe and Germany hard—unemployment was high; the German people were restless and looking for a leader.

The old General von Hindenburg was president. He was almost incapable of running a government at his age, especially when times were so troubled. As Hitler's power increased in the Reichstag, he demanded more power—no one could effectively stop the ruthless Hitler. Although he had only 44 percent of the seats in the Reichstag, Hitler dominated the scene—his opponents were weak and fragmented. Finally, to end the chaotic situation, Hindenburg appointed Hitler to the office of Chancellor; Hitler, in effect, became the ruler of Germany.

Off came the relatively velvet gloves. Overnight, the history of Germany was changed, I believe one can say not for the better. Mysteriously, the Reichstag building burned down; Hitler blamed the Communists. This was the end of any semblance of democratic government in Germany. Hitler was now absolute ruler and dictator of Germany; there was only one party, the National Socialists or Nazi Party.

Thus Adolph Hitler, the penniless street person of Vienna in 1914, became dictator of Germany twenty years later. By guile, by perseverance, by ruthlessness, by unbridled ambition, Hitler had reached the apex of power. He had overcome everything and everyone. His will was unconquerable. While Hitler knew Germany and had some limited knowledge of Europe, he had absolutely no knowledge of the world outside of Europe—in particular, the United States—a flaw, and possibly a fatal flaw. No matter, he set out to avenge the First War and to make Germany the master of Europe—and then, who knows?

He came dangerously close to doing it. There is no doubt that Hitler had a certain demonic brilliance; his oratory, in particular, was hypnotic to the German people. The whole country, except for a few, united behind him. He led them to glorious victories, and in the end to total destruction. He did not deserve their loyalty. Millions of German soldiers and civilians fought and died to perpetuate a man and his policy that exterminated six million people. Many other ruthless acts and atrocities were committed which Hitler encouraged. It was well that Germany was defeated; if they had won, what other unspeakable acts would have been committed, probably the same on a much larger scale—if that is possible to comprehend.

Churchill was the first to understand Hitler and raise the alarm. He was ignored for years, but when desperate times came to England, they turned to Churchill, who was ready. He was mentally brilliant. His values were totally sound. He always had the big picture in mind, and he was tough as nails.

Churchill was a great and good man. Stalin, in his own way, was equally brilliant. Rising through the dark chambers of the Communist party, Stalin succeeded Lenin as First Secretary of the Communist Party. His foes in Russia didn't realize it at the time, but this post became one of the most powerful and vital in the government. Stalin made it so.

As ruthless as Hitler, Stalin ruled with an iron hand; terror and fear were his weapons. Millions of people were executed or starved to death. Stalin wanted a strong industrialized state, and he achieved it at a heavy cost to his people. It is possible to say that Stalin's strength and ruthlessness saved Russia during the war. Only a man such as Stalin in Russia could have stood up to the onslaught of the German Army. Remember, in the First War, Russia collapsed when only a fraction of the German Army was turned against it.

The Red Army put up a terrific struggle against Hitler and the Germans; the Red Army was led by Josef Stalin.

It is strange that at the end of 1945 only one of these leaders was still in power. Roosevelt had died; Hitler had committed suicide; and in a strange twist of fate, the victor, Churchill, had been voted out of office—only the inscrutable Stalin remained.

The Greatest Leader Was . . .

If you consider the four leaders in the war—Churchill, Roosevelt, Stalin, and Hitler—you may well ask yourself which of these was the greatest. Because he lost and because of all of his mistakes, Hitler could not be considered. That leaves Churchill, Roosevelt, and Stalin.

Winston Churchill will probably go down as the greatest man of the twentieth century, and rightly so. In a desperate time, England turned to Churchill, who was the very best man they had for the job—and what a tremendous job he did. Even though he led them to victory, the British people decided they no longer needed Churchill. They preferred the Labor Party to run the country in the post-war years and promptly voted Churchill out of office. This hurt Churchill deeply, and understandably so. Churchill felt this wasn't quite fair, even ungrateful, and the world and history would agree. Undaunted as usual, Churchill became Prime Minister again in 1951.

As to Stalin, in many parts a tyrant and evil man, he put up the greatest fight of the three against a terrific attack from Germany. It is hard to see any other man in Russia who could have accomplished what Stalin did—it was close to a miracle, considering the huge difficulties he had to overcome. Stalin was a bad man, but he was the right man in the right place at the right time.

In the author's mind, Roosevelt was the greatest man of World War II. Consider this: Roosevelt did not make *any* mistakes during the war. He was fighting the powerful Germans on one side of the world and the very tough Japanese on the other at the same time. He was providing a mass of materiel to Britain and Russia, which enabled them to stay in the war. With only 30 percent of America's forces involved in the Pacific, the United States was defeating Japan practically all by itself.

Roosevelt didn't make any strategical mistakes in the war. He realized that Germany was the main threat and used the bulk of his forces against it. He mobilized the United States and executed its power all over the world—decisively. The United States had the greatest industrial complex in the world, and Roosevelt organized it to produce war materiel, planes, tanks, and ships in overwhelming quantities. To some extent, the war was won on the production lines of the United States.

Roosevelt's most singular achievement was in his selection of men, in particular, Marshall, Nimitz, MacArthur, and Eisenhower. These men in turn selected excellent subordinates to aid them. As mentioned, once he had his men in place, Roosevelt, other than making strategical decisions, left them alone to conduct the actual fighting of the war. His confidence in them was not misplaced.

While cooperating with Churchill and Stalin, Roosevelt had his own vision and priorities in conducting the war for the United States, that is, to apply America's power in a direct and decisive manner to reach the heartland of Germany and Japan. While having a huge air force and navy, the United States Army was not nearly as big as Germany's and about equal to Japan's. Roosevelt built an army of 90 divisions plus six elite Marine divisions. Sixty of these Army divisions were on the decisive Western Front—just as in World War I, they tipped the scales against Germany and led to Hitler's defeat. American power was applied at the decisive point.

At the same time, Roosevelt was facing a Japanese army of over three million men—Roosevelt's land forces in the Pacific numbered less than one million. However, the Japanese were spread out all over the South Pacific—Burma, China, and Manchuria in that theater. With a stronger navy and air force and having the initiative, Roosevelt could concentrate his forces at the point of attack, thus overwhelming the Japanese at that point. In organizing his army, navy, air force, and industrial complex, Roosevelt used them to maximum advantage. He was also a great inspirational leader to the American people. He did a great job.

In addition to everything else, Roosevelt organized and developed the atomic bomb, the ultimate weapon—the weapon that convinced Japan to end the war. Again, Roosevelt had the strategic vision and appointed highly competent people to organize and then build the bomb. Roosevelt was making big decisions covering the whole world, and making them right.

In short, Roosevelt conducted practically a perfect war. Hitler had grossly underestimated America and Roosevelt—it cost him the war and his life. He had to learn the hard way, just as Germany did in World War I. It cost them two world wars and the destruction of Germany to learn the lesson.

At the end of World War II, under Roosevelt's leadership, the United States was the world's superpower, and it has been that ever since. The world and its future generations should be grateful that Roosevelt, when he became ill with polio, did not retire to his home at Hyde Park. Rather, he became

President of the United States and led a great coalition in the defeat of one of the greatest menaces of all time—Adolph Hitler.

Churchill, Roosevelt, and Stalin
vs
Adolph Hitler

The coalition of Churchill, Roosevelt, and Stalin worked extremely well as testified to by the results. The person who created this great coalition was one Adolph Hitler. The fear and detestation of Hitler had united the great powers—Hitler was the motivator who caused his own and Germany's destruction. His cruel actions and even his early victories only spurred his enemies on. Hitler's actions proved to be self-destructive.

Hitler kept hoping the three Allies would break up in discord—he even had a fragile hope that a negotiated settlement could be made if that occurred. That was one reason for his desperate attack in the Ardennes. He said to his generals before the attack:

> Never in history was there a coalition like that for our enemies, composed of such heterogeneous elements with such divergent aims. . . . Even now these states are at loggerheads, and, if we can deliver a few more heavy blows, then this artificially bolstered common front may suddenly collapse with a gigantic clap of thunder.

Of course, his attack failed. In any event, Hitler was clutching at straws—straws that did not exist. The allies were never even close to a break-up during the war—they knew they needed each other, and their hatred and fear of Hitler was much greater than their relatively minor disagreements. Beating Hitler was all that mattered to them. Hitler was the most hated man in the world—a negotiated peace with him was impossible. Besides, the Allies were winning—why should they negotiate? Time and everything was on their side.

The purpose of the grand alliance was to crush Germany from all sides. Churchill's and Roosevelt's actions were independent of Stalin's, but they had the same effect—closing in on Germany—putting pressure on Hitler from many directions. Thus, the separate actions of the Allies were in effect coordinated by the same goal and in the same ultimate direction—to overwhelm Hitler's Germany in the heart of Europe.

Of course, Germany was in Central Europe geographically. From its defensive standpoint, this was a distinct disadvantage. It was at the mercy of multi-front war from nearly all directions. This Bismarck had foreseen, but evidently Hitler had not. Also, the attackers coming in from east and west were not faced with any formidable natural geographic barriers outside of possibly the Rhine River, which proved to be a relatively minor obstacle. In its weakened condition, Germany was almost a sitting duck, subject to being hit from all sides—its worst possible nightmare. Hitler had brought them to this.

One big advantage for the Allies was the frequency of communications among Churchill, Roosevelt, and Stalin. It is true that some of the messages from Stalin were tough (he was, at times, in a desperate situation), but they were still communication. All of their communications were vital to the Allies— they helped hold the alliance together and kept each other informed of developments. For instance, Stalin's constant demand for war materiel put pressure on Churchill and Roosevelt to expedite and increase supplies to the Soviet Union, which they did in spite of great difficulty. This helped keep the Russians in the war.

Stalin's and Roosevelt's pressure on Churchill to proceed with the second front in France put Churchill in a position of having to go along despite his reservations. All in all, these differences were worked out in an effective manner to the detriment of Hitler. Their frequent communications kept each other on the right track and all pulling together to smash Hitler.

The two face-to-face meetings of Churchill, Roosevelt, and Stalin at Teheran and Yalta provided further communication and coordination among the Allies. Also, the personal contact drew the alliance closer together. They were three different personalities drawn together by having the same enemy, Hitler, and having the same goal—survival and the defeat of Germany. When the person fighting beside you is helping you in a desperate struggle, you do not ask his political views.

All in all, Churchill, Roosevelt, and Stalin formed the most powerful coalition in all of history. Certainly it was effective and, in the end, successful. (It should be noted that Churchill and Roosevelt did not advise their ally, Stalin, about the development of the atomic bomb. Perhaps they realized that when and if it was developed, it would be a huge political and military advantage for them. Why bother Stalin with it? Why not let it be a big surprise?)

Let us contrast the coalition of Churchill, Roosevelt, and Stalin against Hitler's nonexistent alliance with Italy and Japan. As for Italy, as mentioned previously, Italy was a distinct liability for Hitler. It was a constant drain on Germany's resources beginning with North Africa, then Greece and Yugoslavia, and then Italy itself. With friends like this, who needs enemies?

As far as his ally, Japan, was concerned, there was no coordination of effort between Germany and Japan. Each would fight its own war and be successively defeated. Where communication was frequent and abundant among the Allies—it barely existed between Hitler and Japan. As mentioned, if Hitler had demanded that Japan attack Russia as a condition for his declaring war on the United States—this would have coordinated an attack on the Soviets by both Germany and Japan.

The results on Stalin may have been decisive—no one can tell—but the pressure from both east and west would have made things much worse for Stalin. Germany and Japan, although many miles distant, could have at least coordinated in the war against the Soviet Union. If Russia had been defeated, the whole war would have changed in favor of the Axis powers.

Hitler chose to go it alone. Japan chose to go it alone. This strategy, or lack of strategy, was in striking contrast to the coordinated efforts of the Allies. It was as if Hitler and Japan were inviting their own separate destruction—very convenient for the Allies. As the leader of his loose-knit coalition, Hitler must take the blame for this. Hitler was so self-centered that he felt he did not need anyone else.

Churchill, Roosevelt, and Stalin lived in the real world, while Hitler lived in a world of his own. It was a delusional world based on past triumphs and his egomania—a world that would be shattered by the crush of events.

Churchill, Roosevelt, and Stalin
vs
Adolph Hitler

Starting in 1939, the war went well for Hitler for the first several years. He crushed one opponent after another until he ran into Churchill and the R.A.F. Blocked at this point, he then moved east to strike Stalin and the Red Army. Not satisfied, he then took on Roosevelt, the leader of the number one industrial power in the world. No wonder he lost. Hitler, a seemingly brilliant man, but evidently a man whose vision extended only to the next horizon, had managed to blunder into an impossible situation for himself and Germany. In doing so he pitted himself against three brilliant and resourceful leaders.

Each of these three men—Churchill, Roosevelt, and Stalin—was smarter and thought on a much wider scale than Adolph Hitler. Yes, it was three against one—and as Hitler would find out, in three against one, three always wins. As Churchill would say, "It's simple mathematics."

Great Britain, the United States, and the Soviet Union, under the leadership of Churchill, Roosevelt, and Stalin, were too much for Adolph Hitler. Perhaps by its terribleness, it was the great war to end all great wars. It is conceivable that nuclear weapons have made war between large powers obsolete. Let us hope this is so and that the millions of people that died in this war did not die in vain. Their sacrifices were great but their achievements were beyond measure.

References

Alsop, Joseph. *FDR*. Viking Press, 1982.

Ambrose, Stephen. *Band of Brothers*. Simon & Schuster, 1992.

Ambrose, Stephen. *Citizen Soldiers*. Simon & Schuster, 1997.

Ambrose, Stephen. *D-Day*. Simon & Schuster, 1994.

Ambrose, Stephen. *Supreme Commander*. Doubleday, 1970.

Barnett, Corelli. *Hitler's Generals*. Grove Weidenfeld, 1989.

Bradley, Omar W. *A Soldier's Story*. Henry Holt & Co., 1951.

Brooks, Thomas. *The War North of Rome*. Sarpedon Publishers, 1996.

Bryant, Arthur. *Diaries of Lord Alanbrooke*. Doubleday, 1959.

Burns, James M. *Roosevelt—The Soldier of Freedom*. Harcourt, 1970.

Bush, George. *All the Best*. Scribener/Lisa Drew, 1999.

Butcher, Harry. *Three Years with Eisenhower*. Simon & Schuster, 1946.

Calder, Angus. *People's War*. Pantheon Books, 1969.

Churchill, Winston. *The Boer War*. W. W. Norton, 1990.

Churchill, Winston. *The Second World War*. Houghton Mifflin Co., 1948.

Deighton, Len. *Blood, Tears, and Folly*. Harper Perennial, 1994.

DeGaulle, Charles. *War Memoirs*. Simon & Schuster, 1964.

Eisenhower, Dwight D. *Crusade in Europe*. Doubleday & Co., 1948.

Eisenhower, John. *The Bitter Woods*. G. P. Putnam Sons, 1969.

Gilbert, Martin. *The First World War*. Henry Holt & Co., 1994.

Gilbert, Martin. *The Second World War*. New York: Henry Holt & Company, 1989.

Hart, Liddell. *The German General Talk*. William Morrow & Co., 1948.

Horne, Alisteir. *To Lose a Battle*. Little, Brown & Co., 1969.

Hoyt, Edwin P. *Japan's War*. McGraw-Hill Books, 1986.

Irving, David. *Rommel, Trail of the Fox*. Thomas Congdon Book - E. P. Dutton, 1977.

James, Clayton. *The Years of MacArthur*. Houghton Mifflin Co., 1975.

Lamb, Richard. *Montgomery in Europe*. Watts Publishing, 1984.
Lee, Bruce. *Marching Orders*. Crown Publishers, 1995.
Lochner, Louis. *Goebbels' Diaries*. Greenwood Press, 1948.
Lord, Walter. *Incredible Victory*. Harper & Row Publishers, 1967.

MacDonald, Charles B. *A Time for Trumpets*. Morrow Publishers, 1984.
McCullough, David. *Truman*. Simon & Schuster, 1992.
McNeal, R. H. *Stalin, Man and Ruler*. New York, University Press, 1988.
Miller, Merle. *Ike the Soldier*. Putnam Publishing Group, 1988.
Miller, Russell. *Nothing Less than Victory*. William Morrow & Co., 1993.

Overy, Richard. *Why the Allies Won*. W. W. Norton & Co., 1995.

Perret, Geoffrey. *Eisenhower*. Random House, 1999.

Rigby, T. H. *Stalin*. Prentice-Hall, 1966.
Robert, Brian. *Churchills in Africa*. Taplinger Publishers, 1971.
Rooney, Andy. *My War*. Random House, 1995.

Shirer, William L. *Berlin Diary*. Little, Brown Co., 1941.
Shirer, William L. *Collapse of the Third Republic*. Simon & Schuster, 1969.
Shirer, William L. *The Rise and Fall of the Third Reich*. Simon & Schuster, 1960.
Sides, Hampton. *Ghost Soldiers*. Doubleday, 2001.
Smith, Denis. *Mussolini*. Alfred A. Knopf, Inc., 1982.
Snyder, Louis L. *The War: A Concise History 1939-1945*. New York: Julian Messner, 1960.
Soames, Mary. *Winson & Clemmie*. Doubleday, 1998.
Speer, Albert. *Inside the Third Reich*. MacMillan Publishers, 1970.
Stokesbury, James L. *World War II*. William Morrow & Co., 1980.
Stolfi, R. H. *Hitler's Panzer East*. University of Oklahoma Press, 1992.
Strong, Kenneth. *Intelligence at the Top*. Doubleday & Co., 1969.

Toland, John. *Adolph Hitler*. Doubleday, 1976.

Toland, John. *The Rising Sun*. Random House, 1970.

Tucker, Robert. *Stalin as Revolutionary*. W. W. Norton, 1973.

Townsend, Peter. *Duel of Eagles*. Simon & Schuster, 1969.

Van der Vat, Dan. *The Pacific Campaign*, Simon & Schuster, 1991.

Von Bock, Fedor. *Von Bock's Diary*. Schiffer Publishing, Ltd., 1996.

Von Manstein, Eric. *Lost Victories*. Presidio Publishing, 1982.

Weinberg, Gerhard. *A World at Arms*. Cambridge University Press, 1993.

Weintraub, Stanley. *The Last Great Victory*. Truman Talley/Dutton, 1995.

Werth, Alexander. *Russia at War*. Dutton Publishers, 1964.

Whitney, Courtney. *MacArthur, His Rendezvous with History*. Alfred A. Knopf, 1956.

Zhukov, Marshal. *Memories*. Harper & Row Publishers, 1969.

Index

Air War, 209
Alexander, General Harold, 128, 141, 152, 156
Antwerp, 201
Anzio, 170–173
Ardennes, 72, 202–209
Arnhem, 198–201
Auchinleck, General Claude, 140
Austria, 30
Australia, 234

Bastogne, 205–208
Bataan, 114–115
Berlin, 86, 143, 258, 261
Bismarck, 158
Bizerte, 156
Bock von, General Fedor, 72–73, 95, 96, 133
Bradley, General Omar, 144, 156, 183, 189, 203–208, 257, 258
Brooke, General Alan, 75, 79, 125, 127

Casablanca, 80, 153
Casablanca Conference, 162–164
Chennault, General Claire, 220
Churchill, William Spencer 13, 15; and Boer War 36–40; and Dardanelles, 40–43; in 1930's, 44–48; Munich, 51, 55, 61, 62; at Admiralty, 68–70; becomes Prime Minister, 71; and Battle of France, 75, 79; and French Fleet, 80–81; and Battle of Britain, 81–83; and Greece 91–92; and coalition, 93, 108–109; Singapore, 112; and El Alamein, 139–141; and invasion N. Africa, 153–155; Casablanca Conference, 162–164; and Anzio, 170–172; and Teheran Conference, 175–177; invasion of southern France, 194–195; and Air War, 211–213; and Pacific War, 218; and Yalta Conference, 244–246; achievements of, 272–277
Clark, General Mark, 146, 154
Convoys, 160–162
Corregidor, 114–115

Darlan, Admiral Jean, 154
DeGaulle, General Charles, 65, 77–79; return to Paris, 122
Doenitz, Admiral Carl, 160, 262
Doolittle, General James, 117–118
Dresden, 246
Dunkirk, 75

Eden, Anthony, 91, 128
Eisenhower, General Dwight D., early life, 143; at West Point, 144–145; as MacArthur aide, 145; in Philippines, 145; aide to Marshall, 147; promoted to Europe, 148; heads N. African invasion, 153–155; invasion of Sicily, 167–168; Normandy invasion, 179–187; victory in France, 189–192; Market Garden, 198–201; the Ardennes,

202–209; Germany crushed, 256–264

Enterprise, 121–122

Falaise, 191

Galland, Colonel Adolf, 85
Guadalcanal, 221
Gestapo, 22
Goering, Hermann, 21, 27–28, 66; Battle of Britain, 81–86; 262

Halsey, Admiral William, 121; Leyte Gulf, 227–229
Hamburg, 211
Harris, General Arthur, 246
Himmler, Heinrich, 22, 27; Death Camps, 250–252
Hirohito, 101
Hiroshima, 244
Hitler, Adolph, 13, 14, and early life, 17–19; forms Nazi party, 20–22; Goals, 23–24; and Master Race, 26; and Roehm, 27–28; and Rhineland, 29–30; Austria, 30; at Munich, 50–55; attacks Poland, 66–67; and Norway, 68; compared with Churchill, 70; attacks France, 71–77; against Churchill, 79–80; Battle of Britain, 81–86; attacks Greece, 92; attacks Russia, 92–99; and United States, 105–108; coalition against, 108–109; on offensive in Russia 1942, 133–137; and U-boats, 160; Summer 1943, 165–166; in Russia 1943, 173–175; and Normandy invasion, 179–

189; in France, 189–192; assassination attempt on, 192; Ardennes attack, 202–209; and atomic bomb, 158–159; Final Solution, 249–252; Germany crushed, 256–258; Final Days, 260–262; Mistakes, 265–269; Hitler, 268–272; Churchill, Roosevelt, Stalin v. Hitler, 274–277

Iwo Jima, 235

Jodl, General Alfred, 183–185.

Kasserine Pass, 156
King, Admiral Earnest, 148, 225
Kimmel, Admiral Husband, 102
Kluge, von General Guenther, 190–191
Kliest, General Ewald von, 137
Kursk, 131

Leigh–Mallory, Air Marshall, 181
Lenin, Vladamir, 56–57
Leningrad, 95
Leyte Gulf, Battle of, 227–229

MacArthur, General Douglas, Bataan, 114; New Guinea, 222; at Leyte, 230–231; and Pacific War, 231–235
Maginot Line, 72–76
Malta, 142
Manila, 233–234
Marinas Islands, 224
Marshall, General George C., as Chief–of–Staff, 100; N. Africa,

153; and Eisenhower, 147; and
Normandy, 178; cabled to
Eisenhower, 263

Marsh, Donald, 213

McClusky, Lt. Commander Wade,
122

Messina, 167

Montgomery, General Bernard, in
France 1940, 79; in N. Africa,
141–143; in Sicily, 167; in Italy,
169; in Normandy, 179–180; at
Caen, 189–191; Market Garden,
198–200; in Ardennes Battle,
206–208; crosses Rhine, 257

Mussolini, Benito, enters war, 89–
90; fall of, 168

Nagumo, Admiral, Pearl Harbor,
102; at Midway, 120–122

Naples, 170

Nimitz, Admiral Chester, and
Midway, 121–122; and Pacific
War, 223–224

Norway, 69

Okinawa, 237–239

Oppenheimer, Robert, and atomic
bomb, 242

Palermo, 167

Pantelleria, 167

Paris, fall of, 76; liberation of, 192

Patton, General George, 145, in
Sicily, 167; in Normandy, 190; in
Ardennes Battle, 205–209;
crosses Rhine, 257;

Petain, Marshall Henri, fall of
France, 76; and DeGaulle, 77; N.
Africa, 154

Prague, 260

Remagen, 256

Rommel, General Erwin, 73, in N.
Africa, 140–142; at Kasserine
Pass, 156; in Normandy, 181–186

Roosevelt, Franklin D., 13, 14, rise
of, 31; as President, 33–35; 59–
60; in 1941, 99–100; Pearl
Harbor, 105–107; and Navy, 123–
124; Churchill meeting, 124;
Churchill and Roosevelt, 129–
132; at Casablanca Conference,
162–164; at Teheran Conference,
175–178; Roosevelt and
Churchill, Pacific War, 218; and
atomic bomb, 241–242; Yalta
Conference, 244–246; and
industrial production, 246; death
of, 252; no mistakes, 264;
Greatest Leader Was, 272–274;
Churchill, Roosevelt, Stalin v.
Hitler, 274–277

Runstedt, General Gerd von, attack
on France, 72–76; and Normandy,
184–186

St. Vith, 205–207

Salerno, 170

Singapore, 111–113

Spruance, Admiral Raymond, at
Midway, 121–123; in Marianas,
225

Stilwell, General Joseph, 219

Stewart, William C., Jr., 212–217

Stalin, Joseph, 13, 14, and Munich,
34–35; early life and rise to
power, 55–59; pact with Hitler,
64–65; Hitler's plan to attack, 88–

92; Hitler attacks, 94–99;
Stalingrad 1942, 132–137; on
Stalin, 137–139; and convoys,
161; battles of 1943, 173–174;
Teheran Conference, 175–178;
battles in 1944, 201–202; Yalta
Conference, 244–246; and
industrial production, 247;
mistakes, 265; Greatest Leader
Was, 272–273; Churchill,
Roosevelt, Stalin v. Hitler, 274–
277

Taranto, 90
Tarawa, 244
Tojo, General Hideki, 101
Truman, Harry S., 253–256

U-boats, menace, 160

Wake Island, 113–114
Warsaw, 68, 202
Wray, Waverly, 182

Yalta Conference, 244–246
Yamamoto, Admiral Isoroku, and
    Midway, 120–123; death of, 222
Yorktown, 120–123

Zukhov, Marshall Georgi, at
    Moscow, 98; at Stalingrad, 138–
    139

www.ingramcontent.com/pod-product-compliance
Lightning Source LLC
Chambersburg PA
CBHW032037080426
42733CB00006B/115